Understanding Child Development

Knowledge, theory and practice

Jennie Lindon, BA, MPhil., C Psychol.

THOMSON

LEARNING

Australia • Canada • Mexico • Singapore • Spain • United Kingdom • United States

To Lance – with my love and thanks

THOMSON
LEARNING ™

Understanding Child Development - Knowledge, theory and practice

Copyright © Jennie Lindon 1998

The Thomson Learning logo is a registered trademark used herein under licence.

For more information, contact Thomson Learning, Berkshire House, 168–173 High Holborn, London, WC1V 7AA or visit us on the World Wide Web at:
http://www.thomsonlearning.co.uk

British Library Cataloguing-in-Publication Data
A catalogue record for this book is available from the British Library

ISBN 1-86152-688-1

First published 1998 by MacMillan Press Ltd
Reprinted 2000 by Thomson Learning

Printed by CTPS, Hong Kong

Contents

Acknowledgements

I would like to thank Ann Robinson of the Early Childhood Unit and the staff of Balham library who continue to be such a help in tracking down material for me. Thanks also to Peter Elfer and Dorothy Selleck of the Early Childhood Unit for discussions about research into early communication.

Many thanks to my partner, Lance Lindon, who took all the photographs (with the exception of the photo on page 119 by Patricia George and on page 39 by Marguerite Roberts). Some photographs are from our own collection; others were taken in early years settings. We very much appreciate the support of staff, parents and children who appear in the photos: from the Balham Nursery School, the Balham Family Centre, the Broomwood Methodist Church Parent/Carer and Toddler Group and the Balham Leisure Centre Creche. Thank you to our daughter Tanith for the sketches in the book.

Thanks to our son Drew and to Tanith for letting me quote from the diaries that I kept of both of them for their first five years.

I appreciated constructive comments on the draft of the book from the reviewers.

Introduction

I have been fascinated by children and their development for a long time. I think my interest started when, as a small thirteen-year-old with appendicitis, I spent a fortnight in a children's ward rather than being placed with the adults. I was cheered up immensely by playing with the bored and sometimes distressed toddlers who were also on the ward. As a child psychologist I have continued to be intrigued and often surprised by what children do and how they see the world. As adults we can learn so much by looking through children's eyes. And, for anyone working closely with children, this attempt to move from an exclusively adult view is crucial for good practice.

About this book

The aims of the book

I have written books in the Caring Series which focus on good practice. So it is important to say that this book was written to be of practical use to people working with young children, but it is not a book about your practice with children as such. It is not a 'what to do' book but is much more of a 'think about what you do' book.

In the various chapters I cover the knowledge that underpins what is regarded as good practice and the questions that continue to be asked, because we are still learning about children and their development. You will find discussions about theories of children's development and findings from a wide variety of research about children. Throughout the book I am concerned about what theories and research findings say about good practice with children. You will find many further questions, as well as some considered answers. But nobody is in the position to be complacent and say, 'Now we know all about children' because we do not.

People who work with young children cannot, any more than parents, hang about while researchers and theorists come to some definite agreement. Full agreement will not happen because, as you will discover in reading the book, people who study children (and make practical suggestions on the basis of their studies) sometimes take such different viewpoints that they are never going to agree. I do not see this as a problem, since there is something to learn from all the material that is covered in this book. Even when you feel most in tune with research or a theory about children and child development, you still have to ask that key question, 'So what?'

Who the book is for

This book aims to support early years workers in making sense of information and sharing some of the tools for applying knowledge to practice.

Readers of this book are going to be working closely with young children and their families – either because you are already in a job or because you are working towards an early years qualification on one of the accredited training courses. Your focus in work may be in any of the different early years settings: nurseries, playgroups (many of which are now known as pre-schools), children's and family centres and the nursery and reception years of primary school. The content will also be relevant to readers involved in playwork, with reference to the younger end of the age range that you cover. Readers who work with sole responsibility for children, as a nanny or childminder, will also find the book appropriate to their jobs.

The content and approach of the book is relevant to students on the following types of course:

- NVQ/SVQs in Early Years Care and Education, levels 2 and 3
- NVQ/SVQs in Playwork levels 2 and 3 – with a focus on the younger end of the age group covered within playwork
- CACHE Certificate in Child Care and Education (CCE), Diploma in Nursery Nursing (NNEB), and Advanced Diploma in Child Care and Education (ADCE)
- BTEC National in Childhood Studies (Nursery Nursing)
- GNVQ in Health and Social Care – especially Intermediate and Advanced
- GCSE Home Economics: Child Development
- GCSE Psychology

Appendix 1 gives cross references to specific modules or units from the courses.

The book is organised so that it will support you in personal study or reading for your own interest. If you are attending any of the training courses, then your supervisor will advise you on how to choose topics to support your study programme and in using the many activities and exercises as you build up your portfolio of work. The aim of the book is to extend your knowledge and understanding of child development, but within the context of supporting your practice with real children in ordinary early years settings.

1 Understanding child development – a framework

This chapter covers:

- child development as a whole;
- making sense of child development;
- the main influences on development;
- theories about child development;
- the study of children's development.

1.1 Child development as a whole

Children change visibly and behaviourally from birth through to the onset of young adulthood. They grow in size and strength but they also show many changes in what they can do with their bodies and how they use their minds. **Development** is a term that covers the whole span of changes.

Different areas of development

Researchers who are especially interested in one aspect of development may focus almost exclusively on, for instance, a child's ability to communicate or the physical skills of a very young baby. And when you are observing children your attention will be drawn, in turn, to their different skills and ability to understand the world around them. But the whole picture is that development progresses in different directions at the same time and anyone who is working with young children needs to have a well-rounded view of children.

Children's development covers all of the following areas:

- *Their physical development*: Babies are born with a small number of instinctive reflexes, but after birth all the other physical movements are learned and improved through practice. Children learn the large movements, such as crawling and walking, and the fine coordinations that develop alongside the use of their senses of sight and touch. Children are also growing in size and strength and their general health will affect their pattern of development.
- *Communication*: The development of communication is only partly about learning to speak, although the spoken word is an important step for children. They are also learning to understand what is communicated to

them, both through words and non-verbal language. Some children are learning more than one language in early childhood.

- *Thinking and understanding*: Children's ability to think and to reason develops with their experience and growing age. They are not only gathering more knowledge; the ways in which they make sense of that knowledge continue to change. The word **cognitive** is used to describe the broad range of intellectual development.
- *Social development*: From the earliest weeks, babies show a wish to make contact; they are naturally social from the early days. Children develop attachments to adults and also with other children. Children's social development unfolds as they learn how they are expected to relate to others and how they should treat a shared environment.
- *Personal development*: Babies need to be cared for by adults, but young children are soon motivated to take part in their own care and to be helpful in the daily routine. Children are also developing a sense of themselves as individuals in relation with others. Their sense of confidence is shaped by experiences in their family and other settings.

Further research supports our understanding of how children develop. For instance, social cognition is an exciting branch of study in which children's abilities to think, communicate and relate to others have been seen to link together in their continuing development. (More on social cognition from page 151.)

TO THINK ABOUT

Children are not helped by a fragmented view that divides each stage of development into a separate parcel. However, it is very easy to slip into viewing babies or children mainly from one angle. For instance, children under five years are sometimes referred to as 'pre-schoolers'. This arises in England and Wales because by law children have to start an education in the term after their fifth birthday. Yet this phrase has the unfortunate effect of defining early childhood as the run into school rather than years of great importance for their own sake.

- Can you think of other phrases or ways of talking about young children that risk losing their individuality?

Does development stop?

Psychologists used to study development as if nothing much happened after adolescence. The implication was that adults simply got on with their lives and were not of much interest to psychology unless they experienced serious problems. This situation definitely changed during the 1970s with an interest in the changes in adult life that promote further development.

The **life span** approach to development is now well established. This approach recognises that adults have the capacity to learn new skills or apply existing skills in new ways. Important life events such as becoming a parent or losing one's job are recognised as significant experiences. Adults have to cope one way or another and they can learn and change in response to what has happened.

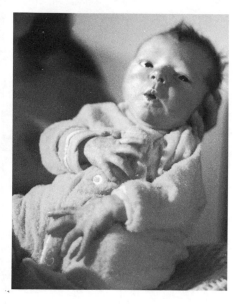

Whole child development

It is more manageable to describe development through separate aspects but, of course, children do not develop in neat and separate packages. Effective early years workers need to have a sound grasp of the different areas of child development but also an understanding of how different parts relate to other areas. A **whole child** or **holistic** approach to children stresses the importance of thinking about and acting towards children as entire individuals. You need to be ready to look for links between different aspects of the development of an individual child, as well as being alert to the overall balance of the experience you are providing for a group. Four examples follow which illustrate the kind of links you can make in taking a whole child approach.

1 Active and alert babies

Research over the last few decades has transformed the view of babies and toddlers – both from a psychological angle and in terms of good practice with very young children. Babies and toddlers undoubtedly have pressing physical needs for care and feeding, which they cannot meet themselves. But the view that babies are passive, mainly physical beings has been well undermined.

Experimental research from the 1960s onwards demonstrated that even very young babies have working senses. Their hearing appears to be the most fully developed but sight, touch, smell and taste are all present. Babies showed clear preferences between different tastes and between pictures or mobiles at which they could stare. Babies also showed an awareness of familiarity and novelty. For instance, a design in an abstract picture that had held their gaze strongly in the beginning seemed to become less interesting to them over time. Babies consistently show greater interest in pictures that have the basic features of the human face, such as two large black dots for eyes. Within their physical capabilities, babies make choices and show the results of previous experience.

Social communication

Anecdotal evidence from parents and other involved carers has always suggested that babies are ready to relate to human faces and the feel of human contact. Before babies produce their first smile, they engage adults with a steady gaze. Research has established that babies' ideal focusing distance from the first days is the distance created between a baby's face and that of an adult when a baby is held in your arms. Young babies show an awareness of different ways of holding, and probably the familiar body smell of a parent or regular carer. They will sometimes protest loudly at unfamiliar ways of holding. The opportunities of video and freeze-frame technology in the 1970s brought new possibilities for research with young babies and their carers. The detailed studies of babies and their mothers changed views about early social communication – more of this topic in chapter 4.

The physical baby

Observation of babies demonstrates their powerful drive for physical control. Before they become mobile, babies spend a lot of their waking time using their current physical skills. Their ability to control their body moves steadily downwards with control of the head being the first task. If you watch babies under a year old, it is very noticeable how much effort they put into moving their limbs, getting hold of objects and in attempting to move themselves by whatever method they can manage. Mobility becomes a key issue for them and for their carers, since an immobile baby is very dependent on what adults, or other children, bring to them or take them towards. A mobile baby or toddler uses the skill to explore with no grasp of possible dangers.

2   Children's physical development

Young children develop their ability to use and learn further physical skills, yet physical development is not separate from everything else that they are learning. Careful watching of babies' and toddlers' physical abilities can often highlight other, less obvious, aspects to their development. You will see their persistence, creative attempts to solve problems (How do I get hold of this? How do I make that work?) and their delight with achievements. The boxed example from my own family diary illustrates how Drew's developing physical skills opened the door for a great deal of learning within other aspects of his development.

Drew: 16-17 months

These are some highlights from my diary of Drew while he was a toddler.

- *Drew is confidently mobile - walking, climbing and running. He moves all over the house, including up and down the stairs. He will go and find Lance when I suggest 'Go and show Daddy' even if that means going upstairs.*
- *Drew now clowns around to make us laugh by standing on tip-toe, twirling, walking or crawling backwards. He falls over deliberately sometimes and gives his loud 'stage' laugh.*
- *Sometimes he clears his toys off the low wooden chest and climbs up. Then he sits or stomps about, calling out in triumph to me.*
- *Lance has started a game with Drew where Lance says 'One, two, three, go!' And Drew runs and throws himself into Lance's arms. Drew now makes sounds in the same rhythm when he jumps on his own or throws himself on to the floor cushions with a 'Da, do, da, dah!'*
- *Drew is safe to let walk into the garden from the back door. He has his little watering can and wants to water the flowers. He is also very interested in the flowers - to smell them and to blow on the dandelions.*
- *He wants to use the J-cloth to wipe up his highchair tray, as he sees me do. He likes putting objects into containers so he is happy sometimes to help in tidying up his toys.*
- *Drew likes to take off his socks and hat. He can finish taking off his cardigan or jacket if one sleeve is already done and can step out of his dungarees.*
- *He can blow into a tissue to have his nose blown and wipes a tissue over his nose on his own. He seemed to be confused for a while between blowing and smelling. He was blowing on the flowers.*
- *He can get out the books he wants from the shelf and has learned to work the pulls in the books with moveable parts.*
- *He is so pleased with himself when he makes something work. He can get all the cones on to his rod and, if one of us engages the mechanism, Drew can press the lever and shoot them into the air. He stamps his feet in appreciation or applauds himself by holding one hand steady and clapping the other against it.*

SUGGESTED ACTIVITY

1 Take some time to observe a child of a similar age.
2 Focus on what he or she can manage in terms of physical skills.
3 Then look for how these skills open up other areas of development.

When you read the short descriptions, can you see how Drew's physical skills were very important to him as a toddler? They were a source of enjoyment and satisfaction, including making adults laugh with his antics. He found pleasure in being helpful within the daily routine and chose to take part in his own care. His mobility opened up the outdoors to him and a delight in natural objects such as flowers.

3 Developing a moral sense

Children's ideas of right and wrong and their understanding of what is expected of them is a blend of several different areas of development.

- A growing sense of morality is partly a social development for children. Rights, wrongs and expectations initially make sense to children because they are grounded in their relationships with other people and children's wish to please and get along with others.
- Morality for children is first about behaviour (what they or other people do). Ideas are harder to grasp and come later.
- Children's behaviour is affected by the understanding side to their communication abilities. Do they hear and follow what adults are saying to them? Adults' ability to say clearly and consistently what they want is also a key issue here.
- Moral understanding is later related to children's growing ability to think and reason (their cognitive development). They begin to follow a pattern of what is expected, of rules about acceptable and unacceptable behaviour. Older children will start to challenge what they judge to be unfair rules or inconsistent application of rules.

So, an area that might seem initially to be mainly about children's ideas can be seen to be related to most other areas of their development. (More on moral development from page 150.)

4 Children's health

Advances in health psychology have illustrated how children's physical well-being cannot be seen separately from the rest of their development. Early psychological approaches to childhood illness treated children as if they were isolated individuals reacting passively to their illness. Study of children with chronic illness and their families has encouraged a more realistic and rounded approach:

- A child's illness can affect her feelings and emotional well-being, but the impact can also be in the other direction. A sad, depressed or frightened child will cope less well with illness or unpleasant medical procedures. Caring and aware adults can take steps to help children with their feelings.
- Young children try to make sense of what is happening to them and, in the absence of other explanations from adults, may decide that illness or an unexplained operation have come about because they have been badly behaved.
- Children do not live alone; they are part of a social network of family and friends. Serious illness or disabling conditions affect relationships within a family for the child who is sick and for any siblings. Repeated hospitalisations for children will disrupt their friendships and continuing illness may well affect children's play opportunities with others.

1.2 Making sense of child development

Developmental milestones

A considerable amount happens as children pass from babyhood into middle childhood. Some of the more striking events, or those that are judged to be especially important, are called **milestones** in development. Some examples are children's first unaided steps, the first understandable words or abilities in self care such as putting on their own coats. The advantages of watching out for the developmental milestones are that:

- Early years workers or parents can feel confident that young children are gaining new skills.
- An alertness to children's learning can mean that you support them when they are nearly able to do something and need help and encouragement.
- There is great satisfaction for you in recognising that children, with your help, are making visible progress.
- It is also possible to help a child sooner rather than later because you realise that she is having difficulty with a skill. Knowledge of approximate ages for a wide range of milestones helps you to know when to become concerned.

The potential disadvantages of a rigid approach to milestones are that:

- Too much emphasis is placed on the actual milestone than on all the learning that builds towards it. For instance, early years workers and parents should not just be celebrating the first recognisable words, but also a young child's ability to understand or their obvious wish to communicate with expressive sounds and gestures.
- Some milestones may be regarded more highly than others. Perhaps self care skills are seen as making life easier for adults but not fully appreciated for the fine physical skills that a child has learned and the boost to self-esteem for a child who feels more able to 'do it myself'.
- A misunderstanding of developmental milestones can also lead adults to focus unhelpfully on what children cannot do, rather than what they can and the important focus for helping children with what they can nearly do.

Developmental norms

Children vary considerably in the age at which they manage all the different skills of their development. It is certainly not possible to make absolute statements along the lines of, 'At 14 months all toddlers will be able to...' However, observation of many children can support descriptive accounts of the approximate ages for skills and levels of understanding. These ages provide a guide to **developmental norms**.

The advantages of having a grasp of developmental norms are that:

- Early years workers have a way of monitoring children's progress. You will be alert to those who are doing well for their age and may need more challenge in everyday activities. You should also become aware, in a constructive way, of those children who are struggling and need some extra help.
- Adults who spend their working time with children who are almost all delayed in their development can find their expectations shaped through everyday experience. Without norms for references, it is all too possible to shift an overall framework of children's development to fit the group

for whom you are responsible. Children who are doing well, compared with their peers in this group, start to be seen as outstanding and children who are having difficulty are viewed as average.

The potential disadvantages of checking children against developmental norms are that:

● Early years workers or parents may become too fixed on the actual age ranges rather than finding satisfaction with the children on what they can manage within their own developmental timetable. A great deal depends on how the use of developmental information is introduced and organised within any early years setting.
● Developmental norms can sometimes be expressed in a narrow way, representing only one social or cultural group. Important developments for this individual child may not be recognised and legitimate family traditions may not fit a restricted view of 'what children should be doing'. There is a far greater awareness of cultural differences in child rearing than a couple of decades ago. But again, much depends on the early years setting in which any developmental information is applied.

Within development, babies and children may share many patterns in the skills they learn and in what way. Yet there are still many individual differences and even an extensive knowledge of child development does not allow you to make detailed predictions about individual children. You would need to get to know and observe each child.

The nature of developmental change

Anyone even slightly involved with children can see that they change over time. A two-year-old does not behave in the same way as a five-year-old; there are significant differences in their relationships with others, their ways of solving problems and their patterns of communication. But what kind of change is involved?

Developmental leaps

If you have the opportunity to observe individual children over a long period of time you will notice that there seem to be periods of rapid, even dramatic change, when a child makes what have been called **developmental leaps**. Then there can be periods of relative calm when children are consolidating their new skill or understanding. Although changes in children's developmental skills can look sudden, a considerable amount of learning and exploration has been going on to support the change.

It is not the case that nothing is happening during these 'quieter' periods. Children are using, practising and generalising from new skills. One of the risks of a rigid approach to developmental milestones is that adults can overlook the crucial fact that skills such as walking or communicating in words have to be practised in many different contexts by children. Children have to learn skills and use them, including seeing the point of using potential skills (a key issue in learning to read and write, see page 113). One of the distinctions between children who are quick and effective learners and those who have more difficulty is how swiftly children generalise a new skill, idea or strategy beyond the circumstances in which they first learned it.

Children may take another developmental leap largely provoked by their own learning through exploration. Or it can be brought on by changes from their social world, for instance, the arrival of a new baby, attending nursery for the first time or even going on family holiday when they have the undivided attention of their parents. Children may be excited by the new possibilities but can also be less sure of their world, because the old certainties no longer work and new relationships, ways of thinking and behaving have to be learned. For instance, children who start nursery or playgroup may be pleased with the new prospects for play but they have to come to terms with unknown adults, new children, different rules and so on.

As children develop, some of the changes that can be observed are **quantitative**. The list of words used regularly by a child grows until it is practically impossible to maintain the list. Children learn more than one strategy when faced with a problem to solve. Their ability to run gets better and faster. So, in one way, developmental change is about more of the same thing.

Yet, change in child development is also **qualitative**. What a child has learned, whether physical or a new way of looking at the world, has opened up new possibilities that were not previously part of her repertoire. Once children have learned to speak, they add words to their vocabulary. But their language development is far more than a rise from a vocabulary counted in tens of words to one numbered in hundreds. A four-year-old is not just learning the word 'rainbow', but is also asking tough questions like 'How are rainbows made?'

EXAMPLE

Andy has learned to crawl and now uses his skill with confidence and none of the frustrating rocking movements that he used to make before he got moving. Andy crawls about his home with obvious delight, using his new skill to get from place to place, to follow the sound of his mother's voice and to chase the family cat.

His mother has noticed the **quantitative** change in Andy's development as he crawls faster, with more confidence and in all possible directions around their home. But the ability to crawl has also opened up new possibilities for Andy. His independent mobility has changed his social world – a **qualitative** change for Andy and for his mother. Andy can now move himself towards objects of interest and sets about exploring drawers and waste bins that were not previously in his sphere of interest.

Question:

You might like to think about how the gaining of a new skill affects a child's development in more ways than applying that specific skill. For instance:

- being able to reach and open a door
- being able to use words as well as gestures to communicate wants
- learning to read

Stages or sequences?

The nature of developmental change was believed for a long time to be through distinct stages. The strongest influence on this position was Jean Piaget, whose theory was that all children went through qualitatively different stages and that the insights of later development had no meaning for younger children, whose attention was focused elsewhere. Many of the ideas that Piaget introduced are still valuable and you will find many references to him in this book. However, the idea of very clear-cut, separate and major stages has not proved a good fit for the pattern of children's development.

Children's development does not seem to follow genuine stages, but equally so it is not a collection of random patterns. Later learning builds on earlier struggles and explorations. In many developments there is an approximate sequence that children follow. For instance:

1 If you watch a very young child in the last weeks before walking, you will see that there has been a lot of focused practice before those first independent steps. Babies do not just get up and walk. They have been strengthening their legs and improving balance with standing, cruising along with hand-holds from furniture or tottering with an adult hand for support. They have taken small risks in crossing an open space by choosing those gaps which they can stretch across with one hand left holding on to a firm surface. (This is another good example of how watching young children's physical development gives you a window into their thinking: planning ahead, risk assessment and actively seeking help from others.)

2 There are a number of steps in a sequence of intellectual understanding before children are able to start reading. They have to grasp that what looks like squiggles in books and elsewhere are meaningful print and that adults are reading the words when they tell a story or look at a signboard. Children also have to realise that writing is a different system from the number patterns before there is any chance of their learning to read. (More on learning about written communication from page 109.)

Understanding and noticing these developmental sequences is important for early years workers and parents too. There is immense satisfaction for adults in enjoying all the learning that occurs between conventional 'milestones' and this awareness helps adults to support and encourage children's learning.

Individual development

Children are not simply batted around by external pressures on their development. Research into young children has supported the rich anecdotal evidence from families that babies are individuals from the beginning. Although adult reactions undoubtedly then interact with the babies' tendencies, the individual differences in children continue as broad themes in how their development unfolds. There is a core of individuality that runs through how a child reacts to the world.

A jumpy baby who prefers gentle handling and is very wary of new experiences may continue as an uncertain child who clings to a parent at the first day of playgroup. Perhaps this child will always be very wary of new situations but she can learn ways of coping, especially if her first experiences of uneasy newness are handled with sensitivity by caring adults.

Research into differences in temperament has suggested that broad differences exist which probably have a genetic component. Temperament is not a strait-jacket and certainly should not be used as a negative label by adults. On the other hand, an awareness of differences in temperament can be a constructive way to look at how individuals learn or cope with problems. This theme can also support making sense of mismatches between adult and child preferences for dealing with situations or frustrations.

1.3 The main influences on development

The most basic question asked about children is whether their development and behaviour are shaped by a pattern that was laid down before they were born, or whether children's reactions and tendencies are the result of later experiences. This question sets the influence of **nature** (inborn reactions) in contrast with **nurture** (the impact of experience) and is sometimes called the **heredity-environment debate.**

The first in a series of answers to the question is that matters are not as simple as a straight 'Is it nature or nurture?' Children's development is influenced by both internal and external factors, but their relative importance is not identical at all times and for every aspect of development. It is not a helpful question to ask whether a particular development is caused by 'nature or nurture' because there is nearly always some interaction between the two.

Genetic factors and biological patterns

Every child has inherited a genetic profile that resulted from the blend between their two birth parents. Some individual characteristics such as hair, skin colour or eye colour are definitely inherited. But even with these apparently simple individual differences, you have to know more family information than the appearance of the parents to predict how their children will look. It is a more complicated process than curly-haired parents having curly-haired children. Some health conditions and disabilities have a genetic component that has been identified through study of families. But again the prediction could be that a child has an increased chance of inheriting a disabling condition, but not a certainty.

A considerable amount of research has attempted to identify which individual differences are due to genetic factors, and to what extent. Until about the mid-1980s the balance was far more on considering how environment shaped children and the adults they became. This emphasis was in its turn a reaction against earlier approaches that had downplayed the impact of experience on children. Greater openness about the possible impact of inherited features and a 'biological programme' influencing development seems to have arisen for several reasons:

- New technology has allowed detailed study of the functioning of the brain. Research has demonstrated individual differences and the tremendous growth of neurones in specific areas of learning, for instance when children are very young.
- New scientific and statistical techniques have enabled a more sophisticated study of genetic patterns.
- No sensible psychologist or biologist now talks in 'either-or' terms about genetic and environmental factors. Patterns which appear to be laid down through biological programming are the beginning of the story of child development and not the end. Discussion of possible inherited tendencies is not the same as placing children into a developmental strait-jacket.

Behaviour genetics is a relatively new area of research and studies have suggested that there is some genetic element in such varied areas as body shape, some aspects of cognitive problem-solving, reading disability, extreme anti-social behaviour and variations in temperament. The newer approach to the impact of nature has been to explore genetics as a possible explanation, to talk about probabilities and not certainties.

The interplay of biology and experience

Tendencies are modified by experience. For instance, an in-built bias towards a particular kind of temperament is modified through how parents and other carers relate to babies and young children and make respectful allowance for differences. As any parent of more than one child will tell you, children raised in the same family can be significantly different from their earliest days. The details of children's development seem, at every point that has been studied, to be an interaction between the impact of nature and nurture.

Two periods in the lives of children seem to be especially influenced by biological programming: the first year of life and puberty. At both these times babies and then adolescents experience substantial physical changes – internal and external – that happen without conscious effort on their part. However, even these powerful internal forces can be further shaped by the environment.

Very early development

Babies do not have to be taught to use their limbs, to try to move and later to crawl or walk; they naturally work on all the skills they possess. Yet poor diet can make babies lethargic and inhibit their physical development. Malnutrition has long-term consequences on the child's later development.

Restricted opportunities to move around can limit babies' physical skills because of the lack of practice. However, even severe restrictions on movement do not have the same impact on all babies. Studies of very poor practice in understaffed residential nurseries in the 1940s and 50s produced distressing descriptions of babies in despair who had given up trying and lay in their cots all day. Yet, other babies, less than a year old, were developing powerful physical skills in their continued drive to escape from their cots and attract any kind of adult attention. Possibly this distinction showed another inherited difference, that of temperament.

TO THINK ABOUT

It is important to consider carefully any assumptions about children and genetic influences. Inheritance definitely plays a part in their development. But sometimes characteristics or behaviours are explained as something that 'runs in the family' when experience is more important. For instance, a mother may say of her child, 'I'm afraid she's inherited my fear of spiders'. This mother may say honestly that she has never said to her child, 'Be frightened of spiders!' But the child has watched her mother's fearful reaction and has not had any support to take a different approach to spiders. The child has learned from her mother's behaviour.

- Can you think of examples in your work with children when 'it runs in our family' has not been a likely explanation for the child's behaviour or current difficulty?
- But you also need to be aware that some developmental problems can be linked to inherited patterns, for instance: continued problems with stammering or having difficulty learning to read. Saying 'He's just like his Dad' is not, of course, reason to ignore the problem. On the contrary, such a conversation with a parent is a sign to you that the child may need some extra help, from you or a specialist.

The experience of puberty

Around the world young people experience puberty at some time between nine and sixteen years old. The exact timing of the onset seems to be a matter of individual biological programming, but puberty can be delayed by poor diet and excessive physical exercise – both environmental factors.

As you will recall yourself, puberty is more than just the physical changes. It is also an emotional experience and one which brings social adjustments. The individual experience of puberty, what it means to each boy or girl, is affected by their social environment. The biological programming does not determine the support, or lack of it, you receive from family and friends or how your social environment helps you to feel positive, or negative, about becoming more grown up.

The impact of environment

Just as the study of genetic influences is far more subtle than previously, so the study of how the environment affects children has developed into a more realistic, complex view of the child's world. Children's environment can affect them through several different routes:

- the impact of very early experience on their health and well-being which includes the prenatal environment and complications of birth that affect the baby;
- subsequent illness or relative good health, which in some cases may have a genetic element. But problems will often be the result of exposure to illness or social conditions of disadvantage such as poor housing that affect babies and children;
- children's social and cultural environment and the people through whom this is communicated. Social factors such as social class, or conditions such as poverty cannot affect children directly. Children's experience, positive or negative, has to be mediated through the behaviour of their carers, whose stress or depression will affect their actions;
- the learning environment, including the opportunities given to children or the restrictions, which are partly the physical environment of possible play space but also the behaviour of adults;
- the broad physical environment and how it contributes to children's health and well being or threatens it. Children who live in seriously polluted environments are at risk and some pollutants, such as lead, have a worse effect on children's development, including cognitive, than on fully grown adults.

The impact of environment on children works in a subtle way and studies do not support any simple line of 'this experience leads to this consequence for all children':

- When the biological programme is strong, then environmental influences have to be very powerful to shift the pattern – as in the earlier examples of the physical maturation of young babies or puberty.
- Some environmental input is necessary even when a skill or pattern of behaviour will normally emerge without help. For instance, muscles will atrophy if they are not used. Children's natural inclination to communicate can be effectively destroyed by extreme environmental deprivation.
- Sometimes specific experiences for children will bring on a particular development earlier than usual. For instance, research has demonstrated that, when parents talk more to their young children and in more complex sentences, those children develop two-word sentences and other early

grammar of language at a younger age than the children who hear less spoken communication. The latter group learn to talk, but there tends to be an average delay of a few months, in comparison with children who have a richer early language experience.

- Talking with young children has another effect, beyond bringing on their spoken language abilities a little quicker. The children in the families whose parents have talked with them from early on have slightly higher IQs, on average, than the other children. And this difference persists, so it is a longer-lasting impact of young children's environment.

- Some aspects of children's development can be purely environmental because, without a particular experience, a given skill would not emerge spontaneously. Many children are potentially capable of learning to ice skate, but their skills will not emerge unless they are given access to an ice rink.

- The impact of earlier experiences leaves a strong trace on how children then approach further experiences. Children whose experience of adults is that they are helpful and supportive are more likely to approach new adults, perhaps in playgroup or nursery, with the expectation that these people will also be a useful resource. On the other hand, adults may have to work very hard to gain the trust of a young child who has already decided that adults are unpredictable creatures, best avoided. So, early experience has shaped expectations in the children, which in turn make meaning for them in later experiences.

TO THINK ABOUT

The positive consequences of illness

We have to approach assumptions with caution. For example, we tend to think of illness as a negative experience for children, something to be avoided if at all possible. But, much as children need to face problems they cannot easily solve in order to learn how to problem-solve, so it seems children's bodies need some early experience of illness in order to learn how to fight it.

For instance, health research now challenges the view that rising rates of allergic conditions such as asthma in the child population can be explained by the worsening of pollution. Patterns of higher levels of asthma seem to be more closely related to children's reduced exposure to a range of everyday illnesses. The suggested explanation is that children's immune systems are not getting sufficient experience in the early years of germs and viruses that need to be fought. Consequently, in later years, their immune system fights off a range of non-threatening substances in an allergic reaction. The research does not claim that higher pollution levels do not matter, but that they are not an easy explanation of increased allergies.

Early experience

People concerned with children are usually interested in whether early experiences for babies and very young children have a stronger effect than later experiences, particularly whether children can get over early bad experiences. As you might guess from the previous section, the picture is not a neat and simple one. Children's early experience does matter, but children

can be differently affected by apparently similar circumstances. Two themes have emerged from research into this area:

1   There is rarely a straightforward pattern of cause and effect. And single adverse experiences seem to be less significant than persisting patterns or a piling up of adverse circumstances for children. For instance, low birth weight or premature birth (which may of course be linked) are potentially negative experiences for babies. However, study of infants in different family settings has shown that the low birth weight babies who live in very disadvantaged circumstances tend to have lower average IQs. In contrast, babies with equally unfortunate beginnings, but who are in families with far less financial or social stresses, have IQs within normal range.

2   From the 1980s a number of researchers became intrigued with those children who did not succumb to disadvantageous conditions. Social deprivation did not seem to have the same impact on all children. Researchers such as Norman Garmezy and Michael Rutter developed the concepts of **vulnerability** and **resilience** in children. The sources of this relative state may be relationships with important carers such as parents but in-born temperament is also thought to be an issue. (More on page 190.)

1.4 Theories of child development

Study of children and their development has included not only **what** happens as babies and children grow but an attempt to explain **why** and **how** development unfolds. This understanding is often the basis for a wish to predict as well as explain what will happen to children on the basis of different experiences. You can think of children's development as a progressive series of changes that follow a predictable pattern resulting from the interaction between nature and nurture. Or, at least the pattern would be predictable if we fully understood what most affects children and in what way. Theories of child development are an attempt to create a framework that highlights what is most important in how development progresses or falters.

What follows is a description of some of the main theories in child development. The essence of a good theory is that it should be provable one way or another and this usually means that it has to lead to predictions that can be tested through observation and experiment. As early years workers, it is important that you have a grasp of the kind of theories proposed to explain child development. Without an awareness of the range of theories, it is easy to assume that the one or two approaches you encounter are the whole psychological view. The main theories have also been communicated through advice books to parents, have shaped approaches to education and influenced the themes in everyday thinking about children and families.

Biological explanations

The focus of all biological theories is that both the patterns of development that everyone shares and our individual differences are based in:

- the instructions laid down in the genes – an inherited pattern;
- the controls exerted by hormones in our bodies;
- the patterns of maturation triggered by messages from the brain.

Biological theorists do not claim that biology is everything and environment has no part to play. They emphasise that genetic programming and the internal workings of our brain are a powerful influence and should not be discounted. There has been a renewed interest in the biological basis to development and behaviour patterns and one of the topics has been that of sex differences (see also page 172).

Maturation

Arnold Gesell and his colleagues, working during the 1920s and 30s, established a maturational approach to child development which still exerts influence today. Gesell believed that the sequence of development for babies and children was controlled by a process of maturation which means the emergence of physical characteristics, shared by all members of a species and triggered by the information in the genes. He believed that the environment has a supportive role but that the push towards change was internal to the child. Gesell and his team studied babies and children in great detail and their descriptions were very specific to particular ages. Their research work was extended into developmental tests for assessing babies and children and the ideas of 'milestones' and 'developmental norms' emerged from Gesell's work.

The maturational approach, as developed by Gesell, influenced advice books in the 1940s and 50s. Some writers were very specific about what 'your child should be doing' at given ages. A related idea that passed into advice for parents was that babies and children would achieve the different developmental stages and skills when they were ready and that certain kinds of behaviour, like two-year-old tantrums, were 'phases' that would pass.

Animal studies

Another influential strand of biological explanation came from studies of animals which established that some patterns of behaviour were innate – animals were born with these tendencies, they did not learn the behaviour. The work of Konrad Lorenz and of E.H. Hess showed crucial periods in the early days of birds and mammals when attachment had to take place between infant and mother. The animal studies have been generalised to human behaviour especially in the understanding of early attachment behaviour of infants. John Bowlby believed that the development of attachment specifically between baby and mother was an innately driven set of behaviours that protected infants at a vulnerable time. Biology offers a good explanation for some aspects of human behaviour but the evidence has not emerged to claim that humans follow very similar patterns as the rest of the animal kingdom. We seem to be more complicated than just animals who happen to talk. (See also the discussion of bonding and attachment from page 36.)

TO THINK ABOUT

Part of the biological approach to human or animal behaviour is the study of instincts and instinctive behaviour. In general conversation, these words are often used loosely, as in 'mothers instinctively know how to care for babies'. Instincts are inborn reactions, driven by biology, that are released regardless of experience. So, if caring for babies were instinctive, women who become mothers would not need to learn anything about baby care and they would all be fully competent. Now, this is clearly not an accurate description of how life works with a new baby. The word 'instinctive' is being used wrongly here and the unfortunate consequence, for this and other examples that you will hear in conversation, is that it leads us to overlook how people learn and what can help.

I offer some alternatives to consider when you are thinking about behaviour and individual differences.

- **Instinctive behaviour** is something you can do without any learning. You are born with this capacity. There are few genuine biological instincts in humans. Babies are born with a number of instinctive physical reflexes. Some reactions, such as the physiological reactions to fear (fight or flight), remain with us throughout life.
- **Automatic behaviour** is something you do without thinking. There will be some actions that you have learned so well that you no longer have to think, 'First I.., then I...' Or else you have modelled your behaviour on someone else and the reaction seems the obvious way to behave.
- Behaviour that feels **natural** is something that comes more easily to you than perhaps to friends or colleagues. Some people are said to be 'natural listeners'. A combination of experience and temperament have suited them to be good listeners but other people can learn to listen.

Biological theories – in summary

- The maturational approach to child development stimulated a tremendous interest in the detail of what children did. This continuing fascination can be seen in current research by psychologists from a wide variety of theoretical backgrounds.

- The focus on children's normal development has been very useful in some ways, especially since some other approaches focus on development more as a catalogue of what can go wrong. However, the original concepts of the 'normal' child or development did not really allow for the great variety within child development. The idea of a 'universal child' has been roundly criticised since the 1980s, at the same time as far greater awareness has grown of cultural variations in child rearing and development, as well as common themes.

- A rigid view of normal development can undoubtedly worry parents and other carers when children's development or behaviour lies outside the normal boundaries. Developmental norms are often of limited use for guidance with children who have learning and physical disabilities. Research and practice development for children with special needs since the 1970s has led to a developmental focus and assessment procedures with a positive emphasis.

- The maturational approach told parents that they were not personally responsible for every hiccup in their child's development. This removal of blame could be a relief. On the other hand, if development unfolded whatever adults did, the maturational approach did not generate ideas of how parents could help beyond sitting out a phase like tantrums. Practical help about what to do has emerged far more from the behavioural and learning approaches to development.

TO THINK ABOUT

The day that I was writing this section there were reports in the media that a team at Great Ormond Street Hospital, London, had discovered a link between anorexia, the eating disorder, and an abnormality in the brain. The details of this finding illustrate rather well how a biological basis to behaviour and development may work.

In a small study, researchers found that anorexic children and young people often had reduced blood flow in the part of the brain that controls visual perception (what you see and the sense you make of it), appetite and a feeling of fullness. The findings point to a possible physical cause why young people who are already dangerously thin remain convinced that they are overweight; they genuinely see themselves as fat. However, as the research team pointed out, this possible biological cause leads to the **potential** to be anorexic, not an absolute certainty. Social and personal factors would tip the balance: a society that admired thinness, a child or young person who strives for very high standards and a time of stress. Biology is not destiny but it may make you vulnerable in some ways.

Theories of learning through behaviour

Learning theorists focus on what children, or anyone else, learns through experience and the consequences of behaviour. So this approach is sometimes called behaviourism. In basic terms behaviour is understood to change following patterns of reward and punishment. The extreme behaviourist stance, which few theorists take now, is that newborn babies start with biological reflexes (nature) but that everything else is then learned (nurture).

The principles of learning theory were first explored in work with animals by Ivan Pavlov and B.F. Skinner. The simple, rather mechanical-sounding explanations of that early work do not make much sense when applied straight to humans and current learning theories are considerably more sophisticated. But it is useful to understand the basics as well as the later extensions of learning theory.

Learning through conditioning

Classical conditioning occurs when a new signal or stimulus brings out an existing behavioural response. A simple example would be that, if you stroke a young baby gently on the cheek, she will automatically turn and begin to suck. She does not have to learn to turn and suck. It is an automatic reflex with which babies are born – and a very useful one if you are trying to get a distracted or lethargic baby to feed. Classical conditioning involves an involuntary response – the response is not chosen, but is an in-built physical reaction.

In classical conditioning terms, the touch on the baby's cheek is the **unconditioned stimulus** and the turning and sucking is the **unconditioned response** ('unconditioned' because the baby does not have to learn either of these). Now, other events (stimuli) can become associated with the unconditioned stimulus of touch. For instance, perhaps the mother talks gently as she picks the baby up for a feed or some babies seem to recognise the mother's familiar smell and the baby starts to turn and try to suck without the touch on the cheek. The sound of mother's words or her body smell have become a **conditioned stimulus** and the sucking is now a **conditioned response** to learned patterns.

TO THINK ABOUT

Classical conditioning makes sense as a process of learning in some instances, especially when feelings and senses are involved as associations are built up for children. People and places can become associated at the most basic, and non-rational way, with both pleasant and unpleasant events for children. These reactions are very personal and can last a long time.

For instance, my stomach still churns in reaction to a distinctive smell of institutional cooking, because it brings back an unhappy memory of being forced to eat what I viewed as a disgusting school dinner at the age of five. On the other hand, the smell of coal dust has positive associations for me, because it triggers happy memories of playing in my grandparents' garden in a Welsh mining village.

Think for a while and you will almost certainly come up with similar personal associations.

The second type of learning is called **instrumental conditioning** or sometimes **operant conditioning**. This process involves linking a new response to an existing stimulus (as opposed to classical conditioning that links an existing response to a new stimulus). The change is achieved through the principles of **reinforcement**. Any behaviour (response) that is reinforced is likely to be repeated in the same or similar situation in which the reinforcement (stimulus) previously happened. In contrast with classical conditioning, instrumental conditioning involves a deliberate action as response.

A **positive reinforcement** is anything that, when it follows behaviour, increases the likelihood that the behaviour will be repeated in that situation. Positive reinforcement might be tangible rewards but, with children, is just as likely to be a smile or hug and encouraging words. **Negative reinforcement** is an unpleasant event that, when it stops, the cessation acts to increase a particular behaviour. Parents, or other carers, usually find that picking up a crying baby will soothe the cries. So parents are more likely to pick a baby up next time he cries. In ordinary life, there is often a pattern of **partial reinforcement** – not every instance of the particular action is reinforced. (More about reinforcement on page 145.)

Social learning theory

Explanations of children's learning do not work well if they depend entirely on classical and operant conditioning and only a few behaviourists still follow that path. Albert Bandura has been very influential in developing his theory of social learning which provides explanations with greater flexibility and which make more sense when applied to the complex lives of children. Bandura introduced important additional themes to learning through conditioning: learning through modelling (adults showing what is wanted by their behaviour), the importance of internal feelings of reinforcement and the link between thinking and observational learning. (More on these in chapter 5, page 118.)

Learning theories – in summary

- An explanation of children's development based entirely on learning through conditioning is neither convincing nor useful. So, it is important to understand that current learning theory (or a behavioural approach) is far more sophisticated than those early ideas derived from animal studies.
- However, some of the 'hard-line' applications of behaviourism to child care still exert an impact. John Watson's firm ideas about the importance of training children and avoiding softer feelings for the good of the child still echo in claims that babies are spoiled by picking them up.
- Perhaps the most useful focus brought by a behavioural learning approach has been an emphasis on what children do and what happens around them, rather than working from guesses about children's mental state and feelings. A focus on behaviour does not have to deny feelings but can be helpful in making sense of patterns in children's behaviour and adults' reactions.
- Learning theory, even Bandura's social cognitive theory, is not an approach which provides a clear sense of development, of how children change over the years. However, the focus on practicalities and the here and now has proved attractive for people developing programmes of learning for children, step-by-step programmes for children with disabilities or plans for guiding children's behaviour.

TO THINK ABOUT

An important practical application from social learning theory is that rewards or punishments are personally experienced. So adults involved with children need to make an effort to view a situation from the child's perspective. The adults' view of reward or punishment is not always the same as the children's.

Adults can be puzzled when children continue in patterns of behaviour that, from the adults' point of view are being punished. For instance, a child who seeks immediate attention by throwing toys or shouting may experience adults who tell her off at some length. The adults judge that they are dissuading her from being so 'demanding' but, from the child's point of view, her behaviour was successful (reinforced); she got the full attention of the adult. Children who have little experience of pleasant adult attention may act so as to attract reprimand and anger.

The same theme, in a different example, was highlighted for me in conversations with older children about reward systems for good behaviour in primary school. Some children disliked having their name read out as 'best behaved child of the week' or similar descriptions. Some children enjoyed public praise but others found it embarrassing and, especially for some of the boys, a threat to their playground credibility. What was supposed to reinforce good behaviour was operating more like a punishment. The conclusion of this example is not that adults should avoid celebrating behaviour they want to encourage, but that they should consult children in order to understand what they find genuinely rewarding!

- Can you think of examples from your work or personal experience that highlight unexpected patterns of reward and punishment?

Psychodynamic theories

The psychodynamic tradition started with Sigmund Freud, which is the reason you may hear this approach described as 'Freudian' (not an accurate term since this group of theories includes many people who have disagreed with Freud). The theory was also linked with Freud's development of a form of therapy called psychoanalysis, which is the reason this group of theories is sometimes called psychoanalytic. Psychodynamic theories explain development as the result of children's struggles to resolve the conflicts arising during different stages of their development. Inadequately resolved conflicts can leave a lasting impact that shapes later development.

Freud believed that energy from the libido (an unconscious sexual drive) was the force behind most human behaviour. He outlined a theory of stages in children's development in which the libido exerted most impact in the part of a child's body that was most sensitive at that age. Freud proposed five psychosexual stages:

- From birth to one year was the **oral** stage, in which sensation was focused on the mouth, lips and tongue. Feeding and later weaning are important aspects of the baby's life.
- From one to three years was the **anal** stage, in which sensation was focused around the child's anus and toilet training features largely in a child's life.
- From three to five years was the **phallic** stage when children's interest and sensations focused on their genitals. During this period Freud believed that children resolved jealousy of their opposite-sex parent and reached a sense of identification with the same-sex parent.

- The period from five to twelve years was called the **latency** period by Freud, because he believed that sexual interest and energy was quiet during these years.
- During the years from twelve to about eighteen children and young people are in the **genital** stage, when sexual energy awakens and a mature sexual identity develops.

Freud believed that, at each stage, children needed sufficient stimulation for the area of their body in which key sensations were focused, but that over- or under-stimulation led individuals to become fixated (stuck at particular stages in a way that distorted their development).

A central part of psychodynamic theory is the assumption that behaviour is influenced by unconscious thoughts and feelings as well as conscious processes. Some material in our unconscious can rise to full awareness if we are prepared to explore the possibility either in personal introspection or through therapy. A further development in Freud's theory was that anxiety gives rise to conflict which children and later adults manage through a range of defence mechanisms. These forms of self-protection work at the unconscious level. Freud regarded them as completely normal and not problematic unless they led to a serious distortion of reality. The defence mechanisms have entered much of ordinary conversation and include:

- *suppression* – an unhappy experience or uncomfortable dilemma is pushed to the back of your mind for a while;
- *repression* – experiences that arouse anxiety are pushed even further into the unconscious and may remain almost forgotten for some time;
- *denial* – someone claims that a troubling experience did not touch them emotionally or, in extreme forms, did not actually happen;
- *projection* – dealing with troubling emotions by pushing them on to another person, that s/he is the one who is worried or unable to cope;
- *intellectualisation* – someone considers an upsetting experience in rational terms but loses all the feelings.

Although Freud emphasised the importance of the sexual drive, he also created a focus, that continues in many psychodynamic theories, on the interaction between children and their environment, between them and the people and objects they encounter. Subsequent developers of the psychodynamic tradition took different directions from Freud, sometimes disagreeing with his sexual emphasis.

Erik Erikson proposed a series of **psychosocial stages**, moving away from Freud's emphasis on the sexual. Other theorists have also challenged a view of children as sexual beings. (The confusion between seeing sexuality in young children, rather than a need for physical closeness and intimacy, continues to provoke difficulties, for instance, in the area of child protection.)

Erikson saw children as experiencing a sequence of developmental tasks that were influenced by the culture in which the children were raised. Children's future development was shaped by the extent to which they had resolved conflicts such as the one between trust and mistrust, which he said was experienced during the first year of life. Some wariness is healthy for a child but too great a mistrust could negatively affect how a child reacted to later experiences. Erikson proposed eight stages in total which stretch into middle adulthood. Unlike Freud, Erikson believed that individuals continued to develop their sense of identity well beyond the end of childhood. (More about Erikson's ideas on page 141.)

Alfred Adler placed a strong emphasis on the dynamics of the family and children's experiences of birth order determining their individual roles. Later theorists in the Adlerian tradition have explored children's emotional needs and how they may relate to behaviour. Further applications to child care and education have been through the use of encouragement as a positive way to guide children's behaviour and distinguishing this from praise and reward.

Psychodynamic theories – in summary

- The striking contribution of psychodynamic theory has been to give a role to unconscious feelings and thoughts; that everything is not described by what we observe on the surface. This focus led the early psychodynamic theorists to be in continuous argument with the behaviourists. But both traditions have since become more varied and complex in their ideas.

- The importance of feelings (children's and parents') was in striking contrast to the fierce training approaches to child care that emerged from the early behaviourists. Benjamin Spock was very influenced by Freud and his best-selling *Baby and Child Care* (over 24 million copies sold!) brought psychodynamic theory into ordinary homes from the 1940s.

- Many psychodynamic theorists and psychotherapists have studied adults and children who are in some way experiencing problems. The belief is that normal development can be better understood from the analysis of what goes wrong. The approach has sometimes led to a depressing view of childhood and family life as a minefield of problems. Some stages, for instance that of adolescence, have been presented as considerably more fraught than is the experience of many families.

- Theorists and practitioners in the psychodynamic tradition contributed an emphasis on the overwhelming importance of the early years. They have exerted a lasting impact on approaches to attachment and the central importance of mothers to young children. The details of some of the claims have been challenged but the importance of what happens to children remains (see also page 40).
- Some of the ideas of psychodynamic theory (such as repression or the existence of infantile anxieties stretching into adulthood) are unable to be proved one way or another – a disadvantage for a good theory. However, some of the suggestions, for instance, those of defence mechanisms make sense from experience and can be useful.

Cognitive theories

The **cognitive developmental** theories emphasise how children think and make sense of their world. They place considerable emphasis on children's experiences with play materials, the evidence of their senses and how they then think about the experience. There was initially much less emphasis on the emotional side to child development or on social relationships with adults or other children. But now many current cognitive theories have considerably more social emphasis.

The cognitive approach to child development was established by Jean Piaget who studied what children of different ages did when faced with a range of situations. He built his theory originally from case studies of his own three children. Piaget proposed that all children pass through the same distinct stages, and sequences within the broad stages, although not necessarily at exactly the same age. Stage theories are hierarchical in that later stages take over from the development of the earlier ones. Once a child moves on to a later stage there is no return, since his/her ways of thinking about the world have changed in a qualitative way. The change in ways of thinking has brought about a permanent change in how children behave.

Piaget had a substantial impact on views of child development but only a minority of psychologists now accept his theory as originally proposed. Lev Vygotsky disagreed with Piaget's view that children were essentially egocentric (only able to see the world from their own perspective). Vygotsky placed more emphasis on children's early language as a social tool. Jerome Bruner was one of the early critics of Piaget in the English-speaking world. Bruner believed that development could be accelerated and adults take a more active role in children's learning. Some theorists have developed different sets of stages, for instance Lawrence Kohlberg extended the Piagetian view to the development of moral thinking and judgements.

Margaret Donaldson and her research team at Edinburgh (now spread in other universities) challenged many of Piaget's claims about what young children do not understand. Donaldson stressed the importance of the context in which children are learning or being asked questions by adults. The constructivist movement accepts the view of children as creating their own learning and the role of adults as enablers in that learning, whilst rejecting the idea that development unfolds through stages.

I have not given much detail here on the cognitive theories since you will find extensive discussion of the ideas in several chapters of the book: the development of thinking in chapter 3, cognitive theories and language in chapter 4 and moral development in chapter 6.

Cognitive theories – in summary

- The power of the cognitive tradition has been to make adults aware of the complexity of children's thinking and of the qualitatively different perspective of young children from older ones and the adult world. Children are not simply smaller, less efficient adults.
- Research by cognitive theorists has continued to illuminate the details of children's understanding and often has practical applications for an effective role for adults, for instance, in schooling.
- Cognitive theorists focus on infants and children as active in their own learning, working to make sense of, to explore and control their world. Disagreements between theorists arise over the appropriate role of adults in supporting children's learning (see page 122 for discussion of this topic.)
- The cognitive tradition has influenced much of educational practice in Britain through the concepts of being child-centred, of a focus on children's readiness to learn and on learning through play exploration. The constructivist position has been especially influential in early years.

An ecological approach

At least some theorists from all the different traditions now emphasise the social or cultural context in which children learn. Children used to be studied as if it was irrelevant where and how they lived, or even the context in which they were observed or asked questions. Relationships within the family might be considered, but much research focused on mothers and children only. Consideration of broader social factors tended to be basic measures of social class or family poverty. But studies would not necessarily consider what these labels meant for children and family life.

Urie Bronfenbrenner has been one of the most prominent psychologists to address specifically the relevance of children's social environment through his approach of the ecology of human development. Bronfenbrenner worked to describe the impact of children's environment, without downplaying the uniqueness of individual children. Instead of treating the environment as a

single whole, Bronfenbrenner has distinguished the different aspects that influenced children in more and less direct ways (more from page 166).

The emphasis on environment in the ecological approach has encouraged an awareness of different settings and how children's experiences can shape their development. Some developments in the work consider especially the impact of cultural differences on the patterns of children's development. The ecological approach is a reminder that children do not develop in isolation and is an important balance to theories that home in on the individual child. One advantage of the ecological approach is the attempt to grapple with parts of the social system that affect children but not directly, such as economic policy, the dominant culture or the demands of the world of work. But as a consequence, some of the other approaches to child development offer more guidance in daily relationships with children.

1.5 The study of children's development

Different kinds of knowledge about children

In early years work, as in many practically-based professions, knowledge is gained from two main sources:

- *Evidence* is gathered from the systematic use of the scientific method, which should be applied objectively and produce unbiased results.
- *Wisdom* is gained through the essentially subjective and changing practice of applying what seems to work.

Either type of knowledge can be of limited value on its own.

Scientific knowledge which is uninformed by the wisdom of practitioners can appear divorced from everyday situations and real dilemmas. Indeed, some researchers may wish to step completely aside from considering any practical application of their studies. Research, especially social and psychological research, is often not as objective as people would wish to believe. However, well-planned research, when researchers take care to examine their assumptions, can test the 'everybody knows' statements about children and early years work that otherwise will continue unchallenged.

On the other hand, wisdom gained through experience, direct or from that of other people, needs to be responsive to scientific findings, otherwise practice can stagnate. Wisdom that is not accountable to any objective evaluation may be misdirected. Claims that 'this is true of children and families' or that 'this is the best and right way to work with young children' can persist with no check on the reasons for beliefs or the support for claims. Experienced practitioners can share the wisdom they have gained, but this will only be really effective when they have reflected on the reasons for what they do and can share those as well as the details of practice.

Understanding research

Objective scientific enquiry has not always been viewed as an appropriate source of information and guidance for early years practitioners. Received wisdom, not necessarily explained, from experienced practitioners used to be the main way of gaining knowledge. In recent decades, the lessons of research have been expected to inform practice. But, for research to be of genuine use, you need to know not only *what* results emerged from the study but *how* they were obtained.

Objectivity in research

Five qualities of well-organised research were identified by Rudolph Schaffer.

Empirical
The conclusions of the research are based on direct observation and not on a hunch or the approach of 'everybody knows that...'. Sometimes you may encounter research studies in which conclusions are only partly based on direct observation. Perhaps a writer can report some current observations of young children's play but then continues to contrast what this generation of children do in play with how the previous generation spent their time. The basis for this historical contrast is nothing but the writer's own childhood memories and convictions about what children used to do.

Systematic
The data are collected according to a clear plan, which is the research design, and this plan is explained in the research report. Such a plan should be followed consistently by an entire research team, so that methods are not altered at individual whim.

Controlled
Good research is designed so that explanations or patterns of cause and effect can be deduced as reliably as possible. For instance, children who experience a hospital stay early in life are compared with children who have not, but who are as similar as possible in all other respects.

Quantitative
Descriptive information can be very useful as can case studies which recount in detail individual experiences or sequences of events (qualitative research). But, much research is an attempt to describe data in a numerical way (quantitative) so that statistical comparisons give a sound basis for concluding that one group is different from another.

Public
All the details of methods and findings of a piece of research should be open to scrutiny. Only then can one make sense of comparisons between this piece of research and another, or consider to what extent the conclusions of the study could fairly be generalised to other groups and settings.

Normal problems in research

Careful attention to the above features makes research more objective. But social and psychological research cannot be the same as research in the physical sciences. The rich variety in people, not to mention ethical considerations, makes this impossible.

Limited ability to control
It is not possible to control all possible sources of variation and good research has to recognise any difficulties. For instance, researchers interested in the effects of different types of pre-school experience do not have, nor should they have, the right to direct families to types of early years settings, according to how it suits the research project. Families will have their own reasons for choosing or avoiding different settings and researchers have to attempt to assess how this variation may create groups that are different at the outset.

The social setting of research
Results may be specific to the particular time and place of the research. Children and their families live within a social and cultural context and findings within one culture, or a particular decade, may not be directly applicable elsewhere, although perhaps still of interest. For instance, study of the separation of young children from their families because of hospitalisation only makes sense with an understanding of hospital practices of that time (see the discussion on page 185).

Assumptions in the research
As much as social scientists believe themselves to be objective, they are all influenced to a greater or lesser extent by the social and political climate of the time. For instance, more than one topic of research has been shaped by prevailing beliefs in society. Rudolph Schaffer points out how the first work

on children and the effects of divorce was started when social attitudes towards divorce were hostile. The investigation plans of this early research focused almost exclusively on finding negative effects. A similar pattern was followed in the early research into day care (see also page 187). The questions being asked were not framed to explore the effects on children of divorce, or day care, in an objective and even-handed way but to identify and quantify negative effects which were believed to be inevitable.

Methods shape results

Different research methods will highlight different aspects of a topic and studies which use only one main method may lead to different conclusions from each other. A case study approach (with a great deal of detail about one individual, family or setting) will lead to different results from a large-scale survey (when many people are asked to reply to the same set of questions). An investigation of families who choose to seek help through counselling will be working with a different group of people from researchers who contact families from school lists.

Short- or long-term research

A further issue is the extent to which the research is focusing on immediate effects or the extent to which longer-term follow-up is included in the budget. For example, there were many studies in the 1960s and 70s of pre-school programmes for children who were judged to be socially disadvantaged. Researchers often relied on measures of IQ and a disappointing pattern emerged of temporary boosts to children's scores which faded within the early years of school. However, more detailed and long-term research, especially on the high quality programmes, has shown long-term positive effects as the children have grown towards young adulthood. (See page 132 for more details on this research.)

Applications of research to practice

Researchers and practitioners have a different focus and it is appropriate that they do. Researchers tend to be interested in extending knowledge on a topic. Practitioners are more interested in guidance on what is the best approach under particular circumstances and generally 'what should we do?' Some researchers are far more interested in the practical applications of their work than others.

In this book, you will find many references to research findings as well as to theories and to useful ideas, which may or may not have supporting research. I started my career as a child psychologist by working full-time as a researcher, so I have a blend of respect for and scepticism about research. I believe that this is a sensible combination. Research can be of immense help and you will read of many examples in this book where carefully conducted research has opened our eyes to what children can do or how we can best support them. But the lessons of research and the ideas generated by theories must be seasoned with wisdom. Questions need to be asked, such as 'Really?', 'Does this apply to everyone?' and my favourite question, 'So what?' (which does not have to sound as confrontational as it looks on paper).

In well-balanced research there will often be 'ifs and buts' in the interpretation and conclusions. For social and psychological topics, single cause-and-effect relationships are rare. The more usual pattern is of multiple causes and of trying to establish how significant one factor may be over another or how two factors work together to influence the outcome. To quote Rudolph Schaffer: '...care needs to be taken about making sweeping generalizations and advancing global solutions. "It all depends" may be an annoying phrase and it does not make good headlines, but it accurately reflects reality.' (*Making Decisions About Children: Psychological questions and answers,* page 235.)

Research does not offer a clear-cut answer to all the concerns and questions that arise in the care and education of children. Studies take time to plan, write up and publicise and children cannot be put on hold to wait for evidence to emerge. Research findings are often of patterns and group trends, whereas practitioners need to make decisions about individual children. Yet studies of groups of children can be very useful if you are careful about generalisations – from a group to individuals or the other way from an individual to groups.

The need for caution – research into Sudden Infant Death Syndrome

During the 1970s and 1980s, parents were told that lying babies on their back put them at risk of choking and that the safest position was on their stomachs or their side. This firm advice was based on research with premature babies which was then, with no further research justification, generalised to care of full-term babies.

By the 1990s, further research identified the stomach sleeping position as a risk factor in Sudden Infant Death Syndrome (cot death). The advice to parents was reversed and the level of unexplained infant deaths dropped significantly. Careful tracking of the level of unexplained infant deaths before and after the change of advice (to lay children on their backs) showed that this change in behaviour by parents had reduced the level of unexplained infant deaths. There was no other obvious reason for the improvement.

This topic is a good example to understand because it raises several key issues about research and practice:

- The change in advice is a sober warning about the possible risks of generalising too widely from small-scale research findings.
- But the link between sleeping position and risk of cot death is not a matter of absolute cause and effect. Many parents, who followed the advice of the 1980s to lie their babies on their stomachs or sides, did not face the tragedy of losing their baby.
- Sleeping position was a significant risk factor but research continues to look at other factors, such as smoking in the family home.

The Foundation for the Study of Infant Deaths (FSID) is a good source of up-to-date information and advice on this important practical area. You can contact them at 14 Halkin Street, London SW1X 7DP, tel: 0171 235 0965.

Caution in generalising – the example of diet

Advice on a healthy diet has become progressively more confusing as small-scale research projects seem to suggest that this food is beneficial or that another food has risks to health. An important issue for any early years workers, or parents, is that even reasonable advice suitable for a healthy adult diet cannot simply be transferred to diets for infants and young children.

Research into diet for children is demonstrating that they are not small versions of adults. Children's diets have to fuel their growing as well as maintain health. But children also appear to have different nutritional requirements from adults because their bodies work differently. For instance, low-fat, high-fibre diets are not suitable for the very young. Babies and children need three to four times as many calories per day in proportion to their body size, in comparison with adults. Low fat adult diets are unhealthy for children because they need the fat content, for instance from milk. Children can be missing vital nutrients and be malnourished amidst plenty of food. Children's bodies seem to be designed to use fat more efficiently than adults, but children are not yet well equipped to process fibre. Excess fibre can also interfere with their body's absorption of zinc and iron.

So, caution is needed in weighing up research evidence. In many ways, children are not simply small adults and the same guidelines do not work for them.

Different ways of studying children

A considerable amount of research has been undertaken with children and their families and many different approaches have been used. These are some of the different types of study.

Longitudinal studies

In a **longitudinal design** the same children are studied over a period of time. Perhaps a small number of children are observed at regular intervals in their early childhood, or one child is tracked in a detailed case study. A large-scale study might include all the babies born within a particular week and follow them over a matter of years, perhaps even into early adulthood. An example is the large group followed in the National Children's Bureau Child Development Study. Or a group of children may be followed who are expected to be at risk and their life experience is tracked.

Cross-sectional studies

A **cross-sectional** design allows you to study different ages without waiting for children to grow up. Researchers might select groups of four-, eight-, twelve- and sixteen-year-olds and study them as examples of that age grouping. Research into children's moral development has, for instance, studied how children of different ages are able to reason about a moral dilemma (see page 152).

Cross-cultural research

Cross-cultural or **cross-context designs** are an attempt to deal with the problem of generalising from one group of children to another who may live in a different social and cultural setting. Children are studied from more than one

social class, culture or country. Studies of Piaget's ideas of conservation (see page 63) have been undertaken in different countries, as well as with different age groups of children.

Experimental studies

Experimental designs are an attempt to control some of the many factors in the variety of children's lives. Such studies might be carried out in a research laboratory or in a natural setting, such as a nursery. One group of children (the experimental group) might be given a particular experience and the impact on their behaviour or learning would be studied. A second group (the control group) would not be given this experience and they would be the check that findings for the experimental group could reasonably be explained by their extra experience.

Some research takes place in a psychological laboratory – for children this is usually an ordinary looking play room with video and a one-way mirror. This method is an attempt to simplify the situation to make observation more possible and to avoid some of the normal interruptions of study in a family home or nursery. The research into early communication abilities of babies is an example of this kind of focused observation.

Some experiments take advantage of naturally occurring differences, such as the choice in child care made by parents and then study the different groupings. These studies are called a quasi experimental design.

Narrative studies

Narrative and **ethnographic research** has become another strand in the study of children. The approach is more subjective in that the researcher records events and experiences as they unfold. The researcher may even be a part of those events and is making a choice of what to record as well as making sense of a wealth of information. Vivian Paley's books, based on observations of her nursery class, are an example of this kind of study. The diaries that I wrote of my own children's development are also in this category, although I wrote them as much for personal as for professional reasons.

In summary

All of the different types of design have some built-in drawbacks, as well as advantages. The question is always 'How safely and how far can you generalise from the findings of any study?'

- Longitudinal designs have the advantage of showing continuities in the lives of the same children and some patterns. But studies over a long period of time may encounter the problem that society has changed since the study began, so how far can the lessons of this research be applied now.
- Small studies and case studies of individuals or places may provide rich detail but have to be approached cautiously because not all children, or all families, will necessarily behave like the ones in the study. Any study has to address the problem of how typical are the children and families in the research.
- Studies have to be honest about the possible limitations to their findings. Study of children from a range of social or cultural groups can highlight the common factors as well as the differences. But a good cross-cultural study can be hard to plan. It may not make sense to ask the same questions in a different setting and assumptions that are valid in one cultural setting may be inappropriate elsewhere.
- Controlled, or partly controlled experiments have the advantage of being more able to produce objective findings but this can be at the cost of authenticity. Real life is more complex and may be better reflected sometimes by a narrative approach, so long as the researcher recognises the limitations of this design.
- Study of children and child development is likely to be best served through a diversity of research designs and methods. The other chapters of this book draw from a wide range of studies, as well as theories and ideas about children. In chapter 8 you will find a discussion of research from the perspective of your own studies.

Reading on . . .

★ Hardyment, Christina 1995: *Perfect Parents: Baby care advice past and present* (Oxford paperbacks). A survey of the advice given to parents over a couple of centuries, with insights into how theories make their way into practical advice books.

★ Karmiloff-Smith, Annette 1994: *Baby It's You: A unique insight into the first three years of the developing baby* (Ebury Press). Descriptions of early childhood, brought alive by following through individual children. A double video set is available titled *Baby It's You*, with the six programmes of the Channel Four series which the book accompanied.

★ Lindon, Jennie 1993: *Child Development from Birth to Eight: A practical focus* (National Children's Bureau). Description of the events in different areas of child development and some of the issues that arise in making sense of what is happening.

★ Lindon, Jennie 'Childhood and adolescence', in Aitken, V. and Jellicoe, H. (eds) 1996: *Behavioural Sciences for Health Professionals* (W.B.Saunders). Some highlights of child development with special emphasis on children and health services.

★ Paley, Vivian 1992: *You Can't Say You Can't Play* (Harvard University Press). One of several books in which Paley explores aspects of her nursery classroom in America. She combines description and reflections on her practice.

★ Salkind, Neil 1985: *Theories of Human Development* (John Wiley). A useful summary of different theories, presented in an even-handed way.

★ Schaffer, H. Rudolph 1990: *Making Decisions About Children: Psychological questions and answers* (Basil Blackwell). A practical approach to research and an honest reflection on pressures away from objectivity for researchers. Schaffer addresses a series of questions often asked about children and families and works through what research can offer by way of an answer.

★ Sylva, Kathy 1995: *Research as a Medieval Banquet – Barons, troubadours and minstrels* (Paper presented at the RSA 'Start Right' conference, London). A discussion of the main research methods used to study children and early years settings and of the contribution of each.

★ Sugarman, Leonie 1986: *Life Span Development: Concepts, theories and interventions* (London: Routledge). Discussion of the theory and findings in the life-span approach.

2 Children's social and emotional development

This chapter covers:

- the development of attachment;
- personal development;
- children's relationships;
- emotional development.

2.1 The development of attachment

Attachment is a central idea in any discussion of children's social development. Unless children develop the ability to form attachments, they cannot develop relationships with adults or other children. Unless parents, or parental figures, develop a close attachment to babies and young children, the care and well being of those children is likely to be jeopardised.

Attachment is a positive emotional link between two people – a link of affection. A sense of attachment can be felt by parents for their child and vice versa. You cannot observe attachment because the link is one of internal feelings. But, you would judge that a child was strongly attached to her parent by observing **attachment behaviours**, for example, that the child was pleased to see her parent and wanted to be close, especially in times of stress, and resisted being separated.

Parents' attachment to their child

There are two parts to the development of a parent's attachment to an infant:

- A first bond may be formed in the period immediately after birth so long as the mother, and father, are able to have this very early contact with the child.
- A second part of attachment, and probably the more important one, is continued opportunities during the early months of a baby's life for a parent to get to know this infant. Strong attachments are established through enjoyable play and communication exchanges and through the pattern of care giving routines.

The concept of bonding

Studies of some mammals have shown that, if animal mothers are denied close physical contact with their young in the hours following birth, those mothers reject their babies and the harm cannot be reversed. The animal studies led two American paediatricians, Marshall Klaus and John Kennell, to propose that equivalent dangers would follow if a similar critical period for bonding between human mothers and infants were interrupted.

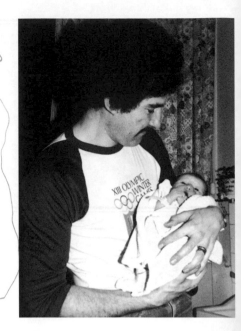

Klaus and Kennell proposed that the first hours, or at most the first few days, were crucial for mothers to develop a bond with their newborn, mainly through close physical contact. They proposed that the hormonal readiness of mothers made this a critical time that could not be recaptured at a later date.

Klaus and Kennell's initial research suggested that mothers who were given more contact with their baby after birth than was usual hospital practice at the time (the first half of the 1970s) emerged as more caring and sensitive mothers on measures taken up to five years later.

Strictly speaking, the word **bonding** refers only to the development of a mother's firm attachment to her baby in the first days after birth. The word is used with this meaning in this section. However, 'bonding' is often used in the more general sense of attachment between parents and very young children.

Changes in hospital practice

The practical recommendations from Klaus and Kennell's research were a radical turn-around of hospital procedure. The importance of the developing relationship between mother and baby became a factor in determining hospital procedure, rather than simply the convenience to the hospital of certain care systems. Changes did not happen overnight and some hospital staff were very resistant. But, steadily, it became more usual that mothers were given the opportunity to hold their baby immediately after birth, rather than having the infant taken away to be cleaned up, weighed and given basic developmental tests. All these important procedures still happened but with less rush. It also became more usual that mothers had their infants in cots beside their hospital bed rather than the babies being removed to a nursery.

Another practical impact of the research was that medical and other caring professions were concerned that bonding should take place. Later difficulties between mother and child were often explained by 'inadequate bonding' in the first few days. When I first starting working with day nurseries, I heard a wide range of problems being explained by lack of bonding. Sometimes, staff were asked to invite mothers in with their young children to ensure that bonding happened, even if belatedly.

Further research on bonding

Other researchers could not confirm Klaus and Kennell's findings or, therefore, their original theory. Following further research, Klaus and Kennell stopped talking about bonding as a strictly time-bound event.

- The process of attachment between human mothers and their infants does not seem to have a critical period in which lack of contact is very disruptive.
- 'Bonding failure' alone has not stood up as an explanation of difficulties in parenting or as a clear-cut explanation of later child abuse.
- Similarly, there seems to be no support for what Rudolph Schaffer ironically calls the 'super glue' interpretation of bonding, namely that the bonding event is a single happening which then ensures attachment and prevents later troubles in the relationship.
- Research suggests that encouraging close mother-baby contact in the early days may help those mothers most at risk of providing poor parenting, but probably only if there is also support in later months.
- A more accurate approach is to see attachment between mother and child as a process that can start during the first hours but which continues.

Fortunately for parents, the significant changes in hospital procedure have not been reversed. A calm post-birth environment and a chance to get to know their baby have been a source of pleasure to many mothers and fathers. The view of bonding as a definite, very early event has persevered with some professionals and you need to be cautious about this idea. It is usually misleading to explain later difficulties between parent and child largely through 'lack of bonding', although an unhappy first few days may not help relationships to start well. Yet it is likely that other difficulties will have continued to undermine the developing parent and child relationship. It may be more straightforward to tackle these difficulties than regret the loss of an elusive bonding time.

The research on bonding is a useful reminder that animal studies may be interesting, but human experience seems on the whole to be different from that of animals.

- A **critical period** in development is a short period of time at which specific experiences have quite different or much stronger effects than at other times. Although some animals experience critical periods in development, there are very few genuine critical periods in human development. One example is the limited period of time within the first three months of pregnancy when the rubella virus (German measles) can damage the foetus.
- A more accurate term for human development is the idea of **sensitive periods.** There seem to be stretches of months, or even years, when children are especially responsive to certain kinds of experience and affected by their absence.

SUGGESTED ACTIVITY

The topic of bonding is a good example of research that makes most sense when you see it in the context of recent social history. You will then understand better why the ideas and the changes in hospital procedure were so radical. Here are three possible activities from which to chose:

- Talk with a number of women who gave birth to their babies in hospital during the 1970s. Contrast the experiences with women who have given birth from the 1980s onwards. Explain carefully your reasons for the conversation since you are asking about a very personal experience. Obviously, you have to be cautious in generalising from a small number of experiences, but it is likely that you will gain a sense of the changes in labour and maternity ward practices.
- Contact the National Childbirth Trust with a view to talking with one of their counsellors who can provide a perspective stretching back to the 1970s. The NCT's head office is at Alexandra House, Oldham Terrace, London W3 6HN, tel: 0181 992 8637.
- Look out for books written by Sheila Kitzinger published in the 1970s or early 1980s, for instance, *The Good Birth Guide* which reviewed the practices of different hospitals.

The developing attachment of parent to child

The early days of a baby's life are not irrelevant, but the first few months appear to be far more important for parents to develop their sense of attachment to their child. Time spent together is crucial for a parent to tune into a baby's non-verbal signals and to feel that a personal relationship is growing through smiles, gurgles, long stares and then the pre-verbal exchanges of sounds between parent and child.

Research using video has shown how babies in the first months are copying the expressions on a parent's face and becoming active participants in an exchange with sound-making, expressions and pauses for the other to reply. Not all parent and baby exchanges are calm and communicative – babies are sometimes fretful and parents are very tired. Research has also tended to focus on the mother–baby pair, excluding the more complex interactions in many families with other adults and siblings. Judy Dunn's observational research has been especially useful in documenting the full richness of daily family life as it unfolds at home.

There is a growing body of research on fathers, although the majority of work still focuses on mothers. Fathers can and do form strong attachments to their young children. The pattern of their attachment behaviour seems to vary and fathers in some studies were engaging in more physical play than care giving. However, it is difficult to distinguish the kind of attention given to a baby from the role of parent as primary caregiver or not. Some fathers in the primary caregiver role seem to behave more like mothers, on average, and some do not. Until there are many more fathers spending as much time with young children as many mothers do, it will be difficult to distinguish to what extent patterns of behaviour are shaped by being female (social and genetic influences) or by the social role of primary caretaker.

When attachment is difficult

The process of attachment between parent and child is not foolproof and some circumstances can interfere with the growing closeness. Attachment is a two-way process: parents are affected by the characteristics of their baby as much as babies respond to the attention, of lack of it, from parents. Any potential difficulties then feed into the interaction between child and parent, as each is affected by the other's pattern of behaviour.

Problems from the infants' side
Some babies may lack the early social skills that engage and reward parents. For instance:

- Babies who cry for considerable amounts of time require great patience from parents.
- Very premature babies may be less able to respond and parents may not be able to have close physical contact with sick premature babies. Many hospitals make great efforts to enable parents to spend time with and to touch their babies.
- Babies with disabilities may respond more slowly or in a different way. For example, babies with visual loss tend to smile less than sighted babies and do not hold a mutual gaze.

Problems from the parents' side
Parents may lack the skills to interact with their babies, for instance:

- If their own childhood was lacking in affectionate contact with key adults, especially if there are no supportive family members now to provide a model of close interaction with the baby.
- Women who view motherhood in terms only of their needs may see a baby as someone who will provide them with unconditional love. They may be insensitive to the baby's signals or require that the baby follows a timing that suits the parent.
- Depression, for instance post-natal, or significant stress in the family can detract from parents' abilities to give time and attention to their baby which is a vital part of building up the relationship.
- Parents' abilities and motivation may be severely impaired by alcohol or drugs – neither of which are compatible with focusing on a baby's needs.

SUGGESTED ACTIVITY

- Talk with a health visitor or other professional from a Child Health Clinic about circumstances in which babies' or parents' conditions can complicate the development of attachment.
- You might, for instance, ask about babies who cry excessively or women who experience post-natal depression.
- The medical professional should not break confidence and talk with you about individual families by name, but could explain in general terms how attachments can sometimes be more difficult.

Not all parents faced with the above circumstances fail to become attached to their babies, but the process can be harder and support may be welcome. For instance, parents of babies who cry a great deal may need encouragement to interact positively with the baby when she is happy and responsive. Worn-out and disheartened parents may miss the opportunities. Parents who have few happy childhood memories of their own can and do find the pleasure in close contact with their baby, but again some considerate suggestions or a model to watch may help.

The development of children's attachments
The nature of attachment

Young children use the people to whom they are attached as:

- a safe base from which to explore;
- a source of comfort when they are upset, uneasy or ill;
- a source of guidance and encouragement.

Attachment behaviours are those patterns of actions that keep a child in touch with another person: smiling, calling out or crying, using physical movements to get closer to the person and touching. Children are usually happy to be in the company of people to whom they are attached and unwilling, especially when very young or in a new situation, to allow them to go out of sight. In a known situation, children may be happily absorbed in play and only glance up from time to time. However, if an unknown person enters the room, or the child hurts herself, then the full attention of a parent may be immediately very important.

The influence of John Bowlby
In the period between the mid-40s to mid-70s the prevailing view on children's social development was that of John Bowlby, whose approach was influenced by psychodynamic theory (see page 21) and by the animal studies.

Bowlby's theories shaped research, policies and practical advice to families over several decades. Mothers were seen as the most crucial ingredient in young children's early life, fathers scarcely rated a mention, siblings were viewed only as rivals for mothers' attention and developing friendships with peers were ignored. The impact of separations on children was seen almost exclusively as an experience of **maternal deprivation**. This term was used to describe the temporary or permanent loss to a child of her mother's care and attention.

From the beginning, some psychologists challenged parts of Bowlby's theory and the interpretations of research undertaken by him and by Mary Ainsworth. But from the mid-70s onwards, the criticisms became more extensive and well supported by research. However, a stress on the exclusiveness of the mother-child relationship and the dangers of any separation are still part of many discussions about mothers in employment and about day care. Although research and theory has moved on, the simple tenet of 'mothers have to stay at home or they damage their children' is still widely believed. You need to understand the greater complexity of what happens in the early years. However, it is also important to appreciate some very positive changes that followed from attachment theory and research (more on this topic in chapter 7).

The first attachments

Babies are social beings. They show a desire for contact from the earliest weeks through looking, touching and later smiling. However, the desire for physical contact does not yet mean that a firm attachment has been formed to a particular person. The existence of attachment between a baby or very young child and a caring adult is usually judged by the baby's reaction to being separated from that adult.

The impact of separation was studied through hospitalisation (when allowing parents to stay with their children was unknown) or temporary separations. The research has shown consistently that it is in the third quarter of the first year, when babies are seven to eight months old, that they are visibly distressed by separation from a particular familiar adult, most often in Western culture their mother. Babies have come to know and recognise their mother; other adults, however kindly, are not an acceptable substitute. Babies vary, of course, and seven or eight months is not a fixed time for all. Some babies show protest at being separated from their mother at a younger age and some do not seem to be troubled until a little later.

At around the same time that babies are expressing their strong attachment to one or two key figures, they also express a wariness of strangers. This reaction is further evidence that babies in the second year of life have learned to distinguish familiar from unfamiliar people. The reaction to strangers varies in intensity and some babies show unease rather than fear. Much depends also on what the unknown individuals do. For instance, insistence on picking up a wary baby or removing him from his parent provokes a distressed protest from most babies or young children.

Mothers are important but...

The strong belief in a primary relationship between mother and child has been based in two assumptions derived from Freudian psychodynamic theory. Such theory claimed that young children were incapable of forming more than one important attachment, and that was to their mother. The second assumption was that young children would inevitably be confused if they had to have more than one caretaker, this confusion would weaken the primary attachment to their mother and undermine their sense of security. These statements, although firmly believed, have not been supported by research.

Babies first become able to form attachments in the second half of their first year when they can reliably distinguish other people. Research studies show that many young children within families demonstrate a strong attachment to their mother. But, there is consistent evidence that infants and very young children also develop strong attachments to others within their family, often to their father but also to siblings and other relatives. The key factor seems to be, not surprisingly, that other family members spend time to get to know the young child and to build a rapport. There is no evidence in these situations that very young children are confused, nor that family attachments to figures other than the mother were 'second best'. On the contrary children seemed well able to distinguish the objects of their attachment and to anticipate and enjoy different care and playing styles.

The cultural context

A consistent theme is that babies and young children want and need to form attachments. Research shows that mothers are extremely important to infants and young children, but that the mother-child relationship is not unique in the sense that it overshadows all others.

It has to be said that theory and argument about the exclusiveness of the mother-child relationship were based on a culturally very restricted world view. In Northern America and Europe, where much of the child development research has been undertaken, it is common for mothers to take responsibility for care of young children. However, exclusive care by mothers is not universal – far from it. Rudolph Schaffer quotes anthropological research indicating that, among human societies that have been studied, only 3% have mothers as the exclusive carers of their children and 60% as the predominant carers. Other carers are usually from the immediate family group, often females, although fathers are involved sometimes. Patterns of care involve grandmothers, aunts, other wives in polygamous societies or older siblings.

Forming several attachments

In families where others besides the mother, for instance, fathers or grandparents, share a noticeable amount of the care, babies may be happy to be left with these adults and distressed at separation from them. Research into fatherhood suggests that fathers who spend more time with their infants are likely to encourage a stronger attachment from the infants. So, not all babies have a single person to whom they are strongly attached, some have more than one. However, it is not unusual that in times of stress the baby may want one caregiver over the others. The majority of infants in the Western family pattern seem to form one intense attachment, often but not always to their mother, and then swiftly expand into other important attachments within the family or with regular caregivers.

The importance of early experience

The assumptions underlying the study of attachment were initially that there was a critical period for young children to develop attachments and consequently the ability to make relationships. This period was believed to be in the first two or three years at most and later experiences could not put

Children also make close relationships with grandparents

the damage right. The hopelessness of any later intervention seemed a reasonable claim, since it was consistent with the dominant Freudian view. Freud believed that the early years of a child's life were crucial and set the pattern for a child's personality with no chance of reversal.

Careful research has not supported this gloomy view. John Bowlby's initial studies focused on residential care and hospitalisations. But even some of his research did not support the stance that children deprived in this way commonly developed an inability to form relationships. The pattern was varied: some children seemed to be badly affected by the experience and some had overcome the negative effects, at least to some extent.

The main themes of some complicated research are that:

- Children's early experience is important, but does not appear to set the course of their later development in an irreversible manner. Children's outlook on the world, their social and intellectual development depends also on what happens after the early years, as well as how any distressing events are handled.
- Negative early experiences do not inevitably doom a child and neither do positive experiences make a child safe from later emotional damage.
- In general, single events have less impact than a continuing pattern of disruption and distress for children, which establish for those children that this is the nature of their social world.
- Research since the 1980s has focused far more on children's coping skills in the face of adversity and how children may develop resilience through learning from difficulties and being supported in the process. (More on page 190.)

2.2 Personal development

There are several themes that run through the study of children's personal development:

- **Self-concept** – that children increasingly have a sense of themselves as a separate and unique individual, although sharing some experiences and feelings in common with other people. This idea is also expressed in discussions about the development of a **personal identity**.
- **Self-esteem** – children's self-concept does not develop in a neutral way. All children develop the sense of whether they are of value, for themselves and to others in their life. Some children have relatively high self-esteem; some experience low levels of self-esteem.
- **Personality** – the idea that everyone has enduring personal characteristics that last a lifetime and shape our approach to other people, new situations, problem solving, stressful events and so on. The concept of **temperament** has been used to explore individual differences in children.

A sense of self

As well as making relationships with others, young children also have a growing sense of themselves as separate individuals.

Babies

For very young babies there is an unclear boundary between their own bodies and the rest of their world. Young babies look surprised, as well as intrigued, when their own hands come into their line of vision. Once they have gained some physical control it is not unusual for them to grasp their own toes, push them into their mouth and, if they have a tooth or two, babies can inflict a painful bite on themselves. Not surprisingly, they then cry but babies cannot make the links that the toe is at the end of their body and biting causes pain. There is so much that they yet do not understand.

Although babies have much to learn about the world, their behaviour in experiments has shown how they can learn that what they do makes a difference. They have some sense of the difference between 'me' and 'not me'. For instance, young babies (well under six months of age) have learned to suck in order to bring a particular picture into focus or to make certain movements to switch on a light. In a range of experiments, young babies have acted so as to bring about a change in their environment. They lose interest after a while and show distress if the established patterns of control are changed.

Anecdotal evidence has also emerged from families that tried alarms which were sensitive to babies' breathing and set off a sound if the breathing stopped. Some babies appeared to have learned to hold their breath and were rewarded by the prompt arrival of anxious parents at the side of the cot.

Toddlers

It is difficult to show that toddlers have developed a self-concept but the two observations often used are:

- when toddlers say their own name when shown a photograph of themselves;
- when toddlers recognise that it is them reflected in a mirror.

Very young children often enjoy looking in mirrors and pressing their nose against the reflective surface. But it is not until well into the second year of life that children realise that a dab of blusher, surreptitiously put on their nose, is on them and not the person in the mirror. The photograph or mirror self-awareness starts with some children around 15–16 months, but by 21 months around three-quarters of toddlers are saying their name to the photograph or touching their nose and rubbing the blusher.

Toddlers have a growing idea of themselves as unique individuals, with a name of their own and a pattern of relationships with parents, siblings and other close family. They have a growing sense of themselves through those relationships and how they are treated. Very young children who are treated as if their natural explorations are intentionally naughty may come to see themselves as unliked. On the other hand, toddlers who are treated with care and encouragement can be starting the basis of a confident outlook on life and learning.

An example of names

Children are learning not only their own personal name and those of other family members, but also the cultural tradition of family or surnames. At 2:2 (2 years 2 months) our son, Drew, had grasped that Mama was also called Jennie and Daddy was also Lance. He was prepared to believe that Lance had another name, Lindon, and that he, Drew, also was Lindon. But he laughed uproariously and gave a disbelieving 'No!' when told that Mama and baby Tanith were also Lindons. He seemed to take the view that there might be two people with the same name in the house but that it was clearly a joke to suggest that there could possibly be four. He reacted in exactly the same way when told that he too had once been a baby just like Tanith.

For you to think over
- Watch out for examples of the children in your care as they build a picture of themselves in relation to others.
- You may also find, as in the example above, that young children's current understanding of the world leads them to believe you are making a joke when what you say makes no sense to them.
- This example illustrates again how different aspects of development link within a child's daily life. Children's curiosity is often provoked by the relationships they have formed. But the explorations, like Drew's interest and disbelief about names, also show the progression of their cognitive and language development.

SUGGESTED ACTIVITY

The second half of the one- to two-year age range is also the time when toddlers become ever more definite about what they want and 'me' and 'mine' can become significant words. Although this single-mindedness can be hard for adults, it is an important step because the young child has become more self-aware.

- You could gather examples of toddlers' behaviour that illustrate that they have a developed self-concept.
- Try the examples of the photograph or the mirror.
- But also look out for events such as young children making a joke by pointing to themselves and saying someone else's name, then laughing loudly.

Social identity

Through experience and the knowledge that is shared by older children and adults, young children come to an understanding that places them by various social labels. These further sources of identity include whether they are a girl or a boy; their age and that of other children; their family; signs of ethnic, cultural or religious identity and later their membership of social groups like school.

Children build their sense of a personal identity partly through how other people react to them on the basis of the various social labels. Children may accept negative associations about their sex or ethnic group if these are communicated on a regular basis or by adults and children important in this child's life. On the other hand, strong messages in the opposite direction can counteract sex or racial stereotyping, at least to some extent.

Children are often far more aware of the relative value given to different social and ethnic labels than adults believe. For instance, research has established that young children of three years and more are perfectly well aware of racial differences of skin colour when they are part of a diverse group or neighbourhood. They can see the differences just as they notice other ways of distinguishing between individuals. Awareness does not become a racist outlook unless children are also exposed to negative views on race, for instance, that parents talk disparagingly about families different from them or other children insist on excluding certain children solely on the basis of race.

TO THINK ABOUT

The area of good practice known as equal opportunities or an anti-bias approach is a good example of how values are also involved in the step from research to practice. Research tells practitioners that young children are aware of the attitudes of adults and older children. The values underpinning good practice are that early years workers should take note of this aspect to a child's world and use their adult skills to counteract negative effects.

So, the task of adults who are concerned to develop an anti-bias approach is not to pretend that children (or the adults themselves) do not notice racial or sex differences. The objective is to create an environment in which negative comments or rejecting behaviour are dealt with promptly and that the whole curriculum gives a positive place for all the social groups represented by children. Children from the groups most likely to be subjected to offensive remarks or actions then have a better chance of developing a positive sense of identity. And children of the dominant group are not building a sense of self-esteem mainly through disdain for others.

Values are involved because adults are taking responsibility to shape events, rather than denying the findings about children's development or taking the view of 'that's life'.

Personality and temperament

The term **personality** has been used more in connection with adults whereas the study of temperament has been a search for individual differences in childhood. The word **temperament** is used to mean in-built tendencies for children's reactions and behaviours that probably build the basis for a more enduring adult personality. Both concepts are a way of describing and trying to explain continuities in how the same child, or adult, tends to approach and deal with their experiences.

The different theories of child development vary in how they approach the idea of temperament or adult personality (for more detail on each of these theoretical stands see chapter 1):

- Biological theories focus on genetic differences underlying individual differences in reacting to people and the environment. There has also been increasing evidence that neurological and chemical differences in the body underlie some of the observed individual differences in behaviour. Biological explanations do not discount the impact of children's environment, but point to tendencies that even very young children appear to bring to any situation.

- The psychodynamic view is that children's and later adults' personality is shaped by the extent to which infantile and early childhood conflicts have been resolved. Children's relationship with important adults, especially in the family, is judged as very significant in early childhood through the process of attachment (see page 39 in this chapter).

- Learning theory or behaviourism stresses how the basic processes of learning such as reinforcement (see also page 145) shape children's behaviour including how they relate to others. Social learning theory builds in the impact of experience on children's expectations for new situations or adults and the extent of their sense of control within their environment.

An interactionist view of the development of temperament combines something of all the theoretical approaches. (The cognitive theories of development have little to say about these kinds of individual differences.) This approach takes the line that tendencies towards particular patterns in temperament are inborn. But that from the earliest days a baby's tendency to a particular type of temperament exerts an impact on her immediate carers. Later development is the result of the continuing interplay between the baby's, and then the child's, natural inclinations and the reactions of key adults. So, patterns can be laid down from early childhood and the quality of the emotional relationship between child and carers is important. There can be positive reverberations as well as negative. This area of research is also useful when looking at children's behaviour (more on page 143).

Self-esteem

Some children have very little sense of **self-worth**, because of how they have been treated by others. Children's level of self-esteem develops as a result of the gap between what they feel they should, or could be and the kind of person they are and their achievements. If the gap is small, then children can have high self-esteem; they feel that all things taken into account, they are a worthwhile individual. If the gap is wide then children have low self-esteem.

There are several sources of children's feelings of self-esteem:

- their direct experiences of whether they are managing or doing well in different areas of endeavour;
- how they feel they line up against other children, especially those they admire;
- the views of adults who matter to them – parents, other relatives and liked carers. What these people think is important and how they judge this child to be doing;
- general influences, communicated through adults and children, that affect a child's sense of whether they are at root a worthwhile person. Prejudiced and offensive remarks, based on race, sex or perceived disability, can undermine a child's level of self-esteem.

Young children playing together

Self-esteem is a further example of the interaction between individuals and their environment. For example:

- Cheryl is progressing very well at school and gets good marks. But she is persistently criticised by her parents who expect nothing but 'A's. Despite the support of her teachers, Cheryl has developed low self-esteem and describes herself as 'pretty stupid really'.
- Matt is not good at sports in a school that places a high value on physical activity. But, Matt has a close circle of friends who also dislike school sports and value Matt's talent for drawing caricatures. Matt puts up with sports and mainly feels good about himself.

2.3 Children's relationships

Children's experience of interpersonal relationships are central to their development. They learn about themselves through close interactions with others and build their self-concept and level of self-esteem from how others treat them. Children generally make close relationships within their family, with parents and with siblings. Such relationships are called attachments because comfort and the relief of emotional distress are usually a part of the relationship. Children develop many relationships within childhood (with other children and with adult carers) but only a few are attachments.

Brothers and sisters

A considerable amount of research into early relationships has been organised as if families only include mother and child pairs but family life is usually more complex than just two people. Judy Dunn opened up the field of looking at sibling relationships in families. She found great variety between individuals as well as some patterns. Although she reports levels of disagreement and resentment between siblings, the normal family situation is certainly not unrelieved sibling rivalry (as implied by some of the psychodynamic theories).

Dunn observed families in which the second child had been born. She found that older children who referred to the baby in their talk also wanted to help and play with the baby; there was a spreading of friendly behaviour towards the new sibling. It seemed to help if mothers discussed the new baby with the older one as an individual person. This kind of conversation helped to encourage the older child's interest in the baby. The older child was then more likely within three or four weeks of the birth to talk about the baby as a person. And at the observation 14 months after the birth, there was more likely to be mutually friendly overtures by both children.

Siblings could be a source of companionship and enjoyment to each other but they could also be a source of aggravation on occasion. More later in this section on 'playing together'.

Only children in families

Some families have one child, either from choice or because attempts to have further children are not successful. Families of only children have been the subject of a great deal of speculation about the development of children without brothers or sisters. It has been claimed that only children will be lonely or unable to make friends, or that they will inevitably be indulged by parents. Ann Laybourn's review of the research demolishes most of these myths and highlights that there is a great deal of variety within the development of only children. Some children may feel isolated, especially if parents do not organise easy contact with other children. But, in the main, only children have as much chance of positive emotional and social development as children with siblings.

TO THINK ABOUT

Ann Laybourn's review of the research on only children brings out a useful general point about how people make sense of their observations. Once the myth of the 'problem only child' becomes established, difficulties in families are interpreted in a different way.

- Brothers and sisters do not always get along; some have volatile and unhappy relationships. But such problems are likely to seen as *particular* to this family, perhaps explained by parents' mismanagement of relations between the siblings.
- Relationship problems of an only child are more likely to be *generalised*, in that the difficulty is explained by being an only child.
- So, an only child who seems to find it hard to make friends is seen as proof of the general rule and support for claims that parents should not stop at one child. A child with siblings who has social difficulties is more likely to be seen as an individual with problems.

Over the next few weeks, try to keep aware of how you, and your colleagues, make sense of observations about children. Are you taking one or two children's behaviour as support for a more general rule (not just about only children)? How can you justify this interpretation?

Making friends

Making social contact

Babies and young children need to have developed secure attachments in order to make later relationships. Their initial attachments develop for them a sense of self worth, of security and of knowing how to behave in a close relationship. Young babies are essentially social in nature and show interest in other people – children as well as adults. Older babies and toddlers seek to make social contact with others of their own age as well as older. The difficulty for babies and toddlers is that their physical moves to contact another child of the same age are inevitably less subtle than those of older children. Touches may be more a poke than a pat and adults tend to become concerned about possible hurt from the whole body clasps and semi-wrestling that toddlers sometimes use. However, the persistent myth that very young children are self centred and scarcely interested in relationships does not survive some careful observation of the under-twos.

Elinor Goldschmied has gathered observational material in England and Italy. Her videos of babies and toddlers exploring materials in her treasure basket show that gazing, touching and offering play materials are regular exchanges between young children. The visual material of babies gazing at one another and making physical contact within an Italian day care centre highlights that even very young children are showing social behaviour. Toddlers and young children develop relationships with their peers that show friendly behaviour, a wish to be together and mutual enjoyment in shared activities, however simple.

SUGGESTED ACTIVITY

Studies have confirmed that mobile toddlers sometimes show preferences, which may persist for months, in their choice of play companion in day care. If you have contact with under-twos, make your own observations over a matter of weeks, following the preferences of a few of the children.

1 When the young children arrive in the morning whom do they go towards?

2 Given the choice, do children sit beside one or more children more often than others?
3 Do they take toys or books to show particular children?

See if there are any patterns of preferences within the group. If you have difficulty in observing very young children, then try to watch Elinor Goldschmied's videos (see page 61).

Playing together

Another persistent myth about very young children is that they cannot play with other children, that they only play alongside them (parallel play). This belief is largely a misunderstanding of research that showed how older children spent relatively more time in cooperative play and less in parallel or solitary play than the younger ones. Recent research into the social and communicative abilities of very young children undermines the misunderstanding or myth.

It is accurate that younger children do not play in the same way as older ones but they engage in playful exchanges. Carol Eckerman observed very young children in contact with each other and noticed the following deliberate patterns:

- Mobile babies establish a joint focus of interest by making physical contact with an object that another young child (or adult) is manipulating. The baby then imitates the 'play partner'. This copying action seems to signal a message of 'I like this' or 'Let's do it together'.
- In interaction between toddlers, imitative acts seem to be the opening moves in an exchange, because they often happen swiftly after the first contact. The other toddler is encouraged to imitate in return. Imitation establishes a connection between the two children.
- Reciprocal imitative games are common between toddlers, for instance, taking turns to do the same action, like jumping off the sofa.
- Toddlers string together a series of imitative acts, but do not copy everything – there is some selection in their play. Through imitation, toddlers playing together develop relatively complex games, often physical play. Toddlers who know each other can have a number of ritualised play sequences.
- From two to three years, words begin to be integrated into the young children's play. Children now begin to be able to coordinate their actions towards new play sequences, not only the familiar rituals. Verbal and non-verbal language is used to guide the interaction.

So, the playful interactions between under-twos form the basis for later, more complex play.

Much of the play research has been undertaken by observing same-age groups of toddlers. Sometimes researchers also seem to take an inappropriately strict line over what can be defined as 'play' and what can not. Eckerman's careful observational research challenges the claims that very young children do not really play. But another perspective is to observe mobile babies and toddlers in interaction with older children, most likely their older siblings.

Judy Dunn's research in families produced examples of younger siblings who were drawn into the play of an older brother or sister. I have certainly encountered a great deal of anecdotal evidence (see the following box for my own observations in my family) that toddlers are often, although not always, given a role in the play of older siblings and become involved in games which they do not initiate with their peers.

Mainly friendly relations with older siblings also give the younger ones a chance sometimes to exercise some direction over the play, perhaps by clowning around and making the older ones laugh. I observed a lovely sequence in which an 18-month-old held the attention of three older children (ranging in age from three to seven years) by running along a hallway and then sliding along on her bottom, cushioned by her nappy. The older children fell about laughing and Anna repeated her run and slide six times, delighted with the full attention of the older ones.

SUGGESTED ACTIVITY

Look out for examples of play between toddlers in your own setting or from opportunities that arise in everyday life.

For instance, my wait in our local health clinic was greatly enlivened by watching two young children in a double buggy. One child looked about two years old and the younger was about eighteen months. They amused themselves for at least ten minutes. The older one usually started a game but the younger one then re-started a sequence once he had played it a few times. The two of them played 'I touch your knee and then you touch mine', 'We stare into each other's faces' and 'we shake our heads hard so our hair swings about'. Pauses were filled with chortles and grins and then one of the children would make the move into a game again.

Playing together – two siblings

The following are excerpts from my family diary. They show how an older sibling can give a lead to a younger and create games that the younger one would not develop alone or with peers. Tanith was born four days before Drew's second birthday. I have included some highlights from their first year together, since playing together comes from reasonably happy early relationships.

<u>Tanith is 1 month and Drew is 2:1:</u> D thinks T is funny when she cries and even funnier when she is sick. He says, 'More noise, baby!'

<u>Tanith, 2 months and Drew, 2:2:</u> D likes to have her on his lap sometimes. He chooses her clothes every morning.

<u>Tanith, 6 months and Drew, 2:6:</u> D is mainly gentle with T. He likes to brush her hair with the soft brush and give her toys. But he is less keen on sitting in the double buggy with her, because she pokes him and pulls his hair hard.

<u>Tanith, 8 months and Drew, 2:8:</u> T is now crawling and got hold of D's books which upset him. We explain how D has to keep his books and toys on the table for safety, whereas he has been happy on the floor. D has discovered how to make T laugh, which made him very pleased. D likes to have a bath with T and shows her how the bath toys work.

<u>Tanith, 13 months and Drew, 3:1:</u> T can now walk confidently. D has started a chasing game with her. Mainly he gets her to chase him along the hall by calling her name. D builds brick towers, says, 'What about this, Tanith?' and then she knocks them down. They both laugh loudly. Sometimes T brings him the brick box to get him to do the game.

<u>Tanith, 14 months and Drew, 3:2:</u> They still play the chasing game but sometimes T starts it now by hovering until D sees her. They spend time together in the playhouse we made out of a huge cardboard box, playing peep-bo through the windows. They wrestle together.

<u>Tanith, 15 months and Drew, 3:3:</u> T sits beside D and hands him Lego for his models. They still play the chasing games and growl at each other as monsters. D has created a rescue game. He lies down and calls out 'Tanith! Help, help!' T comes up, gives her hand and they walk off.

<u>Tanith, 18 months and Drew, 3:6:</u> D has invented more games for him and T. Most revolve around chase and rescue: sharks, traps and something to do with heat. They both chant, 'Hot, hot' and drag the pink bath towel around (I never understood this game, but they loved it). T copies D a great deal in her play - how he handles the play dough, pretending to eat and drink with the tea set, counting like him and trying to jump as he does.

<u>Tanith is 2, Drew is 4:</u> T is as likely now to start their games together as D. As well as jumping about together, they spend a lot of time in the playhouse and they jointly run a pretend cafe from behind the sofa.

I should stress that Drew and Tanith were not content all the time. There were days when they squabbled and I had to give them time apart for everyone's peace of mind.

Brother and sister play

SUGGESTED ACTIVITY

See if you can arrange to visit a family with young children over a period of months and gather information on the games they play together. Alternatively, spend some time talking with parents who have two young children.

1   What do the children do together? Who leads and who follows?
2   In what way is the play environment different for the second child than for the first-born?
3   What strategies do the parents take to deal with squabbles?

Imaginary friends

A sizeable minority of children, up to about one-fifth, have at least one imaginary friend before the age of five. Most children seem to invoke their friend only at home, although some may 'bring' him or her to nursery and playgroup.

Most imaginary friends are not a sign of problems for the child. They seem to be a natural outgrowth for some children of their fantasy play and usually the friend ceases to exist by the time a child is five or six years. (I admit that in my early childhood I had an imaginary friend called Boomer, who lived in the tree at the end of my road.)

Imaginary friends, much like teddies, can usefully be a child's vehicle for expressing concerns and supportive adults will take this constructively. Some adults, after all, seek advice initially through the formula of 'I have a friend

SUGGESTED ACTIVITY

You could undertake a small study of imaginary friends. The questions to explore could be:

● How common are imaginary friends for children?
● What function do imaginary friends fulfil? Companionship? Someone to hear your troubles? Part of a rich fantasy life and story invention? Someone who does all the things this child would like to do?
● How long into childhood are the friends lasting?

You could explore these questions in two possible ways:

1   Gather information on the children with whom you work by talking with their parents. Be sensitive in how you raise the subject, since some parents may be concerned that imaginary friends are a sign of problems.
2   Alternatively, talk with adult friends and acquaintances about their memories of imaginary friends, if they had one. Again, make sure your fellow-adults understand your genuine interest, that you are not making fun of them.

who has this problem...' Adults need to treat the imaginary friend with respect; it is not 'silly'. There would only be cause for concern if requirements for the pretend person were taking over the day, or if the child seemed unnerved by this imaginary friend.

Social skills

Children are developing social skills from a young age but it seems likely that adults notice more when the attempts at contact go wrong than the more successful sorties. It is common to describe young children, especially the under-threes as 'egocentric' – an emphasis largely arising from Piaget's stage theory of development (see page 62). Unfortunately, the word often carries negative overtones, almost as if young children are being criticised as selfish. Babies and toddlers are centred on themselves and the world as it impacts on them; it is the natural way that development starts. But there are signs from early on that they are responsive and alert to others.

Elinor Goldschmied's video material (see page 61) shows the tentative moves that very young children make towards each other on an individual basis. Once children encounter group life, in nursery or playgroup, they are having to learn further social skills and adults can support them. Young children, especially the under-twos, operate socially on a one-to-one basis in their relationships with other children and with adults. It is unrealistic to expect them to see themselves or respond to being treated as a member of a day care group. Group life for older children can have its difficulties and the social complexities of nursery or primary school are often underestimated by adults.

Elinor Goldschmied and Sonia Jackson considered the social skills with which under-threes were coping in a day care setting. But the areas they raised are equally relevant if you consider social skills for older children. In group life, young children need to learn all of the following:

- how to approach an existing group of children and ways of joining the group, becoming a part of the activity without being rejected;
- constructive ways of behaving in a group with other children: how to lead without bossing, how to be part of a group;
- how to leave a group and move on to something else when the child wishes for a change, when the play is boring or the child is unhappy about some aspect of play;
- how to start playing with another individual child, that some strategies of making contact are less successful, for instance, pushing in on the other child's space or grabbing a toy;
- how to handle the stress of rejection by a group or individual and how to deal with persistent rejection or bullying;
- how to cope with children who want to play with you more than you wish to play with them. Some children have others clinging to them, either by staying close or physically hanging on;
- how to manage the intrusions from other children when you want to do something on your own, without being bothered.

Seen from the children's perspective, the learning of social skills extends well beyond adult concerns about sharing and cooperative play. Some of the areas outlined above relate closely to social skills that much older children and adults can experience as problematic. So, when you support children's social learning and acknowledge their feelings about the situations they face, you can be provoked to reflect on your own experiences – current and from your childhood.

Practical work on helping children in interactions with others has focused on attention to children's choices in behaviour, on active and alert adults who model constructive ways of relating to others and on specifically helping children with what they may say or do. Some very practical approaches have emerged from work in the United States to counteract the development of aggressive patterns of behaviour. This effort inevitably takes adults to focus on the behaviour they would like to encourage (more on this topic in chapter 6).

Children who have difficulties in relationships

In many cases, you will be able to see that children who have continuing problems in relating to others are affected by their unhappy circumstances. (See also page 58.) But some children have persistent difficulties in relating to others that are not eased by supportive help from adults.

Autism is a developmental disorder which disrupts children's social development and their ability to form and maintain relationships. Children with autism have difficulties with both verbal and non-verbal communication, which also lead to problems in relating to other children and adults. The children's intense need for a rigid routine, their intolerance of change and likely obsessive interest in particular objects can mean that they need a great deal of specialist adult help and are not attractive companions for other children. The disorder is incurable but specialist education can make the most of children's skills and minimise the behavioural difficulties.

SUGGESTED ACTIVITY

Look at the areas of social skills for children in a group (From Goldschmied's and Jackson's observations) and focus on one or two. Be alert within your own group setting and consider:

1   In what ways do you, and your colleagues, actively support children as they learn this social skill? What do you do in general in your setting?

2   Do you acknowledge the difficulties of some children and how do you plan to help individuals? (You might want to look at the section on temperament on page 46.)

2.4 Emotional development

Children's own feelings

Within their first year, babies show a range of emotions that are only partly provoked by their internal physical needs. Anyone with even fleeting contact with babies will be aware that they cry, but close observation also shows that babies express what can only be described as contentment, happiness and delight. The technical possibilities of video recorded observations (see also page 90 on early patterns of communication) have shown how babies as young as three or four months respond emotionally to the involvement of their carers.

Toddlers show their emotions through facial expression and their whole body movements. They express happiness, excitement, frustration and annoyance. But toddlers also start to show emotions like embarrassment or pride in their achievements, both of which are evidence that they are conscious of their own actions and aware of the likely reactions of important adults in their social world.

Young children learn the words to express their emotions but this is unlikely until after at least two years. The early developments in spoken language are far more about what young children can directly experience through their senses in their environment: the objects they explore and use, people they know and words to express their wants and what they do. But

Getting along together

later on, two-year-olds who are given the words by adults, will become able to express feelings by, 'I'm cross with you' or 'I'm sad. I wanted you'. Observations in families, for instance by Judy Dunn, have noted that the two-year-olds who spoke of their feelings had mothers who had commented on the children's emotions when they were toddlers.

Control of emotions

Two and three-year-olds tend to express straightaway whatever emotion they are feeling. If they are happy, it shows in their face and whole body posture. If they are distressed, the tears will come. Between four and six years, children show an increasing ability to inhibit temporarily the expression of strong feelings. This development of **impulse control** includes children's growing understanding that some situations require peaceful and not highly excited behaviour. You may especially notice children holding back their emotions when they are upset. They sense the situation is inappropriate or they do not want to show someone their distress (the idea of 'being brave').

In early years settings, you will observe children who are trying hard not to cry, although they are distressed. Parents have many experiences of getting home with children and facing the flood of distress that the children have managed to control in nursery or school. A growing awareness of social and cultural expectations is also part of children's learning whether and how to express strong emotions. Cultures around the world vary in social rules about expression of feelings, some being more demonstrative than others.

Children's understanding of others' feelings

Part of emotional development is also children's potential to understand what other people – children and adults – may be feeling. You will find more on the development of children's sensitivity to the feelings of others in chapter 6 (page 156), which also covers how children may behave on the basis of their awareness of others' emotions.

Adult reaction to children's feelings

Adult reactions to children's emotions are an under-researched area in terms of organised studies – with the exception of reactions to babies who cry persistently. My own informal observations and anecdotal evidence suggest that some adults resist accepting that young children have strong feelings, especially that they can be deeply sad or emotionally hurt by how they are treated (within normal daily exchanges, not patterns of emotional abuse). Two processes seem to be at work:

- Some adults resist taking a child's perspective. If that adult does not feel the situation justifies upset, then a child can be told, 'You're making a fuss about nothing' or even 'That doesn't hurt'. In a similar way, some adults act as if children cannot hear them making disparaging remarks about the children, that they, as adults, would find insulting or wounding.
- It is easier to believe that young children cannot be seriously distressed or that they 'get over' upsets quickly. Adults then do not feel responsible for finding a way to support and help children. Adults may also be protecting themselves against their own feelings of distress. This pattern of adult belief and behaviour seems to be at work when they conclude that a child was not 'really upset' because she or he cheered up later. I have also observed the strange reaction of some adults that children's distress is not genuine unless there are 'real tears'.

John Gottman has undertaken longitudinal research with families in order to identify different styles in how parents react to their children's expressed emotions. Gottman's practical applications of the research are equally relevant to early years workers.

Gottman's research highlights that how children make sense of their feelings depends a great deal on how adults react. From the response of parents and other familiar carers, children learn whether their expressed feelings are worthy, whether they should be expressed out loud and the extent to which it is possible to do anything constructive about strong emotions. The most positive approach for children's long-term development was a pattern of adult behaviour that Gottman called **emotion coaching**. He describes this as a pattern of five steps, that parents:

1   become aware of the child's emotion. The adults are alert to children's expressed feelings;
2   recognise that when children express feelings this is an important time between child and adult, when you can be close and children can learn from the experience;
3   listen with empathy, respecting the child's feelings. Adults are prepared to give the child time;
4   help the child to find the words to say what she is feeling and to label the emotion itself;
5   set limits on what is possible in this situation while exploring strategies to solve the problem at hand.

So parents, and other adults, who follow this pattern, accept and respect that children have strong feelings. They do not dismiss the feelings or belittle them, neither do they treat strong expressed emotions as bad behaviour from children. On the other hand, emotion coaching does not stop at helping children to express their feelings. Adults need to help children to problem-solve in a wide range of ways. You will find more on this topic in chapter 6.

TO THINK ABOUT

Undoubtedly changes in practice over recent decades have reflected a greater awareness of children's feelings.

● It is now normal practice for early years settings to have a settling-in period for children and their parents. This is now so usual that it is easy to forget that until the 1970s it was far more likely that children arrived at a pre-school or school setting, with no prior visits, and were expected to wave goodbye to parents at the door or gate.
● Hospital procedure regarding children has changed considerably in recognising that children separated from their families will be distressed (see page 186). Practice now is far more likely to reflect an awareness that sick children have feelings, care about how they are treated and deserve respect and bodily dignity.

Both of these developments also relate to significant changes in the attitudes of service providers to parents. But in many services for children and their families there is undoubtedly still plenty of room for improvement.

Questions
Think over and discuss with your colleagues the ways in which practice in your setting is responsive to children's feelings.

1   How do you settle children into your setting? Do you tend to expect that they will be settled within a given period (be honest)?

2　How do you deal with children's expression of strong feelings? Look at the ideas on emotion coaching. Consider how you create time for individual children to talk (not group time with books or puppet play).

3　Are some feelings from children harder to handle than others – which ones? What do you think is the reason?

Unhappy children

Generally, children are unhappy or distressed for specific reasons and, with reassurance and sympathy from adults, they will emerge from the state. A small proportion of children are unhappy for much of the time and there may be a number of different reasons for this emotion:

- Children may be experiencing persistent difficulties in dealing with group life in an early years settings and in making contact with other children. Temperament may be an issue as well as the organisation of the group.
- Family crisis – perhaps difficulties between parents, divorce or a bereavement. Persistent unhappiness can arise when children's feelings are ignored.
- Serious and continuing problems at home in terms of relationships with their parents. Parents may have great difficulties in relating well to the children, perhaps because of serious family stresses or depression.

Unhappiness may be expressed through tears and sad expressions. But children are individuals and some may express misery by lashing out at other children, by wanting continuous attention or by physical expressions (continued tiredness and lethargy, wetting or soiling).

Children's feelings and family crisis

Adults' inability to acknowledge the feelings of young children comes to the fore in family crisis. Parents undergoing the pain of separation or the loss of a loved family member may ease their own emotional burdens by believing that children neither understand nor feel similar emotions, or will 'get it over' swiftly. Yet, a sense of loss, confusion or distress is not confined to adults. Young children in families where parents are in the process of separating are usually acutely aware that something is wrong and are distressed by events. In the absence of information and family support, young children can be confused and may even conclude that they are at fault in some way. (More on children's experience of divorce on page 183.)

In families experiencing a bereavement, young children can also be distressed. Children by the age of five can have an understanding of final loss and that the dead do not return. Misunderstandings are not only the result of children's level of cognitive development but also that adults often give confusing messages to children about terminal illness and death. The use of euphemisms about death or actually telling lies to children ('Grandad's still in hospital') are sometimes the source of their confusion. Analogies to explain death such as 'it's like going to sleep and not waking up' can lead children to become genuinely fearful that they could die in their sleep.

Children react to family crisis with a range of emotions and behavioural patterns. They may show open distress or an apparent lack of emotion followed by later distressed reaction. They may appear to deny their loss or concentrate on a fear they will lose other members of the family. Children may also experience general reactions such as sleep disturbance or developmental regressions. This variety, in slightly different forms, is exactly what is observed in adult reactions to crisis and loss.

SUGGESTED ACTIVITY

Parents and carers can be confused about how best to deal with children's sadness and reactions to death. Part of the difficulty seems to be concern that what they say could make matters worse or that specialist skills are necessary. On the contrary, what children usually want is someone who will listen to how they feel, at the times when they want to talk, and will answer their questions honestly.

- Explore some of the practical applications of studies of loss by obtaining *Caring for Bereaved Children*, a booklet from Cruse-Bereavement Care, an organisation that has specialised in support for people (children as well as adults) who have been bereaved. You can contact Cruse at 126 Sheen Road, Richmond, Surrey TW9 1UR, tel: 0181 940 4818.
- For a review of the research on children and loss you could read 'Children and Bereavement', *Highlight* series no. 120 (National Children's Bureau).

Talking with and supporting children

Support for children who are distressed or confused has to allow for their level of development, without underestimating children's depth of feeling or their capacity to cope and problem-solve with help. A child's view can be cognitively different from that of an adult and adults who offer specialist help to children have to be aware of children's perspective as well as their possible feelings. This topic is another example of how aspects of children's development are inter-related within real life.

Jean Campion has specialised in counselling children and her observations from practice are equally relevant for those who are talking with and supporting children through caring relationships.

- Children's view can be that their life cannot be any other way, or they may be struggling with the belief that 'it's my fault'. Adults may have the view that change is more possible than children tend to think. Children are less likely than adults to realise that matters could be different and that others have a role in their dilemmas. They may not have considered their difficulties as problems that could be resolved.
- Campion points out that children are likely to be referred to a counsellor like herself because an adult is worried. It is less usual that the child has spoken up and asked for help. Children may be more likely to suffer in silence than adults.
- Children's language development may have progressed to the point where they are articulate in daily life. But in times of trouble, children may not use the same words as adults might and they may struggle to find the words. Any caring adult has to listen carefully and avoid assumptions in order to make sure that they understand what children mean.
- Children are inclined to say what they feel is expected or what they judge adults want to hear. This tendency is worsened if adults use leading questions or keep on repeating similar questions. Children take this as a hint as to what they should be saying or not saying.
- Children's perspective of the world is different and they need adults to respect their concerns and take them seriously. For instance, children can be very distressed by playground troubles or the carelessness of another child who smashes a pot that the first child took ages to make.

Fears

It is not unusual for young children to be frightened or very wary of objects or situations that do not worry adults. The fears come from some source but not necessarily from incidents that parents and other carers could have foreseen. Children's limited understanding of the world combines with their capacity to imagine.

Studies of children's fears show that toddlers can be uneasy or frightened by what seem to adults to be very ordinary events. For instance, some toddlers are frightened by the emptying of bath water or extremely wary of sitting on the toilet. In both cases, the young children seem to be worried that they may be sucked down with the water, although a few children have imagined creatures in the toilet such as snakes. Fear of the dark is quite usual, as is children's powers of imagination making creatures out of shadows or shapes on the wallpaper. Fears of animals, spiders or insects may develop from unpleasant experiences but not all children are, for instance, frightened by spiders appearing from their shoes.

Children's reactions are varied. One child may be frightened by a character in a children's cartoon, another may not be at all concerned. Parents and carers can support children when they:

Sometimes life is serious

- acknowledge children's fears and reassure them;
- do not make children feel silly and certainly do not use the fears as a threat;
- take practical steps to support children such as a low light in the bedroom or a child seat in an adult toilet;
- encourage children to face their fear only as far as the children wish – perhaps standing close to a rabbit or watching a spider;
- encourage a practical wariness so that they gain a sense of danger but lose the fears of what is safe or only the product of children's imagination.

Phobias

For a few children the normal fears of early childhood become so strong that they can be called a phobia. A **phobia** has developed when a child's fear is disrupting normal daily life, for instance, a fear of insects that has led a child to refuse to leave home and to want a parent to check every corner. Phobias could also be said to be developing when children require ever more elaborate rituals to protect them and the original fear, perhaps of the bath water, has generalised to any kind of water. Phobias usually need specialist treatment from a child psychologist, but most children's fears do not reach this level.

Reading on . . .

★   Bowlby, John 1965: *Child Care and the Growth of Love* (Penguin). Worth reading to understand the ideas of maternal deprivation and the social context of the time. Read Michael Rutter and Barbara Tizard for balance (see further down this list).

★   Campion, Jean 1991: *Counselling Children* (Whiting and Birch). A practical book about the special issues of counselling children. You will find some ideas for talking with children and listening as a worker not just as a counsellor.

★   Dunn, Judy 1984: *Sisters and Brothers* (Fontana). Descriptions and interpretations from some of the first research to look in detail at sibling relationships and family life.

★   Dunn, Judy: 'Children in a family world' in Richards, Martin and Light, Paul 1986: *Children of Social Worlds: Development in a social context* (Polity Press). A description of some of the research that highlights the complexity of children's relationships within the family.

★   Dunn, Judy 1993: *Young Children's Close Relationships Beyond Attachment* (Sage). Discussion of research into children's family relationships and friendships with other children. This book is useful because it relates social development to children's cognitive and language development.

★ Eckerman, Carol 'Imitation and toddlers' achievement of co-ordinated actions with others' in Nadel, Jacqueline and Camaioni, Luigia (eds) 1993: *New Perspectives in Early Communicative Development* (Routledge). Not an easy book to read but it is a good resource on the research about very young children.

★ Garmezy, N. and Rutter, M. 1983: *Stress, Coping and Development in Children* (McGraw Hill). Discussion of the research and emerging ideas about how children cope with stressful experiences and what may be learned from those who seem to develop greater resilience.

★ Goldschmied, Elinor – video material in *Infants at Work, Heuristic Play with Objects* and *Communication Between Babies in their First Year.* (National Children's Bureau). Useful visual material for practical ideas within early years settings and for provoking discussion.

★ Goldschmied, Elinor and Jackson, Sonia 1994: *People Under Three: Young children and day care* (Routledge). Consideration of the particular needs of very young children in day care settings.

★ Gottman, John and Declaire, Joan 1997: *The Heart of Parenting: How to raise an emotionally intelligent child* (Bloomsbury). A report of Gottman's research and practical suggestions for supporting children's emotional development. Written for parents but just as relevant to any adults involved with children.

★ Kitzinger, Sheila 1978: *Women as Mothers* (Fontana). Description of how motherhood and mothering is seen differently around the world.

★ Konner, Melvin 1991: *Childhood* (Little Brown and Co). Description of childhood and child development that takes a global perspective. A useful reminder that time and place affects how children are raised.

★ Laybourn, Ann 1994: *The Only Child: Myths and reality* (HMSO). A review of research into only children and their development. A useful book for stimulating your ideas about research and interpretations in general.

★ Rutter, Michael 1981: *Maternal Deprivation Reassessed* (Penguin). A balanced review of the research, issues and social beliefs around the idea of maternal deprivation.

★ Schaffer, H. Rudolph 1990: *Making Decisions About Children: Psychological questions and answers* (Blackwell). Part Two addresses several of the key questions about bonding, attachment and maternal deprivation.

★ Tizard, Barbara 1986: *The Care of Young Children: Implications of recent research* (Thomas Coram Research Unit Working and Occasional Papers 1). A review of attachment research and children's care experiences. This paper gives a useful reminder of the positive consequences of Bowlby's work, even though the exclusive emphasis on mothers was misplaced.

3 Thinking and reasoning

This chapter covers:

- theories of cognitive development;
- children's thinking in context;
- adults' understanding.

3.1 Theories of cognitive development

Children's intellectual development includes their growing abilities to think, reason and solve problems. As children develop their thinking they also become able to understand, and show that they understand concepts that are not immediately obvious, such as number or possible reasons why someone may act in a particular way. This whole area of learning is called **cognitive development.**

Not surprisingly, the theorists who have most to say about children's thinking are those in the cognitive-developmental group. Psychodynamic theory places little emphasis on the development of intellectual powers and behaviourism has considerably more application in the area of learning as a whole (see chapter 5).

Piaget and stage theory

Jean Piaget established a complex theory of how children's cognitive development moves through distinct stages. He built his theory from case studies of his own three children, and later from children of staff working at his research institute in Geneva. In the 1920s and 30s he proposed that young children thought and learned in a qualitatively different way from adults and that they were active in their own learning. This view was very radical for the time, since children were generally viewed as empty vessels that needed to be filled with adult-given information. Piaget described four broad stages, with sub-stages in each.

The sensorimotor period: 0–24 months

This stage covered the first two years of life when exploration and learning occur primarily through physical experiences. Through this medium, Piaget saw evidence of the dawning of memory when babies deliberately repeated actions. Between eight to twelve months babies show signs of understanding

that objects which are made to disappear under a cloth are still there; they search for them. Piaget called this the understanding of **object permanence** and saw it as evidence that babies could mentally represent objects or people. By the end of the sensorimotor period young children are able to invent play activities and not simply repeat them. They have an understanding of play materials as symbols and this development is shown in their pretend play.

Stage of pre-operational thought: two to six years

During this period young children show great interest and an increasing grasp of how the world works. Their explorations are still sometimes through actions, but their learning is now supported by language and their ability to hold images in their mind. Piaget concluded that children in this stage made mistakes, compared with older children, because their thinking was still immature.

Learning to classify

Children become confused about categories of objects and **classification**. Initially, young children may generalise widely from what they learn so that they make mistakes, for instance that any small fluffy animal is a cat. An older child within this stage might be confused about the classification that all cats are animals but not all animals are cats.

Conservation

Piaget also studied children's focus on the appearance of objects and how this could confuse them. For instance, children might agree that two rows of toy cars had the same number of cars but, when one row was spread out, would say that there were more cars in that row. Piaget's explanation was that children had not learned to conserve number and were muddling the concept of number with the visible change of length of row.

The concept of **conservation** is that a characteristic of an object or material remains the same (is conserved), although the appearance has changed. Piaget studied children's understanding of conservation of six properties of objects or materials:

- *Number* – Do children believe that the number of bricks or coins has changed if one row is altered in length?
- *Length* – Two objects, like pencils, are shown to be of equal length by matching them up. Then one is shifted to appear to stick out ahead of the other. Does the child now say this one is longer?
- *Quantity* – Two identical shaped glasses are each filled with the same amount of drink, then one drink is emptied into a different shaped glass. Is there still the same amount of drink? This is the classic children's party scenario when children claim there is more drink in the long thin glasses.
- *Mass* – A child agrees that two balls of play dough have the same amount of dough. One ball is squished into another shape – is there still the same amount in each?
- *Weight* – Two equal balls of dough are weighed and the child agrees they are identical. One ball is squeezed into a different shape – will the two balls still weigh the same?
- *Volume* – Two balls of clay or dough are placed into two identical glasses of water and the child can see that the water level rises by the same amount. One ball is made into a different shape – will the two balls still take up the same amount of space?

An egocentric outlook

Piaget also took the view that young children's thinking was **egocentric**; they could only understand the world from their own perspective and they believed that everyone else took the same perspective as them.

There has been a considerable amount of research on children of this age group and what they appear to understand. The studies have not questioned Piaget's findings that children's answers to conservation and other similar problems are often 'wrong' from an adult perspective. But further investigation has raised interesting questions about how children think and how adults can unwittingly shape their answers in experimental situations. (More on this research from page 71.)

Concrete operations: *from five to seven years until eleven years*

The key feature of this stage is that children become increasingly able to hold an idea in their head while they are thinking about it. They still need relevant materials to see and handle – hence the word 'concrete'. Piaget believed that children were less confused by the appearance of objects and materials. They could now think through issues such as 'there only seems to be more juice in that glass because it's tall.'

The ability to consider possibilities in their minds also helps children to think about how to reverse a situation – 'What did it look like before we...' So children become increasingly able to think in the abstract and to grasp perspectives other than their own. Their abstract thinking is aided by their grasp of general rules, such as addition and subtraction. They also have a clearer understanding of systems of classification, realising that objects can be grouped in different ways: animals, red objects, toys that make a noise and many other ways of organising similar and dissimilar.

Children at this stage have developed a form of thinking that enables them to reason. They use **inductive reasoning**: when experience of specific examples leads to more general expectations about how the world works and predictions for similar situations. So a child at this stage may observe that several wooden toys will float and go on to conclude that there is something about wood that enables it to float, so anything made of wood should float.

Formal operations: 12 years onwards

Piaget believed that from age 12 years onwards children and young people could increasingly deal with systematic reasoning and logic. They could reason in their heads or in conversation, without any concrete reference points. This shift allows children to manage **deductive reasoning**: when young people or adults have learned a number of general principles or rules and can use these to predict what will happen in particular instances. This type of reasoning is used in the scientific method, when a general rule or theory leads to predictions that are tested through investigation of particular events. Young people and adults still use inductive reasoning as well.

Research into the thinking level at formal operations has suggested that children and young people do not inevitably reach this stage within their educational experience or in more general applications of thinking in everyday life. (Frankly, reading what Piaget wrote about formal operations, and trying to understand the concepts are both difficult tasks!) However, the distinction between inductive and deductive reasoning has useful practical applications – see the 'To think about' section below.

TO THINK ABOUT

Piaget distinguished between the inductive reasoning of children from about 5–11 years and the possibility of deductive reasoning, at least on some areas of learning from 11 or 12 years of age. Inductive reasoning moves from specific examples and experiences towards the possibility of working out rules that apply beyond what has happened so far. Deductive reasoning, on the other hand, starts with the more general rule and supports predictions and expectations about what is likely to happen, how you ought to behave in certain situations or likely ways to solve this particular problem.

Younger children need plenty of experience in order to have any basis for rules of problem solving such as 'Our collage won't stick unless we.....' or explanations like 'Maybe Miss doesn't feel well. She's not usually bad-tempered with us.' Good practice with young children stresses their need for hands-on experience and the chance to learn from what they do and observe.

Strangely, this focus on learning from specifics is often lost in discussions about children's behaviour. The adult emphasis is often on general rules about courtesy or cooperation, with the assumption that applications of the rule are obvious. Children think as well as behave and their thinking in this area can only progress through specific experience. They need to see the rule in action through real events and have clear explanations of what adults mean by 'you must share' or the boundaries that an adult draws between 'helping' another child and 'being bossy'.

Be alert to situations in which you, or your colleagues, may be holding unrealistic expectations of young children's reasoning powers. You may find examples in how you approach behaviour in your setting but there will also be other instances – see the discussion about teaching road safety on page 83.

The process of learning

Within all the stages, Piaget believed that learning was guided by two mechanisms:

- **Assimilation** – the ways in which children shape the environment to their own ends, for instance, taking a plastic bowl and pretending it is a hat. Through assimilation children are reorganising and using existing ideas and skills. New experiences are fitted into their current ideas.
- **Accommodation** – a process by which children have to adjust to the environment, for instance, a child cannot reach a book on the table by his usual stretching and grasping movement. After some thought, he drags across a floor cushion to climb on. Accommodation is the process through which children adapt to new information and experiences by changing their ideas and developing new ways of acting.

Piaget viewed development as a continuing sequence of **equilibration** between these two mechanisms.

Current views of Piagetian theory

Piaget had a substantial impact on views of child development, but only a minority of psychologists now accept his full theory as originally proposed. There has been widespread disagreement with the idea that cognitive development unfolds in separate and inevitable stages. It is questionable whether Piaget's last stage of formal operations is achieved or consistently used by many young people and adults. Piaget was not particularly interested in individual differences, nor the impact of culture, and proposed his stage model as a universal pattern for children.

The practical applications from Piaget's stage theory have been highly influential in shaping the approach to children's learning in British pre-school and primary school settings. It has been taken as almost self-evidently true that children learn through personal exploration and that they will discover ideas and skills for themselves when they are ready. The Piagetian role for adults is as an enabler or a facilitator and not as someone who initiates. But this approach has to be seen in context as a reaction to the prevailing view in the early decades of the twentieth century that children did not think independently, they needed to be told by adults. There is a continuing debate about the appropriate role for adults in children's learning – more on this topic in chapter 5.

Despite the criticisms – perhaps because of them – Piaget's work has led to a rich array of ideas and detailed research into how young children think. A summary of some of the main strands are described below.

Lev Vygotsky

Vygotsky was one of the first people to disagree with Piaget's basic ideas. Although he was working through the 1920s and 30s, Vygotsky's work was not well known outside Russia until translations of his books in the 1960s. Vygotsky's academic career was cut short by his death from tuberculosis in his late thirties, but his ideas influenced other key individuals such as Jerome Bruner and there was an upsurge of interest in his views during the 1990s.

The social context

Whereas Piaget studied young children as individuals almost operating in a social vacuum, Vygotsky placed great emphasis on the social context in which children explored and learned. He saw early language as an important social tool for children which brought them deliberately into contact with others. He also disagreed with Piaget's view that children were essentially self-centred and unable to take the perspective of others (egocentrism).

Vygotsky was especially interested in how adults could best help children to learn. He saw the adult task as a far more active role than Piaget proposed, not least because Vygotsky viewed intelligence as at least partly the ability to benefit from instruction. Like Piaget, Vygotsky saw activity as a crucial means for young children to learn, but he saw adults as important resources who would guide children and share ideas and strategies.

Vygotsky's description of the **zone of proximal development** is the key idea for shaping an active role for adults to intervene positively in children's learning. Children's zone of proximal development is the area of possibilities that lies between what they can manage on their own – their level of actual development; and what they could achieve or understand with some appropriate help – their level of potential development. Vygotsky believed that the focused help could come from either an alert adult or from another child whose understanding or skills were slightly more mature. The size of the zone is not fixed; some children may have a larger zone of proximal development than others.

> *The future in this child's development*
>
> **THE CHILD'S LEVEL OF POTENTIAL DEVELOPMENT (NOW, WITH HELP)**
>
> *The zone of proximal development, in which help can be given now*
>
> **THE CHILD'S LEVEL OF ACTUAL DEVELOPMENT (NOW, WITHOUT ANY HELP)**
>
> *All the child's current skills, abilities and understanding*

The zone of proximal development – for an individual child at a given point in time

The word 'proximal' is a translation from Vygotsky's original Russian to give the sense of 'nearby'. Assistance supports children to go slightly beyond their current competence. The help builds on the child's existing ability, understanding or skill, rather than being a means to show completely new ideas or ways of behaving. Appropriate help, grounded in an understanding of an individual child's current, actual level of development helps her to move to a potential level of development through the short distance covered by the zone of proximal development. A sketch further explains the idea in this section and you will find more discussion of a role for adults on page 123.

EXAMPLE

The idea of the zone of proximal development can be a very practical way for adults to think about how they help children forward when a child is stuck in his thinking.

When my son was five years old, a close friend of his moved house and we were invited to tea at Piya's new home. I drove us most of the way and then pulled in to check my London A–Z. Drew and I then had a conversation that went like this:

Drew: How do you know where Piya lives?
Jennie: His Mum gave me their new address. I know it's round here somewhere. I'm just not sure of the last bit.
D: So how can we find it if you don't know?
J: I've got the map. I'm going to find it on the A to Z.
D (looking at the map): But how can you find it on there?
J: It's okay. I know the name of the road.
D: But there's no houses or anything on it (the map). How can you find Piya's house on that?
J: Ah, right. The map doesn't show houses and things. But it shows me the roads. Look. We're here now and Piya's road is there. The map tells me we have to turn right, go straight on a bit and then turn left.

D: But what about his house.
J: That'll be alright because I know the number. We get on to Piya's road and then we look out for number fourteen. The houses will have numbers on the door.

Drew and I talked some more and I understood more about what he needed to know from me, as well as the extent of what he knew already. Thinking afterwards, I realised that Drew had experience of two-dimensional plans that related to three-dimensional settings. For instance, he was able to follow exploded diagrams to make small lego models. But those instructions had drawings that looked like the Lego pieces in front of him. He had a roadway for his cars, but that had the outline of buildings on it. The A–Z was a 2-D representation with even more detail removed.

This example highlights, for one aspect of learning, how a child has a current level of understanding. There is then a gap between that learning and a new idea. The gap is the zone of proximal development, which an adult can help a child to bridge. In order to help effectively you have to understand where and how a child has become confused in trying to bridge that gap without support.

SUGGESTED ACTIVITY

Look out for examples like the one given above in your work with children.

- In my example, I was able to work out what Drew did not understand within the one conversation. But, in an early years setting you may be interrupted. You may need to get back to a child, having realised later where the confusion arose.
- Make some notes on the activity or conversation that you observed, or of which you were a part.

What did the child already understand? In what way was his, or her, previous experience, helping to some extent? Where did the understanding stop? How were you able to help?

You will find a different kind of example in the further discussion about the zone of proximal development on page 123.

Patterns of thinking

Vygotsky outlined three steps in the active process of how children learn to think and their experiences became part of their ongoing way of thinking:

1 Children are helped by the well-pitched and timed assistance of an adult or able other child.
2 Children then work on the idea or skill by talking themselves through it – either out loud, as younger children tend to do, or by silent internal speech.

3   Children fully understand and the idea or pattern of the skill is integrated into their learning.

Vygotsky believed children who supported a confused or less able peer were not only being helpful but could gain in terms of their own powers of thought. The effort of explaining or of showing could help the more able child to understand their own knowledge or reflect on how and why they did something. They might become more able to think about their own thinking processes – a development called **metacognition**. In my experience this is equally true of adults who seek to help children – the example in the box is just one instance.

Vygotsky distinguished two types of concepts:

- **Spontaneous concepts** arise from children's own observations, usually at home and at least outside school.
- **Scientific concepts** develop as a result of formal teaching.

The zone of proximal development also works as children's spontaneous concepts form their current level of development and the intervention of a teacher can guide children towards the formulation of more organised and systematic concepts. An appropriate adult intervention acknowledges and respects the child's existing ideas and helps her on from that point.

Jerome Bruner
Helping children to think

Bruner was one of the early critics of Piaget in the English-speaking academic world. Bruner disagreed with Piaget's view that children's development had to be left to unfold without intervention. Bruner believed that development could be accelerated when adults took a more active role in children's learning. Bruner was especially concerned that children whose circumstances provided poor intellectual stimulation would be seriously disadvantaged without an active role for early years workers or teachers.

Piaget stressed the importance of children's physical environment in stimulating a child to learn. However, Bruner saw language as an important medium for adults to stimulate children to think and understand beyond their current grasp. He was in favour of a child-centred environment and learning through discovery but believed that adults should actively anticipate difficulties and help children directly. Bruner described the importance of supporting children's intellectual growth within any culture as 'a dialogue between the more experienced and the less experienced'.

The spiral curriculum

Bruner thought that children returned again and again to exploring and learning about the same materials or ideas. However, they were able to extend their understanding over the years because of what they had learned previously and through help from adults. Bruner called this circling a **spiral curriculum**. For example, a baby may like bricks to hold and drop but her interest as a toddler will become how to build and knock down. The same child at three years may explore the possibilities of bricks as part of a planned building or as objects for simple counting. In primary school she could be using bricks (or similar materials) to understand about weight or shape.

Bruner also developed the concept of scaffolding to explain how adults could help children to understand and to think. More on this topic in chapter 5.

Margaret Donaldson
Children as competent thinkers

Piaget was very interested in the mistakes that children make and saw them as evidence of their immature thinking. Margaret Donaldson challenged this emphasis on egocentricism and many of Piaget's claims about what young children do not understand. She also argued that the experimental techniques used by Piaget set children up to 'fail', because they concentrated on what children did not know, from an adult perspective, rather than the children's extensive abilities.

The many studies undertaken by Margaret Donaldson and her research colleagues have shifted the focus well away from young children as incompetent and illogical. The studies have shown that young children work hard to understand their world and that they are impressively logical within their current frame of reference. The many different experiments and naturalistic observations have also usefully shown how children can be mis-directed by adult use of language. Children try to make sense of questions from their point of view. For instance, an adult may ask a child to order a family of dolls, meaning from the tallest to the smallest. But a child may, if not asked to order by height specifically, put children with an adult on either side in a protective way that is very common when you take children out on a trip.

Disembedded thinking

Donaldson stressed the importance of the context in which children are learning or being asked questions by adults. She stressed that children are always trying to make 'human sense' of what they experience. Children learn

SUGGESTED ACTIVITY

In a practical setting such as a nursery, playgroup or the early years of school, it can be hard sometimes for adults to grasp where a child's understanding breaks down. And you cannot effectively help a child if you are confused about her confusion.

- A careful observation of a child – what she does and how she goes about a task – can give you insights. But another effective route can be to get a child to talk her thoughts or her plans out loud.
- Try this approach with a child who seems to be confused. You might ask 'Tell me what you're going to do' or 'Show me'. Look also at page 82 for Penny Munn's studies of children learning to count and the usefulness of adults' who talk out loud to explain what they are doing and why.

best in natural settings in which an object or a skill is linked in meaningful ways to their existing experience. Donaldson's view was that the Piagetian approach to children's understanding was an example of **disembedded thinking.** Children were being made to reason without a sensible context for them, and so it was not surprising that they made mistakes. Donaldson's view was that education in school requires children to learn disembedded thinking and this is a necessary skill. But adults should never underestimate the task faced by young children.

Donaldson and her colleagues repeated many of Piaget's experiments and explored the consequences of representing the situation to the child in slightly different ways. For instance:

- If three- to five-year-olds are given some experience of a layout in which a toy figure can see another figure from some positions but not others, then they are mostly able to say correctly when the first figure can see the second and when the latter is hidden from view. Children do not seem as unable to take up the perspective of another person as Piaget claimed.

- Children are also far more likely to say that two rows of the same number of toys are still the same when 'naughty teddy' has pushed one row up tighter, than when the adult has brought about the same change. One possible explanation is that, when an adult makes a change and then asks a question about whether 'It's still the same', children are misdirected into thinking that something must have happened. Otherwise why would an adult ask that kind of question?

In each of the examples, the details of an experimental procedure were shifted towards a context to which children could relate and make sense. This change substantially reduced the 'incorrect' responses as children were able to ground their thinking in events they understood.

TO THINK ABOUT

The less a situation makes sense to children through links with their existing experience, the more they are dependent on making some sense through what they guess the adults want them to say.

A study by Martin Hughes and Robert Grieve explored what happened when children were asked meaningless questions by adults, such as 'Is red heavier than yellow?' In fact, the children worked hard to cooperate with the adults and gave answers that made as much sense as possible out of a nonsensical situation. On the colour question, some children argued that red was the heavier because it was darker, or they explained their answer by reference to red and yellow objects close to them. The children brought in a context to create sense when the only existing sense was that, when adults ask children questions, they expect an answer.

This perspective is very useful to bear in mind when children give you odd answers to questions that seem perfectly clear to you.

1   How can you look carefully at what you are asking and how it links, or fails to link, with children's current understanding?
2   Are you taking the easy way out by assuming that children are being awkward, rather than that they are trying to cooperate and make sense out of a confusing situation?

The constructivist movement

This approach accepts the Piagetian view that children actively construct their own understanding of the world, but rejects the idea that development unfolds through fixed stages.

Thinking by means of constructing reality

The constructivist (or social constructivist) movement argues that few young children learn the same things at the same time and that early years work cannot proceed as if they do. Children, it is believed, construct their own view of reality from personal experiences and use this outlook to deal with new information. Adults' most important task is to understand individual children's understanding and strategies for learning. The constructivist approach stresses the context in which children learn and that adults need to seek ways to make learning meaningful for each child.

Constructivists make a similar distinction as Vygotsky's ideas of spontaneous and scientific concepts (see page 69). They believe children learn informal concepts and strategies at home and bring this rich yet disorganised system to their school experience. Teachers then bring a more systematic and logical approach to help children towards more formal and academic strategies.

Schemas in thinking

Chris Athey developed Piaget's idea of **schemas**: patterns of behaviour that are linked through a theme and from which a child generalises and explores in different situations. For instance, a child may be pursuing interest in a schema of 'enveloping' as she explores many different ways of covering or wrapping up herself or objects, or investigates the schema through craft activities. An awareness of the current schemas of an individual child can then guide adult observation and appropriate involvement in play.

Tanith transporting

Making sense of a child's way of thinking through schemas can also be a more positive approach when children's behaviour seems odd or annoying to adults. For instance, a child who is thoroughly exploring his 'transporting' schema may be busily engaged in moving objects from place to place. From an exclusively adult point of view, the child may be 'messing up' the environment by putting toys and other objects where they do not belong.

EXAMPLE

When my daughter was 18 months old she liked moving bricks and dolls around in her wooden trolley indoors, anything in the small wheelbarrow out of doors and her older brother in his buggy when we went on walks. Tanith had a big handbag in which she carried around a range of objects that were important to her. However, she also added objects that were important to us, such as her father's watch and the remote control for the television. It was crucial that we did not get cross with Tanith: she had not stolen these objects and she kept them safe. So, as well as explaining that Daddy's watch should be left where she found it, we also got used to asking Tanith to open her handbag if we could not find something.

One way of making sense of Tanith's behaviour is to say she was exploring a 'transporting' schema. It was not her only way of exploring at eighteen months, but it was a strong theme in how she worked with and on her environment in the latter half of her second year.

SUGGESTED ACTIVITY

Think about and observe children you know. Can you see the pattern of a schema in their play? For instance, you could look for:

- *Rotation*: an interest in things that turn like wheels, objects that roll or a child's physical exploration of spinning around herself or waving her limbs in a circular motion.
- *Orientation*: a fascination with how things seem from another angle, explored by turning objects around or the child twisting or hanging upside down.
- *Connection*: how things are or could be joined together. A child might explore this in crafts, in stringing together toys or showing connections in a drawing. The opposite schema of separation can lead to havoc when children have the physical skills to disassemble objects that adults would rather they did not!

Make notes and compare your observations with a colleague.

In its application to early years, for instance through the work of Bruce and Christine Pascal, the constructivist movement in Britain influential in encouraging an adult role as enabler or facilitator of c learning. A more active directing role is seen as potentially disruptive of early development – because of the importance of children's own concepts. The power of the approach is in stressing the pointlessness of adults' pushing on with their own plans for children's learning when there are no links to children's current understanding. In its application to school learning there has been less agreement, with writers such as Ros Driver proposing a more active intervention by teachers, that starts from children's existing concepts. Others propose the continuation of a more enabling role for adults through school. (More on the role of adults in chapter 5.)

The constructivist approach – a personal note

The constructivist view, with the adult as enabler, is dominant in the British early years field. I have been concerned that, in some books on child care and education, it is presented as the only way to be sensitive to children's thinking and learning. Other approaches, for instance the behaviourist approach, are sometimes dismissed in a peremptory fashion.

Thoughtless application of behaviourist principles can undoubtedly be authoritarian. But a misapplication of a constructivist approach can lead early years workers to be so concerned not to 'interfere' in children's natural learning that they hold back and take a passive role. I have observed children, who would welcome some help, left to discover everything for themselves – a long-winded and ultimately impossible task. Of course, the constructivist approach does not propose that children should be abandoned in this way, but diluted versions have led to that practical interpretation. Any good ideas can be open to misinterpretation.

Final comment on theories

It is important to realise that not every school of thought on early learning accepts an emphasis on cognitive development at all. The approach that has evolved from the philosophy of Rudolf Steiner, which influences some private nurseries and schools, is critical of the work of people like Donaldson and Bruner. Steiner nursery schools share an early years emphasis on learning through play and discovery and the importance of natural materials. However, the underlying philosophy emphasises spiritual development and does not value an early years focus on intellectual development. Steiner schools judge it is inappropriate to introduce children to abstract ideas like reading until they are six or seven years.

3.2 Children's thinking in context

Section 3.1 covers the main theories about how children learn to think. As you will have noticed, some themes are shared by more than one theory. Exchanges between supporters of different positions sometimes get very heated, but there is no reason for early years workers not to take good ideas from several models of thinking.

This section explores examples of how children, even very young children, show evidence of thinking. My aim is to illustrate the richness of children's reasoning and intellectual problem-solving, without getting mired in which theory is more correct. My related aim is to illustrate how much adults involved with children can learn, and be fascinated, if they give time and attention to what children think and how they understand at present.

Thinking as part of the whole development

Children's intellectual capabilities extend as the months and years pass. The abilities of a four-year-old are dramatically different from those of a two-year-old and part of this change is seen through children's development of language as a tool. But children's remarkable drive to explore and understand should not be seen as isolated from the rest of their development.

Intellect and feeling

It is especially important to bear in mind the link between children's emotional development and their cognitive development in the early years. The increased ability to think and tackle new ideas and intellectual tasks can be undermined

Sam's interest in enclosing was getting out of hand

SUGGESTED ACTIVITY

Research into child development can tell you that children of a particular age are potentially able to manage a given skill or understand an idea. Yet in the practical situation, you will often face 'Maria could do this, but she doesn't seem to want to.'

Observe and then think about one or two of the children for whom you are responsible who seem unwilling to try.

1 Is this child usually wary of new experiences and how could you support her confidence without pushing her further than she is comfortable?
2 Does this child's wariness come from bad experiences when he has made mistakes in the past? How can you make changes in your approach and build up his self-esteem?

by feelings of anxiety or low self-esteem. These issues are covered in chapter 2, but please do not forget them as you read this chapter.

You will not effectively support children's cognitive development if you forget that children's feelings are also involved: curiosity, uneasiness, satisfaction, delight, fear. Feelings and past experience will affect children's motivation: how much they are willing or keen to try. Children whose mistakes have been highlighted, or who have frequently been compared unfavourably with other children, may pull back from taking the many small risks that are part of continued learning.

Children also use their powers of thought and reasoning in their social relationships. This area of study in children's development is called social cognition and you will find more on the topic on page 151.

Cognitive development and health

As well as making allowance for children's feelings, it is important to appreciate that cognitive development can be affected by children's overall health. Poor continuing health and repeated hospitalisations can deprive young children of valuable learning experiences as well as leave them feeling too ill to take notice of their surroundings. A more general point has been raised by claims that giving children vitamin pills will boost their scores on IQ measures.

The research in this area is complex and the results are inconsistent. But general themes emerge which are of practical use to adults responsible for young children.

- It is certainly not the case that taking vitamin pills will boost IQ in a simple way for every child, and these have been some of the advertising claims.
- Severe malnutrition has a long-term effect on development. And poor diet can leave children lethargic, which is not a positive state for learning. So, seeking a well-balanced diet is important for children (see also the comment on diet on page 30). However, deficiencies in diet cannot be corrected simply by taking vitamin pills. Research into nutrients in diet suggests that some of the important ingredients of food cannot be effectively produced artificially.
- Vitamins and mineral supplements seem to benefit psychological functioning in children with a poor diet. However, improving the diet or giving supplements do not guarantee improved school performance. There are a range of psychological and social factors in the learning situation and the interaction of these may prove more important for children.

Talking and thinking

Piaget viewed most of young children's speech as egocentric – personal soliloquies rather than an attempt to communicate. In contrast, Vygotsky took the stance that young children were obviously working hard to communicate with others; it was just that they were sometimes hard to understand. Vygotsky believed that a crucial part of children's development was their increasing ability to control and direct their own behaviour, including their language. Language was so important because it was the means by which children could reflect on and elaborate their own ideas. However, conversation with adults was a powerful shaper of children's learning, since words alone could not carry the meaning of concepts.

Margaret Donaldson shares the view that the origins of language seem to be intertwined with the child's mental life, initially with those activities which occupy the child's mind in the immediate and present. Early in toddlerhood young children discover that adults can inform and help them by telling. The toddlers start to invite and welcome verbal instruction from familiar adults.

Melissa Bowerman, representing a constructivist view, proposes that, as children learn language, the words enable them to express meanings that they have already developed without language. In the central disagreement about 'Can young children think without language?' the constructivists will answer 'Of course they can'.

Support for this approach comes from observations of the play of very young children and their early language development. For instance, symbolic play, in terms of simple pretend actions like drinking from an empty cup, appear at around the same time as a toddler's first words. Then, when a young child shows sequences in her pretend play, the two-word combinations and short phrases appear. So it seems that children are showing a more general readiness to think in a symbolic way. Producing the words, that act as a symbolic representation of an object, is just part of the child's more general development.

SUGGESTED ACTIVITY

Observation of babies and toddlers has highlighted links between how they play and their early language. The pattern is as follows:

When children's play is:	*They will probably*:	*At about this age*:
Exploring objects and people close at hand	Communicate with gestures and sounds	0–10 months
Relating one object with another in play	Produce many patterns of sounds	9–15 months
Simple pretend actions applied only to them	First words	11–18 months
Simple pretend actions that involve other people or toys	2 word combinations, short phrases	12–30 months
Sequences of pretend play and other play involving other people and play materials	3-, 4-, 5-word sentences	19–36 months

Organise yourself to make some observations that start with the play of babies and toddlers and then look at their communication. This observation will be more useful if you can arrange to observe the same young children several times, with intervals of a month or so in between.

You are looking for patterns, not exact relationships. (Please note the wide variation in the ages given above.)

1   What patterns do you observe as you watch and listen to a baby or a toddler?
2   How close in time are your observations of a child's very early pretend play and the first recognisable words?
3   Do you see children, whose language is a little later than average, following the same route?

Thinking in the very young

Over the last few decades there has been tremendous interest in the abilities of very young children. The different areas of study in, for instance early communication (see chapter 3) or social relationships (see chapter 2) have produced detailed descriptions of what babies and toddlers can manage. The observations leave no doubt that the young children are thinking human

(see also chapter 6)

SUGGESTED ACTIVITY

Collect examples of the behaviour of young children that show they remember something, have thought or planned ahead.

- For example, young children show evidence of having learned patterns of how life works in their immediate environment. Patterns of play for older babies often show that they are taking the initiative in expectation of a response from an adult or older sibling. Dropping toys over the edge of a highchair for others to pick up and return is a frequent game.
- Children's ability to think about what is real and not real can be seen when they pretend to be someone else or say something the toddler or young child knows is not true and then laugh.
- Look for examples yourself among the children you know.

beings. The patterns of early thinking are definitely not the same in very young children as they become in four-year-olds or school-age children. And this is an important point for frustrated adults to recall when they are dealing with children's behaviour (see also chapter 6). However, under-twos are alert to what goes on around them and they are working to make sense of their environment and how they can act upon it.

Memory and thinking

There is evidence that older babies and toddlers remember. They do not, for instance, start from scratch every time they encounter the same situation or play materials.

- Toddlers remember where their toys are kept. They can be persistent in searching out objects they are not supposed to have, a source of frustration to parents at home. Even if they do not talk, the behaviour of very young children shows evidence of thinking, planning and use of memories.
- They recall and may tell you that personal objects like a bag or a bracelet belong to a particular person. They show this understanding by taking the bracelet to their mother or pointing to the bag and saying 'Nana'.
- Young children do not remember everything and can be distracted by their consuming interests of the moment. For example, toddlers can collide with furniture which is always in the same place because they are rushing to greet someone.
- Alternatively, young children continue to do something they know is not allowed because their wish to carry on is so strong. So, for adults, the issues of a child's behaviour may become muddled with the conviction that he cannot remember.

Young children's memories seem to operate through links with a specific context and their thinking is also concrete and specific. This focus is not surprising when you consider how much they still have to learn. They do not necessarily generalise outside their immediate experience so far.

Children show pleasure at events they like and enjoy. For instance, older babies and toddlers in a buggy often kick their legs in glee when they recognise the last part of the walk as they reach their grandparents' home or that of their childminder. Their behaviour suggests that they are thinking ahead and anticipating a happy experience. Children use body gestures and early language to register their thoughts about less-enjoyed activities. For instance, we used to wash our son's hair every Friday but he had a bath each evening. Drew did not like having his hair washed and most times that he got into the bath as a toddler he would ask, 'Hair wash?', to be met six days out of seven with 'No hair wash' from us and a grin from him. On Fridays we replied, 'Yes hair wash' and he would try sadly, 'No hair wash' (the tone of his voice expressing a request and not a question).

Even children of three and four years of age tend to recall events as separate incidents and have to learn to use a narrative type structure to help linked recall. You can help to build the narrative with questions – 'What happened next?' or 'What did you do after that?' Genuine interest helps, along with sharing clues from the context and questions to guide children's attention.

3.3 Adults' understanding

Talking and understanding

Babies and toddlers are very specific in how they think about their world. Their actions are based on familiar sequences and situations. By three and four years of age, children are making links between areas of their understanding. They do this partly through active exploration of their environment but opportunities for conversation with adults are also a vital way of extending their thinking.

Children's conversation and especially their questions are an intriguing window into how they think about the world. Their questions illustrate children's thirst for information. But you can also see evidence that children have some grasp of what they do not yet know.

SUGGESTED ACTIVITY

Children are interested to push out the boundaries to their current information and some conversations can put adults on the spot. Margaret Donaldson quotes an amusing exchange between Callum and his mother:

Callum: Is God everywhere?
Mother: Yes, dear.
C: Is he in this room?
M: Yes, he is.
C: Is he in my mug?
M (growing uneasy): Er – yes.
C (clapping his hand over his mug): Got him!
(From *Human Minds*, page 80.)

- Collect some examples of your own to show how children's questions show their keen curiosity and desire to make sense of the world.
- Include some examples of questions that make you think in return, in order to give children a sensible and accurate answer.

Children's mistakes are often logical, sensible deductions based on what they know already (see page 99 in chapter 4) . However, there are large gaps in their knowledge and the framework they have developed will change again. Children do not usually learn an idea or unravel a misunderstanding in one sitting or a single conversation. Their grasp of a complex topic is built up gradually as they fill in the details of what they do not know.

Children are also learning about cause and effect. Three- and four-year-olds ask questions about what follows what, why something has happened and how things work. Children's ability to explain is partly whether they have grasped what is happening and also whether they have the words to communicate that understanding to others. Morag Donaldson found that three- to five-year-olds showed understanding of cause and effect and could communicate their grasp, so long as they were working with situations and materials that were familiar to them. The children used words like 'because' and 'so' correctly and could follow and reply to 'why' questions from adults.

The power of conversation

Children's powers of thinking and reasoning are probably best shown in the conversations that they initiate. But, as Morag Donaldson points out, question and answer exchanges between an adult and a child are very different depending on whether this is a naturally occurring conversation or an adult-initiated

exchange in nursery or primary school. Barbara Tizard demonstrated the same key point in her observations of children's conversations at home and at nursery school. The issues that arise from these studies are as illuminating, and useful, about adult behaviour and options as they are for highlighting children's thought processes.

- When adults are exploring and guiding children's learning (in schools or nurseries), they tend to ask children questions to which the adults have the answer.
- Children's replies are to demonstrate that they know or understand – or do not.
- On the other hand, children's questions are usually, although not always, a request for information. Children are not usually checking out whether the adult knows something.
- So, replies to questions and given explanations in normal conversation tend to have a sharing function. In the school model, children's explanations in reply to adult questions have a display function, showing their knowledge.
- Workers in early years care and education can hold conversations with children but Tizard's research suggests that they tend not to behave in that way.

Research into children's cognitive development has been unbalanced towards thinking and learning in more formal settings – pre-school and school rather than the home. The unspoken assumption seems to be that cognitive development is too complicated for non-professionals and that the caring environment of home is incompatible with stimulating exchanges to encourage children's intellectual powers. (More on this point also in chapter 5, page 131.) Barbara Tizard's work is one exception to the general rule. Penny Munn has also highlighted the extent to which children at the pre-school and primary school stage look towards home as a source of specific and general support. Some children expect that their parents will explain and help in the struggles with concepts such as number and intellectual tasks like reading (see also pages 83 and 113).

Barbara Tizard and Martin Hughes analysed conversations undertaken by four-year-olds in nursery class with their teachers and at home with their mothers. These researchers made the useful distinction that children's thinking progresses along two tracks:

- Children need to learn details and they are hungry for information. Children whose enquiries meet with a positive adult reaction go on to ask many questions.
- But children are also developing a framework by which to make sense of the information. Their questions sometimes show an awareness that something is wrong somewhere – 'But that can't be right because....'

Sometimes children make mistakes because they are missing an item of information, but sometimes they are struggling with the conceptual framework. The boxed example highlights both kinds of potential confusion.

In the absence of vital information, children sometimes turn to what adults see as almost 'magical thinking'. But, from the children's point of view, their (wrong) guess in this instance is understandable in a child's world where much is inexplicable and just seems to happen.

For example, I have a very clear memory of being five years old and learning to knit. I was having trouble with the physical skills of knitting and concluded that my project would grow faster if I simply moved the stitches from one needle to the other. I had assumed that moving stitches across made the knitting grow. My experimental short cut soon showed me that you had to feed the wool into the work to make any progress.

EXAMPLE

One of the four-year-olds observed by Tizard's team was trying to work out the relationship between money and services – a pattern that was initially muddled because a neighbour sometimes paid the window cleaner on other people's behalf. The exchange between Rosy and her mother shows how a child can only explore thoughts through words if an adult gives time.

Rosy: She can't pay everybody's, er... all the bills to the window-cleaner, can she?

Mother: No, she can't pay everybody's bills... she sometimes pays mine if I'm out.

R: Cause it's fair.

M: Mm, it is.

R: Umm, but where does she leave the money?

M: She doesn't leave it anywhere, she hands it to the window-cleaner, after he's finished.

R: And then she gives it to us?

M: No, no, she doesn't have to pay us.

R: Then the window-cleaner gives it to us?

M: No, we give the window-cleaner money, he does work for us, and we have to give him money.

R: Why?

M: Well, because he's been working for us cleaning our windows. He doesn't do it for nothing.

R: Why do you have money if you have... if people clean your windows?

M: Well the window cleaner needs money, doesn't he?

R: Why?

M: To buy clothes for his children and food for them to eat.

R: Well, sometimes window-cleaners don't have children.

And so the conversation continued...

(From Tizard, Barbara and Hughes, Martin: *Young Children Learning* page 120–1).

In the conversations that Tizard and her team observed at home, the children explored many topics of interest to them: how to share out a limited number of cakes, why children cry and scream, how Father Christmas does his job, that clocks tell the time but not the day and many more topics. On the basis of this study and another piece of research on partnership with parents in schools, Tizard challenged the view that children learn most or best in special early years settings. She concluded and some other researchers have supported her view, that:

- Nursery teachers often underestimated the extent to which children explored ideas through conversation at home.
- Learning through play is not the only, or necessarily the best way for children to extend their thinking.
- The most extended conversations at home were often at relaxed times – over tea or during a one-to-one story time. Similar exchanges only happened at the children's nursery school when the adult stayed in one place for some time, for instance, mending equipment and a child stood and chatted.
- Children did not ask questions at school at the same rate they did at home and their school questions were different. Tizard and Hughes concluded that children had taken the message that at school it was the teachers' role to ask questions and theirs to answer. The questions they did pose at school were mainly enquiries, such as, 'Where's the glue?' They rarely asked the curious 'why' questions that were frequent at home.
- Persistent question and answer sessions, in which teachers know the answer, are not necessarily an accurate reflection of what children know nor a good way to extend their understanding.
- Tizard was not saying it was impossible for nursery staff to have useful conversations with children. Rather that the way nurseries were organised, and the way that staff tended to see their role, made such conversations less likely.

SUGGESTED ACTIVITY

Persistent intellectual curiosity is as important to children's development as their active physical explorations. Children need the words to ask adults questions. But they also need to feel confident that an adult will give them time, attention and a useful reply.

Keep a record over several weeks of the questions that children ask you. (Not the questions you ask of them.) Concentrate on questions that require more than a one-word reply from you. Write down in as much detail as you can:

- Exactly what the child asked you – in the child's words.
- The context of the child's question. What was it that the child wanted to know or was showing you she did not understand?

- How did you reply to this question?
- Do you think you answered the child in full? Did she appear to be satisfied with your reply? (Your answer may have been to show a child, as well as a reply in words, or you may have gone together to find out the answer.)

Look over your notes and discuss them with a colleague.

- Are you all making the best of opportunities to hold conversations with children guided by their interests?
- Do the children, or some of them, scarcely ask you questions? How might you encourage this development?

Asking children what they think

Some research into children's thinking has taken the useful approach of directly asking children for their thoughts and opinions about an area of intellectual discovery. Two examples are given in this section: understanding about number and children's making sense of road safety.

The example of number

In terms of adult understanding, young children's ability to deal with number breaks down at three crucial points:

1   Children sometimes lose themselves as they count and forget where they began or count the same object twice.
2   Young children judge rows of objects visually. So a row of toy cars placed close together will be judged as less than a well spread out row, even when each row contains the same number of cars. This conflict between a child and adult viewpoint is described, from Piagetian theory, as a failure in conservation of number.
3   When children are asked to judge the relative quantities in two rows of counters they usually judge by sight and do not count each row unless the adult specifically asks them the key question, 'How many?'

From an adult viewpoint, the children's behaviour in each of these examples has been seen as illogical, as evidence that young children do not really understand number. However, as Penny Munn and others have pointed out, the 'failures' of young children are more usefully seen as evidence of the egocentric thinking of adults, who look only from their own perspective as very experienced users of number.

Penny Munn spent time talking individually with children during their last year in nursery and their first term of primary school. On each of four visits she asked the children the same basic questions including 'Can you count?' and 'Why do you count?' This approach elicited children's beliefs and gives an insight into how children's understanding grows. Penny Munn's research confirmed the findings of other researchers, who have focused on children's rather than adults' perspectives to show that:

•   Children generally learn to recite a number sequence at a younger age than they are able to count a given number of objects, or to select a limited number in answer to the question, 'Can you give me three bricks?'
•   It was rare for young children to understand the adult purpose of counting until they went to school. Then the children more and more gave an answer to 'Why do you count?' that focused on 'to know how many'.

SUGGESTED ACTIVITY

- Look for opportunities to make your purposes clear to children by speaking your thoughts out loud.
- You might muse out loud about how thick the paint should be for this particular craft activity, or talk through your ideas for re-organising the book corner for two children who are helping you.
- Penny Munn gives the example of the characters in Sesame Street who speak their thoughts out loud and this seems to help young listeners.
- Compare notes with your colleagues.

- Children of nursery age seemed to view counting much more as a playful and social activity. This is not surprising, since they mainly experienced counting as part of songs and games like hide and seek. Adults are usually the ones who keep score or make a tally.

Penny Munn's research, and studies like hers, point early years workers towards a respectful approach to how children currently see their world and assign meaning. She draws four practical conclusions from her work and these are applicable beyond the learning of number:

- Adults should take time to understand the children's beliefs about counting before they start activities designed to help learning about number. So long as children see counting mainly as a playful activity, they will not think to count when it would be useful for them to do so.
- Adults should take children's counting seriously and not dismiss it because children use their abilities in a limited context. Children view their counting as meaningful, so should adults. Early counting provides a framework for future learning.
- Adults often assume that their purposes are clear to children, that their thoughts do not have to be expressed out loud because adult goals are obvious from their behaviour. This is not the case here, and in many contexts other than counting. Adults need to make their purpose clear to children in how they use counting – by speaking out loud or by explaining why they are counting up the children, the books or the chairs.
- Encourage children through daily activities to develop their own goals for which counting is a useful skill to apply. Give children a reason to check on 'how many' or 'are they the same?' Children do not necessarily see the point, unless adults explain it.

Road safety

The practicalities of teaching children safe behaviour on the roads is a useful illustration of how adults need to understand children's thinking and their perspective, rather than assume that the adult view is shared by children. Crossing the road safely is a complex task and a good example of cognitive development in action.

A number of research projects on young children and road safety have highlighted that the traditional approach of sets of rules (like the Green Cross Code) or guidance to children (like 'Find a safe place to cross') fail to transfer into children's behaviour at the roadside. Several issues arose when researchers looked in detail at what children thought about road safety.

- Young children think by starting from specific examples and then generalising to other similar situations. Yet, road safety training has frequently worked in the opposite way, by stressing general principles and expecting children to apply these rules to specific road crossing situations. This example is a good illustration of Piaget's distinction between inductive and deductive reasoning (see page 65).
- Children had difficulty applying a rule like 'Find a safe place to cross', because they do not yet share adult ways of thinking about what would be safe or dangerous. Under eights had not usually developed a way of thinking that helped them to distinguish what was relevant and irrelevant in deciding if it was safe to cross. Adults might believe this distinction was common sense, but they had learned through experience.
- Research with five-year-olds illustrated that they had a low awareness of potential road dangers and underestimated the importance of finding a safe location to cross (a key point made by adults). Yet in teaching road safety, adults were not explaining how to choose a location for crossing.

General rules for crossing safely were of very limited use if children chose an unsafe place to cross – perhaps because it was the shortest distance between two points.

● Children also had difficulty in judging the combined effect of the speed of vehicles and their distance from the crossing point. Children might look along the road. But they did not 'see' the vehicle, in the sense of thinking of it as an immediate danger to them if they crossed.

● Children were also unlikely to allow for their own relative invisibility, especially in their tendency to cross by coming out from between parked cars.

A series of studies have looked at training children in the behavioural skills of safe road crossing by taking into account how children think about the situation. Practice at the roadside or with computer simulations seems to be more effective in stimulating children to think in a safe way so that they can adjust their behaviour at the kerb.

Reading on . . .

★ Athey, Chris 1990: *Extending Thought in Young Children: A parent-teacher partnership* (Paul Chapman). Discussion of the idea of schemas in children's thinking. How this can be applied in early years settings and in helping parents to be alert to their children's development.

★ Donaldson, Margaret 1978: *Children's Minds* (Fontana). A lively discussion of children's thinking and how they are expected to think by adults. Illustrated with descriptions of experiments with children and children's comments.

★ Donaldson, Margaret 1992: *Human Minds: An exploration* (Penguin). This book is for dipping into the discussion of how children think and an appropriate role for adults. Some of the book is less easy reading as Donaldson builds a more general theory of mind.

★ Grieve, Robert and Hughes, Martin (eds) 1990: *Understanding Children: Essays in honour of Margaret Donaldson* (Basil Blackwell). Covers a range of topics on children's thinking and communication. The book is useful because the chapters place experiments with children in the broader context of our learning about how children think.

★ Munn, Penny 'Children's beliefs about counting' in Ian Thompson (ed) 1997: *Teaching and Learning Early Number* (Open University Press). A very readable account of the research described on page 82 of this chapter.

★ Sutherland, Peter 1992: *Cognitive Development Today: Piaget and his critics* (Paul Chapman). A useful resource for summaries of different theories in this area – more manageable than some of the original writings of the theorists covered.

★ Thomson, J.; Tolmie, A.; Foot, H. and McLaren, B. 1996: *Child Development and the Aims of Road Safety Education* (HMSO). Discussion of some of the road safety research outlined on page 83 of this chapter.

★ Tizard, Barbara and Hughes, Martin 1984: *Young Children Learning: Talking and thinking at home and at school* (Fontana). Very readable account of the research described on page 80 of this chapter, with plenty of examples of children's conversations.

4 Communication and language

This chapter covers:

- theories of language development;
- the development of communication;
- variations within language learning;
- learning written communication.

4.1 Theories of language development

Language as part of communication

Communication is a broader term than language. **Language** is most often used to mean spoken words and is part of the larger process of communication between people. **Communication** is normally used to mean all the ways that we convey our ideas, feelings, reactions, questions, objections (and so on) to other people. We communicate partly through spoken words, but also by the many ways in which we can say our words through tone, volume and different patterns of emphasis. But we also communicate without words, in the messages expressed through facial expression, gestures and whole body movements. This unspoken channel of communication can support and perhaps further explain our words. But sometimes body language may be giving a different and contradictory message. For instance, the words may say 'I believe you' or 'I am interested in what you have to say' but the body language shows doubt or inattention.

An understanding of children's development in communication has to cover the full range of communicative behaviour. You need an awareness of what children can and are doing and an alertness to how you use both your spoken words and all the supporting body language. You will find all these aspects of communication in this chapter. However, the theories discussed tend to focus on the developmental task of learning to speak. The descriptions later in the chapter of what actually happens as children develop cover a more rounded view of communication. On page 89 you will find explanations of the more usual terms in discussion of communication.

The vast majority of young children learn to speak and many around the world learn more than one language in their early years. Unlike some of the developments in thinking, you can directly observe and note down the ways in which children's power of speech extends over the months and years. There can be no disagreement over the fact that young children manage what, from the outside, looks like a very tough task. The arguments have arisen among psychologists and linguists over how to explain satisfactorily what children are clearly managing to do.

Behaviourism and learning theories
Learning through imitation

The first attempts to explain children's acquisition of language were through basic principles of behaviourism (see page 19) which included imitation. The ability to imitate explains partly how babies' sound making moves towards the language that they are hearing and that children's accents become those of the people they hear around them. The babies who show most interest and motivation to imitate gestures and sound patterns are also those whose spoken language develops earlier.

But simple imitation does not work as a complete explanation. Toddlers soon produce word combinations that they have not previously heard, and their logical mistakes in grammar ('I goed' rather than 'I went') show the results of over-applying a rule system and not of copying. Imitation is clearly of some importance, but children are soon very creative in using the results of their imitation.

Patterns of reinforcement

Behaviourists such as B.F.Skinner proposed that young children learn to speak because their parents systematically reward correct versions of the language and do not reward mistakes. Again, young children seem to flourish with positive feedback for their early attempts at language. But most adults are considerably more flexible than a reinforcement explanation would predict. Parents and carers respond meaningfully to a wide range of constructions and pronunciations from toddlers. Correcting all or most of children's mistakes seems to inhibit communication rather than encourage it.

Environment and experience

Some explanations of language focus on children's early experience of language. In order to talk, young children definitely need to hear spoken language and have opportunities to use what they learn. Children who have experienced a severely deprived childhood, with very limited human contact or care, do not learn to speak in isolation.

Children who hear plenty of language seem to develop their vocabulary slightly faster than those whose experience of language is limited. Toddlers also seem to develop slightly faster when adults communicate in a responsive way, dependent on what the young child has said. Babies and toddlers who have experience of infant-directed speech (see page 92) also seem to develop some facets of their language slightly faster.

Children also seem to be helped by later developments of child-sensitive language from adults, for instance, the effort to expand children's sentences by adding to the stem created by children's small number of words, or by slightly recasting what they say. For instance, the child says, 'Moggle village – little houses, little mans, little boats'. Her parent expands and gently corrects with, 'Yes, we went to the model village, didn't we? And everything was so little. There were little people and even the little boats. And the little train, do you remember the little train?'

Yet, all of these results are of the 'slightly' and 'a bit' variety. And children whose early experience of language is less rich still learn to talk, although early years intervention programmes are often built around concerns that such children's use of language can be very limited. Responsive patterns of communication with babies and toddlers are well worthwhile, because they build close relationships as well as foster language development. However, they do not stand alone as an explanation of how children learn to talk.

One of the puzzles of explaining children's language development is that their rate of learning language and their later use of language both appear to be influenced by the communication behaviour of their parents, or other important carers. But research does not point to particular aspects of what adults do and prove that 'this is the really important way to behave'. There does not seem to be a simple relationship between what adults do and how children develop in language.

Biological theories

Since language development is not well explained through the details of individual children's experience, some theorists have proposed that some innate biological system must be involved (some process within the brain that is present when a baby is born).

Noam Chomsky first proposed the explanation that language is not learned, but emerges as part of the process of maturation (the unfolding of characteristics programmed by a genetic code). Children need to hear language spoken to trigger the system and the innate readiness has to be for language in general, not a specific language. Dan Slobin has expanded the idea that every child has a basic *language making capacity*. He proposes that the system works through a set of operating principles which programme infants to listen into sounds and rhythm, to the beginnings and ends of sound sequences and to how sounds are stressed.

The idea of an innate language device overcomes the difficulties of explaining how infants home in on language so successfully. However, such a system would predict that the pattern of learning language is very similar from one language to another. When innate theory was first developed, it looked as if children who were learning different languages did follow very similar patterns. But more recent and detailed research has also found many differences.

Language as part of cognitive development

Innate models of language development allowed for the abilities of children themselves and not just the input of speaking adults. Theorists, whose interest in language started from cognitive development, focus much more on how young children apply their growing capacity to think towards language, in the same way as they have worked hard to make sense of their world without words. Language is then seen as a vehicle for expressing thoughts and as a way of directing and extending thought patterns.

Jean Piaget thought language was important, but more as a way for young children to think out loud than as a form of communication with others. Piaget's approach was to describe and explain children's development shorn of much of the everyday social framework in which they learn. But his view of their egocentricism is not supported by more recent observational research which shows young children's pressing wish to communicate with others.

Lev Vygotsky questioned Piaget's view of the relationship between language and thinking. Vygotsky proposed that children first use their tools of communication in social interaction. But speech also becomes a highly personal medium for learning – firstly as words spoken out loud and later as silent inner speech. Vygotsky suggested that children solve problems with the help of their speech as well as their hands through active exploration.

Vygotsky observed that young children's use of speech started as a means to guide themselves as the words accompanied their actions. Then language began to precede the actions, with a function of guiding and planning what the child might or would do. Language freed children's mental processes from the immediate experience. Vygotsky pointed out that children and adults might use the same words, but that did not mean that the children yet fully understood the concept represented by that word. He was making the useful practical point that concepts are not given to children ready-made with the words – development in thinking also has to take place.

Other theorists and researchers in the cognitive developmental approach share the stance that the beginnings of language are related to children's mental life. And the constructivist view stresses that children learn words primarily because they connect with what the young child is already thinking. Words do not introduce new meanings but give expression to thoughts that the young child has developed pre-linguistically. Look back to page 76 in chapter 3 for more on this approach.

In summary – so how do children learn language?

All of the competing theories have some merit. But none of them offer a full explanation of how young children make the impressive leap between what they hear and the sophisticated language they eventually produce. Margaret Donaldson summed up the situation with: 'How this level of skill is achieved so quickly is a puzzle that has occupied many minds, especially in the last few decades of active research in developmental psycholinguistics. Yet the achievement remains essentially mysterious. We do not know in any detail how it is done.' (*Human Minds: An exploration*, page 106.)

It is possible that several themes are intertwined in language development. There may well be some innate device that programmes babies towards the acquisition of spoken language. However, children's learning is also shaped by their experience of language, especially from the key adults in their environment. But it is equally important what children do with this experience; they are active linguists, just as they are active thinkers.

4.2 The development of communication

We may not fully understand *how* children learn to speak, but there is a rich array of information about *what* happens as their abilities develop in the broad area of communication. Language development is so important because the capacity is closely related to children's cognitive development (chapter 3) and to their emotional development (chapter 2). An emphasis on the full range of communication, and not only the spoken words, is an important reminder that even very young, non-speaking children show evidence of feeling and thinking. Adult awareness and close involvement with children's communication is an effective way of supporting their learning and finding a window into the children's world.

You need to look at two sides of the coin:

1   what children do and say as they communicate with someone;
2   what they understand of what is communicated to them.

Both of these aspects of communication include verbal (spoken) and non-verbal communication (body language). From the earliest months it is possible to look at the development of communication from both these perspectives.

Some useful terms

Speech or **expressive language**: what children themselves say in words and later in phrases and sentences.

Babbling: the early sound making, often very tuneful, of babies who are stringing together a series of sounds in a deliberate way.

Jargon: the term used for the very expressive flow of almost words that many, but not all babies, make around about their first birthday. The stream of sounds has many of the intonations of speech but there are no real words yet.

Articulation: how children manage the sound system that makes up the words in their language. It is not unusual for children to have some difficulties with some sounds as they learn their language.

Fluency: how easily a child's speech flows. The speech of young children often falters for a moment as they search for a word or find a way to express a thought. Persistent problems in fluency, such as **stammering**, may need specialist help.

Bilingual: children and adults who can communicate in more than one language. Children may learn two languages at the same time (simultaneously) – or a second language some time after the first (successively).

Understanding, **comprehension** or **receptive language**: children's grasp of what is said to them. Young children regularly show through their behaviour that they understand words, in context, that they do not yet say themselves.

Non-verbal communication or **body language**: the forms of communicating without words. Children with no or very few words need to use non-verbal forms to convey meaning, but fluent speakers still continue to communicate non-verbally. Some gestures seem to be almost universal but there are many cultural variations in body language.

Children learn to talk – even if we cannot understand exactly how

Early communication as interaction

Detailed observational research has shown just how much babies are primed to interact with adult carers from the earliest weeks and months. The technical opportunities of slow motion and the double video system (one camera focused on each person) have allowed fine-grained analysis of communication exchanges.

For instance, when a baby or young toddler hands an object to his mother, it is not just a case of 'child stretches out hand' and 'mother takes the object'. Watched frame by frame on video, the exchange is shown to be a whole series of subtle moves by baby and mother. In this interaction, and similar ones, the moves of both baby and adult are responsive to changes in signals coming from the other. Such sensitivity seems to be an important part of how babies make and sustain contact with caring adults and how those adults support and make a communicative and affectionate relationship with the baby.

Colwyn Trevarthen has studied early infant communication in great detail. In a study with Lynne Murray, he looked at the reactions of babies of six to twelve weeks under different conditions: when mothers gave their babies full attention, when the mothers gazed without reacting and if they turned away. When babies had the full attention of their mothers, they reacted with smiles, coos and away-from-their-body gestures. When mothers gazed but did not react, the babies made similar efforts of communication, which became more tense until they looked away from their mothers. If mothers turned away, for instance to talk with the researcher (a planned interruption in the experiment), babies looked less at their mothers, gazed at the researcher and made vocalisations and gestures that seemed to be an attempt to regain their mother's attention. These very young babies were active in relating to their mothers and their behaviour changed in response to varied conditions.

The precise and sensitive interaction was further highlighted when Trevarthen and Murray played back to the babies the video sequence of their attentive and smiling mother. This experience led to distress in the babies. Although their mother was gazing and smiling, what she did was not tuned into the babies' behaviour at the time the video was running. Babies were aware of this mismatch and their upset reaction shows how attuned they are to seeking a genuine exchange with important carers.

Researchers who study very early communication have described patterns in the shared interaction:

- **Co-regulation:** the way in which baby and adult continue to adapt to one another, through very subtle and small changes in behaviour.
- **Matching:** when the adult or child makes their actions more similar to those of the other.
- **Imitation:** when adult or child deliberately copies the other.
- **Attunement:** a subtle form of matching in which one person adjusts their actions and words in tune with the emotions of the other person. In very early exchanges, it is the adult who adjusts. But toddlers and young children start to show deliberate shifts in behaviour depending on the visible emotions of others (see also page 156).

TO THINK ABOUT

- Study of the communication of babies is a useful reminder of the importance of body language. But this non-verbal form of communication remains very important even when the words come.
- Adults regularly underestimate the importance of body language, which continues to carry a substantial proportion of the total message between two people who are completely fluent in verbal communication.
- Children seem to be very sensitive to non-verbal signals and are aware when the body language of another child or of an adult seems 'wrong' or does not fit the words they are speaking. When the verbal and non-verbal messages do not match, children (and adults) seem to trust the non-verbal communication.

Questions
- Observe toddlers and young children with a caring adult. How much do they look at an adult as well as use their growing language skills?
- You may have valuable memories from your own childhood that illustrate a child's sensitivity to the non-verbal messages. Perhaps you had an aunt who said, 'So, how is school going then?' But as you started to tell her, her body language communicated that she was not really interested (nodding in the wrong place or interrupting you to catch the attention of another adult). How did you feel about this sort of experience? How can this insight help you in your practice now?

Blind babies

A great deal of what has just been described depends on babies and parents looking at each other. But a blind baby does not have this option. Research into the development of blind babies, for instance, by Selma Fraiberg, established that the babies smiled less often than sighted babies and they did not establish the mutual gaze that is the basis for many enjoyable exchanges between baby and parent.

Without practical advice, sighted parents of blind babies could be saddened by the baby's apparent lack of response or assume that the baby was miserable. Blind babies may be denied the use of sight, but they have touch and hearing and these are the important channels of early communication. Blind babies learn the social smile by reacting to their parent's familiar voice. Parents learn to notice their baby's gestures rather than seeking an alert look. For instance, a blind baby may stop moving when she hears the sound of footsteps or a toddler shows by hand gestures, rather than facial expression, that he realises his parent is close and he is pleased.

How adults communicate with babies

Observational research has also established the positive qualities in adult communication with the very young. Babies seem to prefer to listen and will respond to a special kind of modified language. This version of adult talk is:

- higher pitched than adults' normal speaking voice;
- at a slower pace, with more pauses;
- much simpler in structure;
- full of simple repetitions and a circling quality to the phrases ('Hello... have you woken up then?..... have you just woken up?.... come on then, let's have a cuddle... a nice warm cuddle... it's good to have a cuddle when you've just woken up..');
- often said with more expressiveness than normal conversation.

Babies have been found to prefer listening to this kind of adjusted talk, even when the language spoken is not their family language. A modified form of language is also used with toddlers but often with far more links into what the adult and toddler can both see. For instance, an exchange can circle with 'Where's Asha's foot? .... Where's your little foot then? ..... Has it gone? Has it gone forever?... No, I can see it. I've got it now... I've got Asha's little foot...'

Because most researchers studied mothers and their babies, this modified speech was called 'motherese'. But it is more accurately called **infant-directed speech** because its use is not restricted to mothers, or even to women. Men, as fathers or carers, modify their speech in the same way and so do some children, for instance, with younger siblings. I have watched children of seven

and eight years use simple, circulating forms of speech with a baby or
The older children are encouraged to continue by the chortles and gesture
replies of the younger child.

The use of simplified infant-directed speech has been found in a considerable
number of cultures, although not all. Modified speech seems to help young
children towards learning language but it is not essential. Observation of very
depressed mothers has shown that they are considerably less likely to use
infant-directed speech, but their children still learn to speak. This finding
supports the point made earlier that adult behaviour can create a more positive
environment for children to learn to speak. Yet even in very discouraging
circumstances children still start to talk – evidence perhaps of some internal
drive towards spoken communication.

Infant-directed speech seems to exert a broader effect, because adults who
adjust their speech patterns for babies and toddlers are also paying close
attention to the children. This kind of behaviour supports a warm relationship
with young children and a happy atmosphere in which they can learn.

Practical application

The intense, uninterrupted exchanges described by Trevarthen and other
researchers in this area are not, of course, descriptive of all interaction between
adults and young babies. In family life and elsewhere, communication with
babies is sometimes interrupted and parents of more than one child have to
share out their time and attention – a reality explored by Judy Dunn in her
research with families. But the results from very detailed observation of mother
and baby pairs are a crucial reminder for anyone involved with babies of just
how much is possible. There are important practical applications in day care
of babies and young toddlers, that:

- Communicative exchanges need to be sustained and not rushed. There
  should be a relaxed pattern of give and take that provides time for babies
  to respond.
- Exchanges with babies should not be interrupted regularly, as if they do
  not matter.
- The routines of physical care provide rich opportunities for close and
  sensitive communication between adult and baby.

The research also provides a possible explanation of why babies of depressed
or very angry mothers often do not thrive, even if they are cared for physically.
The babies' keen efforts at warm communication are constantly thwarted.
Sensitivity operates also in the opposite direction. For instance, mothers of

---

SUGGESTED ACTIVITY

Spend some time watching the communication efforts
of babies of six months and younger. You may find
opportunities in your place of work but there can also
be chances to watch in daily life: babies with their
parents on the bus, in the supermarket or in the park.
Watch out especially and make some notes on the
following:

1 Those early 'conversational' exchanges when baby
and adult take turns.

2 How the baby reacts if the adult turns away or
does not respond.

3 How babies use a range of sounds and actions
to get and hold others' attention, for instance:
squeals, yells, blowing raspberries or vigorous
hand gestures.

4 Listening and watching the adults in the exchange,
can you observe the qualities of infant-directed
speech (see page 92)?

infants, who are later diagnosed as autistic, have often been distressed and confused from the early months at their babies' lack of responsiveness (see also page 108).

The early communication of babies and toddlers
The development of sound making

Young babies undoubtedly cry quite a lot; some cry a very great deal. But close observers of the early months of life have documented how, between birth and three to four months, babies develop a range of different cries reflecting their emotions. Parents and familiar carers distinguish the following:

- cries of distress and pressing need;
- the slower build-up of cries of need, such as for hunger, but not yet desperate and for company;
- contented sounds such as coos and gurgles;
- sharp cries for attention, to bring a familiar face or voice;
- protests and complaints, accompanied by vigorous movements of the limbs;
- delight beyond quiet contentment – throaty chuckles.

In the early months, babies are able to make the open vowel sounds of 'aa' and 'oooo'. Their ability to shape sounds moves to the back of the mouth ('eee'), then to the middle and behind the teeth ('oh') and to include use of the lips ('bababab') and the tongue. The sounds gradually become more like those that the baby hears from adults and older children.

TO THINK ABOUT

The universal baby

Babies are born potentially able to produce all the possible sounds and sound combinations. But by a year old, they have lost the ability to discriminate sounds that are not in the language spoken around them. And their babbling has taken on the sound patterns of the language that they hear.

Japanese, for instance, does not make a distinction between 'la' and 'ra' sounds and English-speaking Japanese people tend to sound, and sometimes write, an 'l' as an 'r'. (I know this from personal experience: the Lindon family from London visited Japan some years ago.) Japanese and English babies all start by being able to distinguish the two sounds. Then in the early weeks and months babies' brains develop with subtle differences, depending on the sounds they hear from the adults around them. In an English-speaking home, babies hear short sounds (phonemes) that include sharp 'ba's and 'da's, elongated 'ee's and 'll's and soft, sibilant 'ss's. When babies hear the same groups of phonemes many times, the messages from their ears stimulate the formation of specific connections in the brain's auditory cortex. The baby's brain is becoming specialised for the language that she is hearing.

Babies' sound-making abilities gradually become more obviously deliberate and reflect their moods as well as the specific situation. By six months it is clear to any observer than a baby makes different patterns of vocalisation under different circumstances. If you watch a baby of between six months and a year you will, over a period of time, observe all of the following:

- distinctly different patterns of vocalisation when the baby is annoyed from when she is contented;
- vocalisations that deliberately accompany actions, such as sounds the baby makes on giving an object to someone, or accepting an interesting toy or a liked item of food;
- vocalisations that communicate a distinct message, for instance, using a sound or sound pattern to call for the attention of a familiar adult or indicating that the baby wants something she cannot reach;
- patterns of sound that are stimulated by a known routine such as a game of 'peep-bo'.

The importance of gestures

Gestures are an important aspect of early communication and form part of babies' body language – sending messages long before the words have come. The ability to gesture is linked with babies' increased physical control. But gestures are also a clear sign that babies are trying to gain and direct the attention of others. They use gesture to communicate a range of messages. Some examples follow; you could watch out for all of them within different settings. Babies and toddlers use gesture along with sounds and later with their early words.

- *Requests* – from the age of about five months, babies use hand gestures to indicate wants. A hand stretch and a whine or a look at an adult can communicate 'I want that and I can't get it'. An open and close of the hand can say 'Put it in my hand'.
- *Refusals* – babies and toddlers use a variety of limb and full body gestures to indicate reluctance or full refusal to cooperate. They pull away, turn their head (for instance, to refuse a spoonful of food), push away or whine. Then they add a head shake for 'No'.
- *Social contact* – gestures and sounds are used to attract and hold the attention of adults and other children. Pointing, which starts from about eight months, is a direct way of requesting adults to fetch something for a baby who is not yet mobile. Babies use pointing to direct attention to something interesting or surprising or to ensure that an adult gazes in the same direction as the baby. Patterns of gestures and sounds, like blowing raspberries, are often repeated by babies and toddlers, if they amuse other people.
- *As commentary* – expansive gestures, with sounds or words, are used by young children to acknowledge the presence of an object or a person. The same combination, with increasing presence of words, is used by toddlers to comment on what they are doing, their wishes or needs for help. Toddlers use rich non-verbal communication to say what they cannot yet express in words. At 16 months, my daughter used to fetch her outdoor shoes and wave me them at me when she wanted to go out for a walk. If I was slow to react, Tanith would then get my shoes and push them at me until I cooperated.

Babies and toddlers develop a wide range of meaningful gestures, increasingly accompanied by facial expressions that can be interpreted by parents and familiar carers. Adults often encourage social gestures such as the wave for 'bye bye'. All of these subtle developments in communication depend on vision and close relationships. If you look back over this section, you will get the sense of the interplay between areas of development.

TO THINK ABOUT

Pointing continues as a valuable aid to communication when children learn to talk and is also used as a directing device by adults. Pointing is one of the many gestures for which children learn cultural meaning. For instance, cultures vary in the acceptability of pointing, especially at people rather than objects (I clearly recall being told in school, 'It's rude to point!'). In some cultures it is also important to learn the appropriate combination of hand and fingers in order to avoid offensive gestures.

Meaningful signs

Linda Acredolo and Susan Goodwyn studied the way that toddlers who have no words, or just a small number, use specific signs to communicate an association that they cannot say in words. The signs are a reflection of the child's personal experience, so children do not necessarily make the same signs as each other. For example, Acredolo's interest in signs was stimulated by realising that her young daughter made a blowing motion when she saw a fish and rubbed her hands when she saw a spider. Both these signs were the result of the toddler's alert observation: her mother used to blow on the fish mobile over Kate's cot to make it revolve and the rubbing motion was from the hand movements in 'Incey Wincey Spider'.

Acredolo and Goodwyn found many such personal signs in the toddlers they studied. If parents took the signs seriously as communication, this approach encouraged the development of spoken language. The key was that parents who responded to their toddlers' signs, and took the trouble to work out the links, talked with their toddlers about the focus of the children's interest. Taking children's gestures seriously does not make them stay with signing; it stimulates communication as a whole. In the same way, it has been found that children with learning disabilities that affect language development (for instance, children with Down's Syndrome) can be helped by teaching them to communicate through a sign language like Makaton and talking at the same time as signing.

From sound making to words

The conventional developmental milestone in early communication is the appearance of real and recognisable words. Parents are understandably excited by this development and developmental screening tests include the appearance of speech as an important benchmark. However, a full understanding of the communication of young children has to include the whole framework around the words.

From six to thirteen months, babies engage in a lot of deliberate babbling, which may be repeated syllables such as 'nana' or vocalisations that do not involve repeated sounds, like 'mam'. Babies are practising their repertoire of sounds and they react to the enthusiasm of adult carers and older children by repeating sounds close to real words.

The first recognisable words emerge on average any time from 12–19 months. Before the actual words appear, you will often hear young children use the same sound combination to refer to people or objects. The first single words are likely to be drawn from a young child's familiar environment and from experiences that hold his interest. So, all children do not produce the same first words (or later an identical pattern of phrases). But they may produce the same kind of words, like:

- names of people or family pets;
- familiar objects that are of importance to a child, like a cup or spoon;
- animal noises ('woof-woof' to mean dog) or sounds associated with an object of interest like a car.

The first words carry a great deal of meaning and are used broadly, although in a logical way. For instance, the family dog may be 'dog' or a shortened 'do' but so may any other animals that the toddler sees. Single words are used very flexibly by young children, so that one word, supported by tone of voice and gestures can convey potentially several different messages. These single words heavy with meaning are called **holophrases**. For example, a toddler may use the word 'teddy' in different ways to mean 'Where's my teddy?', 'He took my teddy from me' or 'I'm glad to have my teddy back'. Only adults familiar with a toddler and her routine are likely to understand these associations.

For a while, young children restrict rather than over-extend their use of some words. For instance, drink may be used to refer only to the kind of drink that this child has: juice and milk but not water. Children are learning about specific and general applications. Eventually they learn the symbolic use of language to refer not just to their 'cup' but that the word can be used for any cup. At this stage, as well as later, children make mistakes compared with adult speech, but their mistakes are logical (see the boxed examples on page 99).

As well as words that name objects and people, young children learn words that are useful to them. For instance:

- 'more' or 'na'one' (another one) can be used to ask for more food, the repeat of an enjoyable play action or be a comment on a similarity;
- 'gone' or 'no more' can be a simple statement that something has gone, a request for help in finding something, a description that the toddler has made something disappear and other possibilities;
- following the social gestures, toddlers often also learn social words such as 'tank you' or 'ta', 'hello', 'hiya' and other greetings.

Words and phrases

With encouragement from adults or older siblings, toddlers add many more words so that by 20–24 months, sometimes younger, the first word combinations appear. The earliest short phrases tend to be communicated as if they are one word: 'here'y'are', 'nomorenow' or 'allgonenow'. One word may be used as if it is a movable prefix: 'moremilk', 'nomorebikky' or 'nobyebye'.

Many of the early two-word combinations only make sense in context to a familiar adult who pays attention to how a child is saying the words, using tone and non-verbal clues was well as the words. The first combinations are not a random putting together of words; children show the beginnings of a grasp of basic grammar for the language they are learning. So, the early combinations are not the same structure in every language. In English, the first combinations are often:

- one noun and a second noun – 'Mummy ball' – which might mean 'please get me the ball' or 'Mummy's got the ball now' and so on;
- noun plus a verb – 'car gone';
- verb plus noun – 'give ball'.

These are combinations that support the child's desire to act on her environment. Other words that add descriptions, such as adjectives, will come later and be

SUGGESTED ACTIVITY

Keep a record of the language development of one or two toddlers whom you can observe at regular intervals.

1 Note down what the children say and how they say it.
2 In what ways do the toddlers' early words and phrases reflect their direct experience and matters of interest in their lives?

the words that have meaning for the child's experience (perhaps 'hot', 'broken' or 'nice'). Children's early spoken language homes in on the essentials of speech. Prepositions such as 'on' or linking words such as 'and' come much later.

CASE STUDY

These are highlights from the notes I made of my son's language development from 12-30 months.

<u>12 months</u>: Drew is using a definite word-sound of 'a-ca'. He says this reliably to the family cat, a picture of a cat in one of his books and a cat ornament in his childminder's home. He has a range of sounds to express requests and a pleased sound of 'a-da' when he has managed to do something. He 'chats' to himself when he is playing but no words I can recognise.

<u>15 months</u>: Cats are now definitely 'ca'. 'Mama' for me and as a cry for help if Drew is unhappy or having difficulty. 'Dada' for Lance and as a happy chant to himself when all is going well. 'Og' for his childminder's dog. 'Bir' for bird. Also 'here y'are' when he hands something over, 'look' to call attention to something and 'ta' for thank you.

<u>16 months</u>: Drew has added 'baby', 'teddy', 'more' and 'Daddy' (said to items that belong to Lance).

<u>18 months</u>: Drew has 30 words. Some are clear like 'milk', others you have to listen for, like 'tchu' for train. 'Daddy' is now also the word for any motorbike (Lance rides a motorbike). Drew shows that he understands considerably more words than he uses. If we ask him questions like, 'Where's the . . . ?' he can point to many of the pictures in his books, to choices of food for his meals and to some parts of his body ('Where's your toes?').

<u>22 months</u>: Drew has over 90 words covering people, animals, objects, pictures in his books and food. Some words are almost phrases – 'situp' and 'getup' – and real word combinations are starting – 'more bird' and 'a-a dump-dump' (no more dump trucks).

<u>24 months</u>: Drew now has a total of at least 115 words and has started to make two-word combinations. He uses key words to make these combinations: 'more', 'nomore' and 'lotsandlots' are added to a second word. 'No' added to a second word can mean 'there's no more . . .' or 'I don't want . . .' or as a negative ('no dark' or 'no hot'). A few combinations are for regular events: Drew's excited 'Ada post' is because his minder's son Adam always checks the post when they return from picking Adam up from school in the afternoon. Drew adds a name to an object to show possession ('Mama shoe') or someone's name after 'hello..' and 'bye bye. . .'. We have also heard a few three- word combinations: 'more lello (yellow) light', 'say bye Mummy' (wanting to say goodbye to me) and 'no eye house' (Drew has become interested in which of the pictures on his jigsaws have eyes).

<u>26 months</u>: We have stopped trying to count Drew's words because he now works in combinations and short phrases. He asks questions with 'What's this?' and 'Why?' Drew uses verbs in phrases, sometimes with an all-purpose 'this' or 'that': 'Make this', 'Sit down', 'Get up'. Drew made his first joke, saying and laughing 'Daddy did that' when everyone knew it was not true. He adds 'too' in a meaningful way: 'too high wall' (for him to walk along), 'too big ball' (to go into a small box) and 'too dark kitchen' (asking for the light to be switched on).

<u>27-30 months</u>: It is now a hard job to keep notes on Drew's phrases. He comments on his own feelings, wishes and experiences. He starts conversations about the present and recent past. For instance, 'Little boy no like these' (a new flavour of crisps), 'Drew found that in the bath', 'Baby milk. When finished, hold her' (his baby sister was being fed and Drew wanted to have Tanith on his lap), 'Tell daddy. Saw digger', 'Daddy glasses. To watch TV' and 'Mama go yoga – like Yogi Bear' (a joke about my evening class).

Comments

Any record shows an individual pattern reflecting a young child's experience and interests. Some of Drew's words and phrases make little sense without the explanations in brackets. So, the early language development of toddlers will never be identical in the details.

I kept a similar record for Drew's younger sister and, although there were some similarities (they both used 'Mama' as an all-purpose cry for help and not just as my name), there were many differences. One of the noticeable changes for Tanith was that she copied many of Drew's phrases, including a firm 'I know that!' and Drew deliberately taught her some words. Tanith's words and early phrases also reflected their joint activities, as well as what Lance and I did with them both.

EXAMPLE

Children's mistakes in their early language development are a reminder of how alert they are to what they hear and see. Familiarity with a child and some adult observation will often highlight the source of a mistake. You can understand that children are very logical; they reach sensible conclusions from what they have heard.

- At 18 months Drew used the word 'more' for water. This puzzled me, until I heard myself saying to him, as he waved his watering can at me, 'Do you want some more?'
- At 23 months Tanith used two words 'helpme' and 'helpit' which communicated different messages.

'Helpme' was said with a questioning tone and was an offer to help an adult, whereas 'helpit' was said with a pleading tone and used when she could not manage something. I traced these special words to my own phrases of 'Do you want to help me?' – often said when we were in the kitchen and 'Do you want some help with it?' when Tanith looked stuck with dressing or in play.

- I have encountered individual examples in talking with parents: 'sky' for planes as a result of 'Look at the plane in the sky', 'gorgies' for flowers ('Look at the flowers, they're gorgeous') and many more.

SUGGESTED ACTIVITY

Keep track of the logical mistakes that you hear from young children for whom you are responsible (see the example above).

1 Note down what the children say and the context.
2 Then observe and reflect on the words or phrases.

3 Can you track down the source of the logical mistake?
4 Discuss your observations and ideas with the children's parents.

Understanding of language

The development of children's language is not just what they learn to say themselves. An equally important side is how they tune in to and increasingly understand what is said to them. A considerable amount of what children say and how they say it may not make much sense to an uninvolved observer. You need knowledge of the language to which children have been listening and reacting for months.

Analysis of children's receptive language has shown that young babies are attuned to human speech, possibly even before they are born. Very young babies turn to look towards the sound of a familiar voice and older ones start to move their glance between people as the conversation shifts from one person to another. Babies and toddlers are alert to non-verbal clues of gesture, facial expression and following the gaze or the point from an adult.

Within the first quarter of toddlers' second year, they show that they understand a number of uses of speech in a familiar context with a known adult. Toddlers are likely to come when called by name, hand over a familiar object on request and to reply by gesture if they want a drink. Over the next few months they show a grasp of simple requests to fetch something, take an object to someone else or to stop doing something. They learn the routines, what usually happens, in familiar settings such as home or a day care centre. Toddlers also like and learn from simple rituals within a home or day care setting. The familiar rituals may be play but toddlers are also very motivated to help in the domestic routine.

So, toddlers are able to make sense of simple requests because they are knowledgeable about what their parents and carers usually mean and how they behave. Very young children only need to recognise one or two words and they grasp the remaining meaning from context and not from the actual words. For instance:

- 'Put your tissue in the bin': used tissues always go in the bin.
- 'Can you get Ben a new nappy from the bag?': when the baby is being changed, he always needs a fresh nappy.
- 'Let's tidy up now': it is routine in the day care centre that children put their plates and cups on the trolley when everyone has finished a meal.
- 'No, don't touch the video': a young child knows from experience that this is not allowed. (As toddlers start to control their own behaviour, they often use the same intonation and attempt the same phrase that has been said to them.)

Throughout their second year of life, toddlers show an ever increasing scope of understanding for requests to fetch, show, give or find. Initially toddlers' understanding is limited to the real object, but later they accept that pictures stand for objects or people and can point out familiar things by request. By close to their second birthday, toddlers can often run very simple messages (for instance, to request something from an adult) and fetch familiar objects from other rooms, which shows the operation of their short-term memory.

All these important developments have to occur before children can understand and respond to more complex uses of language. Two- and three-year-olds have gathered enough language experience that they are able to respond more to the words and are less dependent on context and non-verbal clues. Their understanding has extended from an exclusive focus on the immediate and the present and has stretched to the recent past and events that interest them and to following through sequences.

Practical applications

Children learn to speak through experience of spoken language from others and interest and attention shown to what young children themselves express. It helps to see children's language development as intertwined with their social development, since this acts as a reminder that it matters what adults do. Children learn to speak because people speak *with* them, not *at* them. So, play materials, however inventive, cannot substitute for real adults and older children. One of my more numbing experiences in recent years was wandering round a large toy warehouse and finding an electronic console toy that claimed to 'teach your child to speak'. Children were supposed to press picture buttons to start a mechanical voice, with a strong American accent, which then intoned the words.

Young children need to hear words used clearly in a relevant context so that they can:

- understand the word and link it to reality as they know it;
- imitate the word, with understanding;
- spontaneously use the word in context.

In this way, new words and phrases become part of the active vocabulary of young children.

There is considerable flexibility for young children's personal experience but some themes are consistent:

- Babies and toddlers need to be able to get adults' attention. So adults have to make themselves available to babies.

SUGGESTED ACTIVITY

Keep a record of the development of a few individual children's receptive language: how they understand what is said to them. Or keep a separate note of this side to language as a full record of the development of communication.

Remember that young children show through their reactions that they understand the message, but you cannot conclude that they understand each and every word. Young children's grasp of meaning through context and gesture is a very important part of their development – in every sense it is real communication.

Let your observational record reflect this exciting development, with notes of routines and personal rituals that seem to support this child's growing understanding.

- Adults do not need to use 'baby talk' ('bikky' for 'biscuit' or 'gee-gee' for 'horse') but infant-directed talk does seem to help (simpler words and shorter sentences – see page 93.)
- You are having a two-way conversation, even with the youngest babies. So pace yourself for the child, give her time to respond. Look expectant as you wait for the reply in sound, gesture or words and do not turn away.
- Speak directly to children and talk with them about matters of relevance and interest to them. Young children are focused on the here and now.
- Young children like experimenting with language in sound games and enjoyable play with rhyme and rhythm.
- Children will make many mistakes in pronunciation and usage of words. It does not help to correct them in a critical way but children learn from accurate language feedback. Say a word clearly and correctly and give children words if they are struggling ('Is it the … that you want?')

SUGGESTED ACTIVITY

Look at how your setting is organised, especially with reference to time spent with the younger children.

- What kinds of exchanges do you have with the under-threes? Note down five exchanges that you have had in the last week with children.

- Are there some times of the day when it seems more possible to have uninterrupted exchanges with young children?

- How are you using the physical care times? For instance, changing a child's nappy can be a personal time for conversation, as well as showing affection through respectful physical caretaking.

If you do not work directly with the younger children, arrange to visit an early years setting which takes babies and toddlers. Spend some time observing the ways in which this setting offers language opportunities to younger children.

Language development of older children
Understanding of grammar

Young children learn new words at a fast rate between the ages of 20 to 30 months and they combine these in simple sentences. From about 30 months of age, when they have a sizeable vocabulary, children start to learn and use a very wide variety of grammatical structures and inflections that are particular to their language. Children learn both the regular and irregular grammatical forms by listening and being corrected by adults. Many of children's logical mistakes are now about generalising a regular grammatical rule to constructions that do not obey the usual rule. For example, children may say 'badder' rather than 'worse' or 'I eated' rather than 'I ate'.

Children, of course, learn the grammatical forms that they hear. Different versions of English, including dialects, often use variations in the basic grammar ('we was..' rather than 'we were..' or 'me' instead of 'I'). Children will later learn that people speak differently, depending on the version of the language used. During the school years, children are capable of learning to distinguish the different versions, as well as the differences between more formal speaking and informal chat and that written language conventions are often different from spoken. It seems to help children when the differences between versions of English are made explicit and their preferred spoken language is respected, rather than simply criticised as wrong.

Use of language

Children use their now substantial vocabulary in many ways. They form sentences that serve different purposes, use questions and create negatives. They use their communication skills to seek information and their skills of listening to gather new knowledge. Children are also using their language to think out loud. You will hear two-year-olds guide themselves in an activity with 'No, not 'dat' or 'Put in there'. Older children talk themselves through a task as well as using their language in pretend play. This type of self-directing speech becomes less loud as it develops into a low mutter that older children, and even adults, tend to use when they are tackling a new or difficult task. Otherwise this type of language goes silent as **internal speech**.

Children continue to learn new words and now know enough to ask the meanings of words or speculate on fine differences. For instance, by three and a half, my son Drew was asking me questions like 'What's the difference between a forest and a wood?' and 'Are a bridge and a tunnel the same?' (both of these formed a gap through which you travelled).

Children as young as two years can adjust their language depending on the listener. You will observe that young children talk in a different way among themselves, in contrast to their words and intonation with an adult. By four years, children are usually clearly discriminating between different forms of speech. For instance, they will simplify their language when talking to a much younger child. Five-year-olds will usually explain in more detail to an unfamiliar adult than to a friend. The children have grasped that adults do not necessarily know everything that they do.

Children of two and three years have learned a great deal about the functions of language and gained an impressive vocabulary. Research studies of children in natural settings, such as the family home, has shown some child-oriented uses of language which are often not directed at adults. From my own observations, I describe these as 'nonsense talk' and 'naughty talk'.

- Children will play with words: putting words together in a way that sounds funny to them or saying something that they know is wrong and laughing. This 'nonsense talk' is often between children, but may be shared with adults who show a capacity to have fun and take a joke.
- Children also delight in conversations amongst themselves that they tend not to share with adults. The children show a subtle understanding that the topics of 'naughty talk' (usually bottoms, smells, 'poo' and related issues) do not hold adults' attention. This type of talk does not usually arise in formal experiments on children's language and thinking, precisely because children have already grasped that adults are either uninterested or disapprove of such conversations.

By three and four years of age, children's vocabulary and their use of language is sufficiently complex that keeping a record would be a very challenging task. Their language both reflects and extends their thinking and is a reminder that the different aspects of children's development are interrelated (look also at chapter 3 on thinking and reasoning).

4.3 Variations in learning language

Bilingualism

Until recent decades the prevailing view in England was that 'normal' language development was to have one language and then to learn one or more 'foreign' languages through study at secondary school. This limited perspective led to very negative approaches to families who became resident through immigration from the 1960s and whose first language was not English.

Parents were told that they must speak only English to their children, otherwise the children's language development would be muddled. Approaches to children's language abilities often ignored competence in the family language and took children's emerging English as their only language, leading to reports of speaking children as having 'no language'. The first approach has been discredited through research and the second is a reflection of ethnocentric practice (a blinkered view only from a single cultural perspective).

In fact, bilingualism has a long history in the UK and is not simply the result of recent population changes. As someone whose grandparents were Welsh-English bilingual, I continue to be amazed by the extent to which enthusiastic writers on bilingualism regularly ignore the active language movements in Welsh and Irish or Scottish Gaelic, which for decades struggled against attempts to suppress daily use of their language. Bilingualism is the normal state of affairs in many countries around the world, including mainland Europe.

Depending on their experience, children learn to be bilingual in one of two ways:

- **Simultaneous learning**: children's family experience is such that they learn two languages at the same time when they are very young.
- **Successive learning**: children, who have a good grasp of their family language, encounter and then learn a second language – most likely when they join an early years setting.

Simultaneous learning

The evidence suggests strongly that, in families where two languages are spoken by fluent speakers, children should be given the opportunity to learn both. There is every evidence that young children are capable of learning two languages at the same time. Indeed, the assumption that it will cause developmental problems only comes from cultures in which monolingualism is the more usual pattern.

Where it is possible to compare bilingual with monolingual children, study shows that bilingual children may be slightly slower in the early stages of learning words and putting together sentences. Children also sometimes muddle words or grammar between the two languages. However, bilingual children soon reach the same level of language ability as their monolingual peers and they have, of course, achieved this competence in two languages.

The main practical suggestions from studies of simultaneous learning of two languages is that children need to have the languages clearly distinguished. Perhaps one parent or another relative is consistently the person who speaks one language to the child. The second language is consistently spoken by another member of the family. Children, not surprisingly, become muddled if adult speakers switch language in mid-conversation or one parent joins in at random with their less fluent language. It also seems to help for children to have experience of child speakers of the language as well as adults; children use language in a different way from adult speakers.

Children's recognition that not everyone speaks the languages they hear is shown by evidence about bilingual children in families where one language is only spoken by one parent. I have anecdotal evidence of several families in which young children did not use one of their languages at all until a situation arose that seemed appropriate to them. For instance, we are good friends with a family in which the father is monolingual English and the mother bilingual English-Turkish. They live in an English-speaking environment. The mother spoke in Turkish to her son from babyhood but he spoke only English until they went to visit his Turkish relatives. Then the three-year-old sat down with the other children and started speaking in Turkish.

Successive learning

Many children are introduced to their second language in pre-school settings or on entry to school. Approaches to supporting the development of bilingualism at this age have varied around several possibilities:

- Should pre-school age children be given specific language instruction or should they be allowed to learn their second language in their own time and their own ways?

The confidence of some writers that young children will 'pick up' a second language with little effort are not supported by studies of young bilingual children. Children need adequate input on the second language, encouragement and the motivation to learn. Children are capable of the learning task but they still need help.

- Should pre-school children, or school age, be taught exclusively in their first language (their home language)? And then learn the second language as a separate strand of their education?
- Or should children be immersed in the second language for all their pre-school or school activities?
- Or is there some appropriate combination of these two?

Weighing up the research findings is difficult because bilingual programmes may be called similar titles, but the pattern of instruction and support can vary tremendously. However, a consistent theme for school age children is that a genuinely bilingual combination approach seems to work best. Children whose fluent language is not that of the classroom are given some lessons in their home language, but other lessons are taught in their second language. After several years children have usually made the transition to full instruction in their second language. Rather like the pattern of simultaneous learning for very young bilingual children, the best route seems to be not to combine both languages within the same lessons.

It appears that a similar approach works best for pre-school children. Where children are not yet bilingual, their learning is best supported when they enter an early years setting that runs their day or session in the child's most fluent language. Then the second language is introduced later. This level of flexibility is often not available for children, especially in neighbourhoods where there are many different languages.

Whatever the particular approach, adults need to understand the task that children are tackling if they are to support young children who are becoming bilingual. Successive learning is different developmentally from the simultaneous pattern. Young children, who are learning a second language after their first is established, have the capacity to think and wish to communicate at a more complex level than their second language will initially support. Three- and four-year-olds learning their second language in nursery or playgroup are not the same individuals who learned their first language as toddlers at home.

Observations of young children fluent in a different language from most of their peers have raised useful hints for how adults can support. The details of how young children tackle this learning task is a timely reminder of the social context of language. Several themes emerge:

- Children need the opportunity to establish friendly relations with speakers of the second language – adults and children (remember the earlier comment that children use language differently from adults).
- Once they have joined a group, children use all the non-verbal clues and their first words or expressions to give the impression that they know what is going on. As they become established, they can turn to their friends for help.
- Children need to feel comfortable to use plenty of non-verbal communication as well as a few useful phrases (verbal formulae) with adults as well as children. Children learning a second language are cognitively well beyond the naming stage of communication. They need to be given useful, everyday phrases.
- Children generate meanings in the second language through using new combinations of the formulaic words and phrases. They often come up with creative combinations that communicate meaning and show you that their thinking is way beyond their current ability to express themselves just in these words.
- Children will assume that the language they hear is directly relevant to the situation in hand. So adults can help by ensuring that their communication follows this pattern.
- Children need to be in a setting that encourages them to start talking and not worry about correct forms until they have plenty of the second language on which to work.

SUGGESTED ACTIVITY

Read through some of the themes that emerge from observation of young children who are becoming bilingual. And think through how adults could best help in this situation:

1   How might you encourage and support a child to make social contact with her peers who speak a different language?
2   Listen in to your daily talk with children. What phrases do you, and they, use a great deal and so would be useful to teach a child who is coming

new to the language? Make a note of these phrases – depending on the age of the children you might be noting 'Do you want a…?' or 'I've got a…'

3   Adults often overlook the importance of non-verbal communication once children are talking. Be alert to how you introduce daily activities in your setting, ask children questions or make requests. In what ways could you use gesture to highlight your meaning, but still communicate appropriately with a child who is three or four years?

Difficulties in communication
Fluency

When children are learning to talk, their speech does not run smoothly all the time. They may stop to search for a word or lose track and start at the beginning of their thought once more. If children are put under pressure by adults with

'Come on! I haven't got all day!', then the fluency difficulty may worsen. But for the majority of children, their speech becomes more steady and flowing. Any remaining stop-start quality is close to what you can observe in adult speech: sometimes stopping to clarify a thought and a sprinkling of 'um's and 'er's.

A minority of children do not overcome their disfluency and will not manage without some specialist help. The British Stammering Association (see the following box) estimates that about 5% of under-fives have fluency problems which are sufficiently marked to be described as stammering and that about one-third of these children do not improve over the months.

Stammering is a difficulty with fluency in speech and you will observe some or most of the following in a child who is struggling. Stammering is about four times more common in boys than girls, so I have used 'he'.

- The child looks to you as if he is having trouble getting his words out. Sometimes there is a visible silent struggle for several seconds before the first words come out in a rush.
- His speech emerges in a jerky way or he gets out part of what he wants to tell you and then stops.
- Sounds are repeated – like the first sound of a word (t-t-t-teddy) – or stretched out like verbal elastic (sssstory).

Stammering can become more than a speech difficulty, since the problem of fluency can undermine a child's confidence. Stammering sometimes runs in families and is found in many different languages and cultures. Although harsh and impatient adults can make matters worse, there is no evidence that suggests parents cause their children's stammering.

Applications to practice

You would not assume that all children with fluency difficulties will develop stammering. Giving children time, attention and patience will usually work well. Children should be referred to a speech therapist for help if:

- there is a family history of stammering;
- the child is having more general problems in learning to talk;
- he is distressed by his difficulties or showing severe struggles to get his words out;
- he is learning a second language and is stammering in his first.

You can find out more by contacting the British Stammering Association, who offer advice and practical leaflets. You can reach the BSA at 15 Old Ford Road, London E2 9PJ, tel: 0181 983 1003.

Disabilities and communication

Children with physical disabilities can have a harder task to learn to speak when their disability directly affects their ability to form sounds through control of their mouth and tongue. If you concentrate on how your mouth and tongue move in different ways for different sounds, you will become more aware of the subtle physical tasks of learning that are involved. Conditions such as cleft palate can give children difficulties because they have a gap in their mouth where there should be none.

Partial or total deafness means that children have limited or no feedback on the sound of language. The majority of deaf children are born to hearing parents and there may be delays in assessing the children as deaf. It seems to be very important for children's communication and later written language that they are taught sign language as early as possible – ideally at the same time that their peers are learning to speak. Hearing parents, and other hearing adults, should speak and sign simultaneously. Children who have not been taught to sign have more difficulties in learning to communicate and in later reading and writing.

Children who have many ear infections and heavy colds can develop the condition of glue ear. The consequence is that their hearing can be variable, there may be good and bad days. Adults need to be alert to the patterns of children's apparent inattention or limited understanding of what is said to them. The children may not realise that something is wrong.

Mild or severe learning disabilities can mean that children take longer to learn to talk because they are finding the task of decoding the meaning of sounds that much more difficult. Use of sign language as well as spoken communication seems to support the development of language for children with learning disabilities, for instance, Down's syndrome.

Autistic conditions

Spoken language is a means of communication but also has a social function in the building of relationships and of play amongst children. It is easy to overlook the related network of learned social behaviours until you see a child whose communication behaviour is 'breaking' the rules.

Children with autism have difficulties in learning to communicate through a spoken language and children with severe autism may never speak. But they also find it very hard to learn and apply the social cues which we take for granted. Autistic children often do not make eye contact in the usual way and, when very young, do not respond to the sensitive interactions described on page 90. When they do learn words, the children show little evidence of adapting what they say to other people, adults or children. Other children can find it hard to play with even mildly autistic peers because these children do not behave within what the non-autistic children have come to see as normal boundaries. Autistic children also show repetitive use of play materials and very focused interests which border on obsessions, neither of which communicate a welcome to their peers.

Children with Asperger syndrome usually have far fewer difficulties with learning a spoken language. They tend to be fluent but their delivery sounds formal or rather stilted. They are unlikely to take notice of the non-verbal clues from other people, such as facial expressions. So children may talk on and on, despite what seems to be obvious evidence that their audience has lost interest or is trying to interject.

An awareness of how children with autism and Asperger syndrome react, and their communication and social difficulties, highlights the wide range of subtle non-verbal clues and learned rules of communication that most children have learned by the age of five or six years.

SUGGESTED ACTIVITY

Find out more about autism and Asperger syndrome from The National Autistic Society, 393 City Road, Islington, London EC1V 1NE, tel: 0171 833 2299.

4.4 Learning written communication

Building the understanding

Children who have learned to speak then have another substantial task to manage: understanding the written system of language through learning to read and to write. Children need to be helped towards the key discovery that you can 'draw' words and not just objects. They are learning another step in language as a symbolic representation. Since cracking the written code is also a difficult task which will take them some time, it is important that children are shown that reading and writing are necessary and useful skills in life.

Research into how children learn to read, and those who manage this task more easily, has shown that children's knowledge of the sound and the structure of language are both very important in supporting their move into coping with written language. Two specific areas of knowledge are especially significant:

- children's ability to recognise individual letters;
- their awareness that spoken and written words are composed of individual sounds that make words when they are placed together in a deliberate way. This understanding is called **phonemic awareness**. (Phonemes are individual sounds.)

This level of awareness about language and how it is put together has arisen from a broad range of experiences in early childhood. Children are undoubtedly also using their skills of thinking to reason the general rules from their experience. Research has shown that children with good logical skills may follow close on the heels of children with high language awareness in learning to read. However, the ability to recognise letters and high phonemic awareness are the best predictors of whether children will learn to read with relative ease.

The importance of early experience

Children who learn to read more easily have had a well-rounded experience of language, both spoken and written. Research has identified a range of related activities with children. Many of these are done by parents at home with their children; it is certainly not the case that building the basis to literacy is an exclusively professional or educational task. The following have all been shown to support children's later literacy.

Talking with children
Children need to hear, experience and use language from an early age. Conversations with young children support their learning of words and boost their motivation to make themselves understood, with ever more complex ideas.

Reading to children
Research consistently confirms the importance of reading to children from a young age. The most effective approach is to share books in a way that engages children's attention, their interest and invites them to respond (for more details, see the following 'To think about' section). Books are then an active experience for children and part of what Cathy Nutbrown calls **literacy**

talk: encouraging young children to talk about the books they like and why and to discuss characters and plots in a simple way.

Story telling is a bridge between speaking and reading and can be a source of listening and talking for children. Effective story telling for children has good plots that can be supported by expressive body language and repeated phrases in which children can join. Children who have become enthused and confident are able to tell the story themselves or to re-tell the story from a favourite book.

Awareness of sounds

Children benefit from activities that alert children to the sounds of words. Phonological awareness is important to help children to make the link between how a word is said and how it is written. They need to tune into the beginning of a word and its sound and to notice when words begin with the same first sound (when words alliterate). Children need also to be aware of how words end (the rime) and to be able to hear the difference between two words that are very similar, except for the ending. Words with the same end sound (the rimes) make a rhyme.

Teaching children nursery rhymes seems to be an effective way of alerting them to slight differences in sound patterns. Children who know and say more nursery rhymes tend to have higher phonological awareness which supports their later reading.

TO THINK ABOUT

Applications to practice

Research studies have pinpointed the key features of adults' reading to children, if the experience is to extend their vocabulary. Reading books to children without encouraging them into an interaction is significantly less valuable than what has been called **dialogic reading** – encouraging a dialogue with individual children.

As well as reading the story, adults (or older children with siblings) need to ask questions that young children cannot answer through pointing. So, questions such as 'What's that there, in the corner?', 'What's the little girl doing?' or 'What'll happen next?' all engage child listeners to use their skills of spoken language linked to heard written material and books.

Dialogic reading is not achieved by simply reading a story to a group of children who sit and listen. The process is ideally an individual interaction between a young child and an attentive adult and certainly is not possible with more than two or three young children.

Suggestions

- Think about and watch how you share books with children in your setting.
- Look at ways to create individual sessions with children. This approach will be especially important if you are working with very young children and crucial if you are aware that their language development is slow.
- You could tape a book or story telling session with children. Listen to the tape later and see where and how you could make the session more interactive for the children.

CASE STUDY

Children really seem to benefit from early exposure to books and to a shared pleasure in books with parents. The following excerpts from the diary I kept of my son, Drew, highlight the pattern for one child.

11 weeks: Drew is very interested in pictures, especially shiny ones. We hold him in our arms and he stares hard at the pictures on our wall that most reflect the light.

14 weeks: Drew is sitting on Gramps' lap (his grandfather) and reaches out to grab a mail order catalogue. Drew looks hard at the shiny pictures.

4 months: Drew likes looking at board books with us. He touches and scrabbles at the pictures as well as staring. We talk with him and say what is in the picture.

5 months: Drew is still keen on brightly coloured catalogues. He scrabbles at the pages and looks. He enjoys a repetitive game when Gramps tries to turn the page and Drew holds it down and Gramps says, 'I thought you'd finished!'

10 months: Drew still likes sitting with one of us and looking at books. But he now also likes to look at his books himself, going forwards and backwards through the pages.

12 months: Drew is listening to simple stories as well as liking the pictures. If a book has only pictures, then we make up a story line that we stick with each time.

13 months: Drew now definitely has favourites. He picks out a book from his shelf, brings it over and gestures at one of us to sit down and look at it with him.

15 months: He has managed to work the pulls and flaps on his special books. We have learned to keep a watch on these - a lot of cellotaping yesterday!

16 months: Lance gave Drew his first book as *part* of bedtime. We have now made this his settling down routine.

17 months: We left a few board books in the cot with Drew once he was asleep. He looks at them first thing in the morning. We can hear him 'chatting' to himself. Then he throws the books out of his cot and shouts for us.

18 months: An exciting event for me - Drew made the link between pictures in his books and what he sees outside. We saw a fire engine when we were out shopping and Drew was very excited, going 'Da-da da-da'. But then, when we got home, he went straight to his books, picked the one with the picture of the fire engine, turned to the right page and came over to me, waving the book delightedly.

21 months: As well as the stories, Drew likes spotting things in his books with the detailed pictures. He likes long games of 'Where's the lorry?' and 'Where's the flower?' He looks carefully, points and then looks expectantly for the next question.

23 months: Drew knows some phrases in his books. With Peace At Last he chimes in with Mr Bear's refrain with his own 'Oh, no! I can't 'tand 'dis!' We now leave him with some board books when he settles in his cot and we can hear him telling himself the story line we use with his Mealtime book.

24 months: Drew's love of books has been a real help since Tanith was born. When I sit to feed her, Drew sits beside us in the wide chair and I usually finish one of his favourite longer stories.

Drew continued to enjoy books, either by himself or to want to be read a story. He learned to read quickly when he started infant school and has continued to read for pleasure as well as for study.

Awareness of the written system of language

The importance of giving children broad experience of writing is illustrated clearly by the consequences for children without this experience. Jessie Reid interviewed children who were having difficulty in learning to read or write. She discovered the extent to which the children were unaware of writing as a system. Children had not realised that the marks in books represented different letters, nor that there was a separate letter and number system. Their attention had not been drawn to the writing all around them, on buses, shops or street signs (what Cathy Nutbrown calls environmental print) and so they remained puzzled about the point of reading or writing, except that teachers seemed to want them to do it.

In contrast, children who learn to read more easily are those who approach the actual reading with a clear idea of the components involved. They have

had their attention drawn by adults – parents or early years workers – to how print is all around them and is used practically through written messages, reading road signs or instructions and placing children's names on their paintings. A set of separate plastic letters (in lower case) seems to be especially helpful for children to learn the shape and orientation of letters and to see how they make up recognisable words such as their own name. The great advantage of the plastic letters is that children can move them about at will and do not have to face the initial physical task of writing the letters. Children who are read to as individuals or in a very small group also benefit when adults show, perhaps by running a finger under each word as it is said, how sounds relate to what is written.

A personal note

When I was working as a consultant with day nurseries in the mid-1970s, I was told very firmly by one officer-in-charge to stop discussing pre-writing and pre-reading activities with the staff for use with the children. The O-I-C's view was that literacy was the job of schools and no arguments on my part that written material was all around the children in the nursery could dissuade her. To give the O-I-C her due, she had been given a severe ticking off by the head of the local primary school that nobody other than teachers knew how to approach reading and writing with children.

   It is a measure of how the view of good practice has changed in early years that I cannot imagine any manager of a centre taking that view now, nor a school head being so blatantly disrespectful to an early years setting. But, workers who are not in a specifically educational setting can still feel uneasy about supporting children in the skills that lay the foundations for reading. Yet, as the research reported in this section shows, the best practical approaches are not complicated.

Learning to read and write

Research has established that specific early experiences can direct children's attention and learning in ways that support later literacy. Children are facing a possible, but still a tough, task and a sense of confidence and competence will help them through it.

Penny Munn interviewed children about their understanding of reading several times during their final year of pre-school. She found that:

- Children's behaviour towards books did not alter much, but their beliefs about the process of reading were undergoing change.
- Most of the children changed from thinking that reading was basically turning pages and telling a story to grasping that the process involved decoding print in a specific way.
- Children needed to understand that they could not yet read; it was a learning task they were going to tackle.
- However, children who had gained familiarity with books at home and experienced helpful adults were less daunted by this realisation. Children with a family background low in literacy expressed less confidence and seemed likely to avoid a situation of potential failure.

Children have to grasp several important features about written material. This understanding is built up over time and through focused experience. Helpful, active adults need to understand what children have yet to learn. Steadily children need to grasp the following:

- It is an intellectual leap for children to understand that the letters of the alphabet are symbols that stand for the sounds that children already know from spoken language. And these letters are put together to form words that build into sentences and which communicate meaning in books and other forms of written material.
- Children need to understand the communicative nature of print; it is saying something. Words carry meaning and may support the pictures in a book, but it is the words that are read for the story.
- Children have to learn that print follows certain rules of format and layout; the pattern is not immediately obvious. Print is made up of letters, words, punctuation and spaces. The letters that initially look like meaningless squiggles are used in a predictable way; the marks always stand for the same units of speech. The word system is different from the number system, although they can both be written.
- Print is read in English from the front of the book to the back, from the top of the page to bottom of the page and from left to right. Readers follow the print in a certain order – line by line and word by word. These are not universal text rules and bilingual children may have encountered a different system in their home language.
- There is a spoken language associated with using books – terms such as page, word, letter and front of the book.

Children learn all these important features of the written language through experience with written material, ideally starting very young. A varied programme of activities in which children continue to encounter and work with written material works most effectively, with adults taking an active role to help children.

Teaching methods

Learning to read successfully is key for children's later learning and achievement in schools, but there has been considerable disagreement about which possible approaches are the most effective.

Part of the difficulty has been the insistence of some educationalists that there is one right method. Such arguments were especially rife in the 1980s, both in Britain and the United States, and focused on whether children should be taught through an emphasis on the sound and letter system (**phonics**) or on patterns of letters that make up actual words (**whole word**). Careful study of the impact of different methods has confirmed that adults do not have to, indeed should not, make a choice between the two methods. Both phonics and whole word are needed for a complete approach to teaching children to read.

In order to become fully literate children need to learn in two broad areas:

- They are grasping at the making of meaning from written material and that books convey ideas, descriptions and the sequences of entire stories. Jeni Riley calls these the 'top-down' or meaning-driven print-processing strategies. Written material all around them serves a practical function of communication, reminding and instruction.
- But as well as the skills for deciphering meaning, children are also tackling the skills of de-coding the written or printed word and how sounds are represented on the page. Jeni Riley calls these the 'bottom-up' or decoding strategies.

No single method will meet these two areas of needs. Studies have shown that focusing on just one part by adults does not serve the children well. For instance, simply teaching the alphabet does not support later literacy unless the symbolic nature of the letters is closely tied to the meaning they convey within the context of books. It is well worth familiarising children with the alphabet but alongside other activities.

Restricted approaches to literacy that expose children to many books, but fail to help them to decode the link between letters and sounds, are only doing half the job. Children may come to like books but tend to see them as an activity that adults do with them. Learning to read is not the same as learning to speak a language and it is ineffective to leave children to try to work out the rules from unorganised exposure to books. The now discredited 'real books movement' was influential in some British schools in the 1980s and took this ultimately unhelpful approach.

Literacy and the family

Study into how children most easily build the understanding for later literacy highlights that all the most helpful activities are equally well undertaken by parents as by early years workers. Not surprisingly, therefore, the most practical projects concerned with literacy have looked at how to encourage parents to work with their children and to boost the parents' confidence that they can make a difference. Cathy Nutbrown's Raising Early Achievement in Literacy (REAL) project identified four main strands of literacy in working together with parents who were uncertain of their abilities in this area:

- encouraging awareness of environmental print – that writing is all around us and used in everyday life;
- encouraging parents to use and enjoy books with their children;
- making writing a practical and central part of activities with children and encouraging them to see that adults use their writing skills;
- using oral language to promote phonological awareness through song and nursery rhymes.

Dyslexia

Some children have more difficulty than they need with reading and writing because their early experience has not helped them. But some children experience continuing difficulties which largely remain, even if they are given careful attention in all the ways described in this section. In this situation the children, more likely boys than girls, may be dyslexic.

Dyslexia comes from Greek and means 'difficulty with words or language'. However, dyslexic children do not only have difficulty with the actual reading and writing. The problem is also one of organising and memory in addition to word recognition. In brief, children with dyslexia will have some or all of the following difficulties and, like many learning disabilities, dyslexia may be anything from mild to very severe.

- Children may have broader difficulties in communication, perhaps being slower than average in learning to talk.
- They may find it hard to pay attention, to stay still and focus on what they are doing.
- It is often hard for children with dyslexia to organise themselves and plan ahead. They have trouble with sorting out a sensible sequence in actions. Older dyslexic children often need help with general study skills. (I have known children, who had appropriate help, to be considerably better organised than their non-dyslexic peers.)
- Children may have problems with physical co-ordination, including being muddled between left and right.
- The most obvious problems, or the point at which somebody (beyond the child's parents) acknowledges there is a difficulty, will probably focus on reading, writing and spelling. There will be an obvious gap between what a child can manage, in tasks that include writing and those which do not.
- Some dyslexic children also have difficulties with mathematics, but certainly not all of them.

Early identification of dyslexia is not very easy as, when children are younger than 5 or 6 years, some difficulties may be shared by their peers as part of early development. Dyslexia cannot be 'cured' but early identification and appropriate help mean that a child's intellectual development can be encouraged and self confidence protected.

Reading on . . .

★ Acredolo, Linda and Goodwyn, Susan 1997: *Baby Signs* (Hodder and Stoughton). A description of the research described on page 96 in this chapter, with examples of how signs are a personal part of early communication.

★ Arnberg, Leonie 1987: *Raising Children Bilingually: The pre-school years* (Avon: Multilingual Matters). A practical book about the development of bilingual children, with suggestions for parents and carers.

★ Munn, Penny 'What do children know about reading before they go to school?' in Owen, Pamela and Pumfrey, Peter (eds) 1997: *Emergent and Developing Reading: Messages for teachers* (Falmer Press). An account of the research described on page 113, which brings alive the ways in which children come to understand this difficult task.

★ Nutbrown, Cathy 1994: *Threads of Thinking: Young children learning and the role of early education* (Paul Chapman). An approach to the development of young children which recognises the importance of parents' input. A description of the literacy project discussed on page 114 of this chapter.

SUGGESTED ACTIVITY

Find out more about dyslexia and possible early identification by contacting the British Dyslexia Association, 98 London Road, Reading, Berkshire RG1 5AU, tel: 01734 668271.

★   Quilliam, Susan 1994: *Child Watching: A parent's guide to children's body language* (Ward Lock). A stimulating book, with plenty of illustrations, that alerts adults to the unspoken side to communication. Written for parents but just as useful for early years workers.

★   Ostler, Christine 1991: *Dyslexia: A parents' survival guide* (Ammonite Books). A very practical book about dyslexia and what caring adults, not only parents, can do to help.

★   Reid, Jessie 'Into print: reading and language growth' in Donaldson, Margaret; Grieve, Robert and Pratt, Chris (eds) 1983: *Early Childhood Development and Education* (Blackwell). Research that illuminates the difficulties of children who have not cracked the code of written language.

★   Riley, Jeni 1997: *The Teaching of Reading: The development of literacy in the early years* (Paul Chapman). A practical approach to all the skills that children have to master in order to become confident readers and writers.

★   Trevarthen, Colwen 'The function of emotions in early infant communication and development' in Nadel, Jacqueline and Camaioni, Luigia (eds) 1993: *New Perspectives in Early Communicative Development* (Routledge). A description of some of the research discussed from page 90. This book is not an easy read, but this chapter, and some of the others, are a good source of information on the detail of research into very early communication.

★   Whitehead, Marion 1996: *The Development of Language and Literacy* (Hodder and Stoughton). Descriptions of how language and grasp of literacy develops for children and the applications for good practice in early years settings.

5 Helping children to learn

This chapter covers:

- theories of how children learn;
- an appropriate role for adults;
- aspects of children's learning.

You could look upon all of child development as a process of learning. In their physical development as much as their intellectual, children are coming to terms with what they do not yet know or are wondering how to do. They face the prospect of dealing with experiences when they are confused or have made mistakes, just as much as revelling in the delight when they manage a new skill. Yet, learning is often discussed largely in terms of cognitive development and more formal settings, such as school and the various early years settings. This restricted view is neither accurate nor very helpful to adults who are working closely with children. In this chapter I have attempted to hold on to a broader view of learning, although you will find more discussion of learning within organised settings, since this focus has been the main thrust of research.

5.1 Theories of how children learn

Both behaviourism and the cognitive theories have a perspective to offer on how children learn. Psychodynamic theory has focused on personal rather than intellectual development.

The behaviourist approach

Behaviourism was originally called 'learning theory'. This term acted as a contrast with psychodynamic theory, which was the main competing theory when the behaviourist approach was first developed. Psychodynamic theory was far more concerned about the roots of later personality.

Practical applications of the behaviourist approach have been most widely used in carefully structured programmes for children, including those for children from socially disadvantaged backgrounds and with children who have physical or learning disabilities. A focus on the step-by-step learning has been valuable in illuminating all the finer developments that are very important to notice, teach and reward when children's development may be slower. You will find more on the behaviourist approach in chapter 6 where the ideas are discussed in the context of how children learn to behave. This chapter focuses more on children's intellectual learning.

Social learning theory

Bandura's more sophisticated approach to behaviourism has practical implications for learning, both about ideas and ways of behaving. He developed several key ideas.

Learning through modelling

Bandura believed that human learning does not always require the kind of direct and visible reinforcement described in operant conditioning (see page 20). Children learn through observation of others – children and familiar adults. If you watch children you will be struck by the extent to which they copy others; the motivation to imitate seems strong. In family life especially, the wish to copy is fuelled also by the strong attachments made by many children to their parents. Children do not copy everything they see – either those behaviours you would wish to encourage or those you fervently hope that they will not imitate.

Intrinsic reinforcements

Bandura also emphasised that feelings shape behaviour through internally experienced rewards such as a sense of personal satisfaction and pride in managing something. These feelings are unlikely to emerge spontaneously and familiar carers have an important role to play. Adults not only share their own delight in what children manage but, through their own adult behaviour, can encourage children to relish a sense of personal achievement and work for that, not just tangible rewards. Indeed, an over-emphasis on rewarding

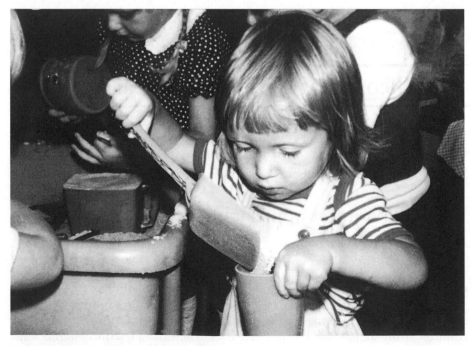

Concentration and satisfaction in a very young child

children for specific 'good' behaviour can persuade them they are only working towards the reward and internal satisfaction is lost. (More on these practical issues in chapter 6.)

Thinking and observational learning
Bandura further extended his version of learning theory to cover how children are not passive observers, or unthinking imitators. He now refers to his approach as social cognitive theory. The extent to which children learn through observation of others does not depend only on what there is to observe around them. The end result will also be affected by:

- the exact focus of children's attention;
- what they are able to remember;
- what children can physically copy, given their skills at the time;
- what they are motivated to imitate. Children are far less likely to copy an adult whom they dislike (unless it is in mockery).

Bandura also proposes that children develop abstract ideas from observational learning: working out what is admired or disliked behaviour, developing attitudes and a sense of their own worth.

Learning as part of cognitive development

The theories of Jean Piaget provoked a radical change in thinking about learning. He shifted the perspective towards children as individuals actively involved in exploring and understanding: the child as young philosopher and young scientist. (More about Piaget on page 62.) The twenty-year period between the 1970s and 1990s saw a move away from study of children as if they were the more solitary learners of Piaget's theory towards looking at how children learned in their social and cultural context. Developments in thinking about how children learn have also highlighted the particular nature of children's learning in formal settings like school.

Vygotsky

Vygotsky, like Piaget, observed children as active learners who were working to make sense of their experience. However, Vygotsky saw this learning as taking place in far more of a social context than was Piaget's approach. Vygotsky described children's learning as part of a specific, social nature and saw the process as one through which children grew into the intellectual life of the more mature children and adults around them.

Vygotsky distinguished between **spontaneous concepts** (or everyday) and **scientific concepts** (see also page 69). He stressed the different nature of school-based learning to children's own explorations. Vygotsky not only believed that formal learning for children *was* different but that it *should be* different from children's own discoveries.

- The nature of school-based learning was that adults bring in systematic knowledge beyond that which children can directly experience for themselves. Instruction from more knowledgeable or experienced people precedes the development of new concepts, such as arithmetical concepts.
- The point at which the new concept becomes clear and part of their overall thinking will vary between individual children.

Vygotsky argued that the absence of a system was the key difference between children's spontaneous concepts and scientific concepts. The peculiarities of child thought described by Piaget arose from the fact that spontaneous concepts were not set in a system that allowed children to generalise. Children were describing what they saw rather than standing back from the immediate experience. So children see no problem with saying that object A dissolved because it was small and object B because it was large. Children do not struggle with the contradiction (which seems obvious to adults) because they are simply describing what they see. They are not proposing a broader rule that links size with whether materials will dissolve or not.

Children start with the rudiments of a system and then, through instruction, the concepts they are learning in a formal setting like school carry with them the relationships of generality. Vygotsky saw the experience of formal learning as transforming the structure of children's spontaneous concepts and helping to organise them into a system.

Margaret Donaldson

Donaldson and her research colleagues have offered another constructive alternative to Piaget's approach to how children learn. Donaldson developed the concept that the experience of school learning required a particular way of thinking from children, which she called **disembedded thought**. By this term Donaldson meant a kind of thinking in which ideas were separate from the context to which children had become accustomed. Her view was that a different kind of thinking will be required of children for their education. Her practical concern was that children had greater difficulties than necessary when adults failed to recognise the kind of intellectual process they were requiring.

The research into thinking and learning by Donaldson and her colleagues over the years has illustrated very well how adults need to tune into how young children think in order to be effective supports in children's learning.

EXAMPLE

Disembedded thinking

Martin Hughes made a series of studies of early mathematical understanding. He shows that well over half of the three- and four-year-olds could manage hypothetical ('what if...') counting, so long as the imaginary situation made sense and related to their own experience. So this age group could often give the correct answer to a question such as, 'If there were two girls in a shop and another one went in, how many girls would be in the shop now?' However, as the following exchange shows, without the context, adult questions made no sense. Martin Hughes was talking with a boy called Ram who was then 4:7.

MH: What is three and one more? How many is three and one more?
R: Three and what? One what? Letter? I mean number? (They had used magnetic numerals in an earlier game.)
MH: How many is three and one more?

R: One more what?
MH: Just one more, you know.
R (sounds disgruntled): I don't know.
(Quoted from Martin Hughes 1986: *Children and Number* (Blackwell.)

Questions
Watch and listen to the children in your setting over two or more weeks. Keep notes of ideas that seem to confuse them, especially of those times when you were surprised they were confused. Use your notes to think over the incidents and ideally discuss with a colleague:

● What were you trying to help the children to learn?
● Or what were you assuming they would understand without specific help?
● Where did the children's understanding seem to break down?
● What does this tell you about how you could better help their learning?

As Donaldson explains, all thinking is abstract to some extent, but the experience in nursery and the early years of school requires children to learn how to step back from concrete experiences. Adults need to understand what they are asking and to ensure that there are plenty of steps between the concrete experience and a purely abstract application of the same idea. (More on this theme from page 71.)

Jerome Bruner

Bruner studied children's thinking and learning through the way in which they process information. His approach is to look equally at two aspects:

- how children's experience affects their cognitive development – from external events to internal thinking;
- how children's ability to think can then shape their experience – inside to outside.

Bruner considered that integration was crucial: how thoughts and actions were organised in different ways that continued to change depending on children's experience. Children's learning therefore depended on their increasing ability to make sense of and use their experiences of the environment. Bruner was concerned that, in a formal learning situation, children can be asked to understand events outside the context in which they occur. Like Vygotsky, Bruner disagreed with Piaget's emphasis on waiting for children to be ready to learn and believed that educators should take the initiative to encourage and stimulate children towards new learning tasks.

Bruner pointed out that children can enjoy **solving problems** but that they are not necessarily very skilled or motivated at **problem finding**. And, of course, in order to identify a problem that needs solving you also need some grasp of the gap between what you currently know and do not know, what you can and cannot do. This kind of identification and guidance is the crucial role of adults who can challenge children without daunting them.

5.2 An appropriate role for adults

Views on adults' and children's learning

The influence of Piaget

Much of the research into early learning in formal settings and children's later development has raised tough questions about how adults should behave. Early years care and education has been significantly influenced by Piaget's theory of how children learn. Two main strands of practice were the result:

- A strong emphasis on children's active exploration of objects and on learning through doing. A focus on the power of discovery for children's continued development.

- In contrast, Piaget had an under-emphasis on how adults could contribute to children's learning. (He allowed for a limited adult role in stimulating children to realise that they held contradictory ideas.) In some educational philosophies, this approach was stressed to the extent that adults were largely relegated to the sidelines. The impression was given that adult input would far more likely interfere with children's learning than help.

New approaches on learning do not undermine the importance of children's active involvement in the learning process. They do, however, place far more emphasis on an active role for adults.

The positive legacy of Piaget's approach has been:

- the importance of focusing on children and their current state of understanding;
- the sense of a progression in learning, that some ideas or skills will make little sense until children have grasped earlier understandings;
- that children are actively trying to make sense of the world. They are not simply passive receivers of adult information.

However, practical applications of Piaget's ideas have led to a situation in early care and education when adults could be wary of offering ideas and help. The reason was that they had been led to believe that this action would disrupt children's natural learning processes. A further unfortunate result of applying Piaget's ideas was an over-emphasis on children's understanding of concepts, such as number, with sometimes a downgrading of practical skills. I have certainly heard early years workers and educationalists dismiss parents' efforts to teach their children to count as 'just parroting' or children's pleasure in factual knowledge as 'rote learning'.

A more active role for adults

The zone of proximal development

Fresh approaches to a positive and active adult role draw on knowledge of children but take a perspective on development and learning more influenced by Vygotsky, who in turn was a strong influence on Bruner and Donaldson.

In contrast with Piaget, Vygotsky's view of intelligence included the capacity to benefit from instruction and so he placed an emphasis on adults' ability to instruct. His idea of the zone of proximal development was built around an active role for adults (or more capable peers). He saw a key role for experienced learners sharing approaches with the less experienced. The combination of an awareness of children's current understanding with a respectful use of greater adult knowledge makes an effective combination, creating a genuinely

SUGGESTED ACTIVITY

- Be alert to examples in your practice with children which can highlight the zone of proximal development for individual children. Look for pointers towards a constructive way to help children move from 'I can't' or 'I don't understand' towards 'I can' and 'Now I see what you mean'.

- With individual children, try to home in through careful observation on not only what they can do but what they can nearly manage. Look for this learning gap between 'can' and 'can't'.

- Look for ways that you can help and try out some strategies. Be very encouraging as the child tries.

helpful adult. The research in early communication and relationships (see chapters 2 and 4) has generated many examples of babies and toddlers who actively engage adults to help them and answer their queries. You will see many instances yourself in everyday life with young children.

Vygotsky's practical approach to the role of adults in instruction is expressed in his idea of **the zone of proximal development.** This idea is discussed in relation to children's thinking on page 67 and you will find a diagram within that section. Vygotsky explained his idea of the zone as being the distance between the actual developmental level of an individual child (determined by his or her skills of independent problem solving) and the level of potential development. This second level could be reached through problem solving with adult guidance, or in collaboration with more capable peers.

So the zone of proximal development includes skills and knowledge that are in the process of maturing. It is, if you like, the leading edge of learning. So instruction, especially that organised by adults, should be looking ahead through the zone. Educationalists are concerned that children should not be discouraged by an overemphasis on what they cannot do rather than what they can. The zone of proximal development is a practical way of thinking about children's continued learning, through what they could manage, with a little help. The approach is also focused on individuals, since every child will have a different zone of proximal development.

EXAMPLE

Perhaps five-year-old Nathan is having difficulties in learning how to tie shoe laces. Left to his own devices, he gets very muddled and upset. The limit of his unaided development is that he cannot manage his laces. But suppose his mother or a patient older sibling gives Nathan a strategy to think his way through the steps

('First we do one lace over and under, pull it tight, now we bend this one back..' and so on.) And Nathan also has company to encourage him as he practises the steps. With this encouragement and specific help, Nathan's potential development may be realised and stretch to doing up his laces so they stay done.

Scaffolding

Bruner developed the concept of **scaffolding** to explain a positive way for adults to intervene in children's learning. The visual image is that of scaffolding on a building. When children are learning an idea or a skill, they benefit from adult support and suggestions. Bruner is never suggesting that adults should take over. Then, as children's understanding or their practical skill grows, adults can steadily 'remove' the scaffolding. This process continues with children's learning at different ages and the adult task is to be alert to the nature and extent of the scaffolding required for individual children.

SUGGESTED ACTIVITY

Jerome Bruner's idea of **scaffolding** has been described as not so much directing children but more a case of 'leading by following'. The key point is that you have to watch an individual child with care before you can judge how best to help.

- Choose one or two children you know and focus on an idea or a skill that they are currently learning.
- You might choose a physical skill such as learning to button up their coat or how to handle a tool like a egg beater in cooking. Or perhaps focus on an intellectual task such as learning about shapes.

- Watch individual children carefully to assess how far their learning has progressed. What kind of help might be most useful now: general verbal encouragement? specific verbal instructions? pointing out specific parts of the task? demonstrating?
- Try different ways of offering help and keep some notes of how far your input seems to help the child.
- What have you learned about: these individual children? the specific learning tasks? the way you tend to offer help?

Contingent teaching

David Wood describes a similar process to scaffolding in **contingent teaching** – an approach in which the adult's input is contingent on (or dependent on) the child's behaviour – specifically whether children show they have understood or not. The two basic rules of contingent teaching are that:

- If, after some help, a child shows she does not understand or cannot take through a given task, then this is a clear sign that greater help is needed from the adult.
- If, after some help, a child shows that she does understand or can do the task, then this is the signal for adults to reduce the help.

These two rules express simply what is hard work for any adult in practice.

If children are struggling or baffled, they do not need a repetition of verbal instructions or demonstrations that have not worked so far. Adult inclination is often to repeat the same help, but this approach is unlikely to be effective unless the child failed to attend first time round and, on the second attempt, you have successfully captured his attention first of all. In my conversations with primary and secondary school children, I have heard many complaints of this nature ('If I'd understood what she said the first time, then I wouldn't be asking for help, would I!'). The essence of contingent teaching is to make the help directly appropriate to an individual child. So, five children of similar age in a small group activity might all need slightly different kinds and levels of help. This type of help is a challenge to adult skills and awareness and, although very satisfying, is hard work.

An essential part of being a useful adult to children has to be an awareness (and recall) of the nature of learning in childhood. Some approaches to children's learning seem to underplay the difficulties that children can face. (See my comments on page 130 about the cultural/educational tradition of the 1980s and 90s insisting that all learning is fun.) David Wood allows for the position of uncertainty in which children regularly find themselves during the learning years of childhood. When adults are facing unfamiliar situations or problems, they can feel great uncertainty. The resulting uneasiness can affect our ability to attend, remember and reason – all important parts of learning in a new situation. Life for children is full of new ideas and required skills and the uncertainty can overwhelm them, if adults do not offer genuine help and a great deal of patience.

Thoughtless adults can discourage and dishearten children. Yet, as Wood points out, they can really help by:

- organising activities to reduce uncertainty or confusion;
- breaking down a complex task into more manageable, easier steps;
- directing children's attention to key features;
- working to grasp where a child's understanding currently stops and offering appropriate help to move the child onwards.

Involved adults

During the 1980s, observational research on adults in early years settings focused on comparisons between the different settings and types of training. The strong belief underlying some of the projects was that teachers would be more effective than workers with other training backgrounds, such as nursery nurses. Projects consistently failed to find clear-cut results and highlighted many unsupported assumptions about what was best for children's learning. However, the long-term result of such projects has been positive. The emphasis has shifted to study of what kinds of behaviour seem best to support children's learning, rather than assuming that certain types of adult will necessarily be better.

One example of this detailed and descriptive approach is the Effective Early Learning (EEL) project, run by Christine Pascal and Tony Bertram. They have developed the work of Ferre Laevers who studied how children's involvement in learning was encouraged by challenges that were neither too easy nor excessively hard. The challenge needed to be at the edge of their children's current competence (Vygotsky's zone of proximal development).

Pascal and Bertram have focused on a range of adult behaviours summed up as **engagement.** They define this term as a set of personal qualities of adults involved in supporting children's learning. Their observational research has worked to ground these qualities in what the adults actually do and in differences between adults working with children. Pascal and Bertram have identified that the key features of more, or less, constructive behaviour with children are:

- *Sensitivity* – of the adult to the feelings and emotional well-being of children. The term also refers to empathy and genuineness on the part of the adult. Sensitive adults' actions show respect and attentiveness to the child. They acknowledge the child's sense of (in)security and offer praise and encouragement.
- *Stimulation* – the way that an adult intervenes in the learning process. Pascal and Bertram have observed how adults introduce or offer an activity. Adult behaviour can be in a more, or less, stimulating way, for instance

in giving information, intervening in an ongoing activity to stimulate action, thinking or communication.

* *Autonomy* – describes the degree of freedom given to the child to experiment. Effective adults support children to make judgements, choose activities and express ideas. The dimension of autonomy includes how adults deal with conflicts, rules and other behavioural issues. A positive approach includes the participation of children in rule-making.

A child-centred approach

The view that good practice in early years care and education should be **child-centred** is now a sufficiently strong tradition that it tends to be expressed as a self-evident truth. Practice does not remain good without reflection and understanding on the part of practitioners. So, this section looks at what a child-centred approach can mean in practice: when it would work well and what are the potential drawbacks. (The importance of 'learning through play' can also slip into an empty truism and some comments are made on page 135.)

Any approach to learning with the young should be child-centred in so far as adults will be limited in their effectiveness if they refuse to take the child's perspective. Adults (early years workers, teachers and parents) need to look through children's eyes and make that imaginative leap back to when they, the adults, had not yet gained their current understanding and skills. This task is not always very easy, even when adults have the motivation and respect for children to attempt it. You cannot help children to learn unless you are grasping where and how they need appropriate help.

Yet, learning should be a shared enterprise to which adults bring their own contribution. If adults are exclusively child-centred then they are restricting children to their own discoveries based on their own current knowledge base and refusing them the adult perspective. Margaret Donaldson has been one of several child psychologists to question an unthinking, child-centred approach. She describes the need for educators to **decentre**, by which she means to avoid being bound to a single point of view. Donaldson's comments are another way of saying that, in some learning situations, perhaps it is the egocentricism of adults that is the problem, not an egocentric viewpoint from children.

The risks of adult-dominated care and education are that children will be less creative and confident in their abilities to explore and solve. When children have little or no say in the enterprise of learning, they can become bored, passive, disruptive or a combination of all three. However, the risks in a child-centred extreme are that:

* It overestimates young children's powers of self-direction, especially if there is no relief. The pleasure in 'doing it myself' becomes the drudgery of 'having to do it myself with no help'.
* Children enjoy making choices and following their own absorbing interests within a theme. They enjoy making discoveries but they also enjoy and benefit from the explanations and insights of adults who have an alternative perspective (but still respect children's viewpoint). Even toddlers show a keenness to recruit adults to help them as well as enthusiasm sometimes to 'do it myself'.
* Children do not want to find out everything for themselves and they generally become irritated, or take the line of passive resistance, if forced back on their own resources all the time. They may also feel overwhelmed by uncertainty (David Wood's point, see page 125).

- Children need systematic, well-chosen help. An excessively child-centred approach underestimates children's wish and appreciation for help, so long as it is not pushed at them. Children ask questions and appreciate clear and honest answers, which can in turn provoke the wish to inquire further.

Donaldson points out that: 'Young human beings have a remarkable fitness for the role of novice. They can enjoy accepting new goals and challenges from other people and can experience great satisfaction from the achieving of conscious mastery.' (*Human Minds*, page 257).

Berry Mayall, taking a sociological perspective on childhood experiences, has also criticised the unthinking application of 'child-centred'. She points out that, when 'child-centred' is more a form of words than a thought-out approach in schools, any problems can be seen as the child's fault. By definition, the difficulties are believed not to be the school's fault, because they are offering a child-centred environment.

TO THINK ABOUT

Would you say that your own early years centre is 'child-centred' in its approach?

- Think over and discuss with colleagues what exactly you mean by this. Collect some specific examples of daily practice that illustrate what you believe to be the child-centred nature of your setting.
- In what ways is some of your practice 'adult-centred'? What would be good reasons for focusing on adults and adult concerns? For instance, do you allow the children to do anything they want, do they have completely free choice? So, what is the balance that you try to reach between children and adults in your setting?

Feelings and learning

Children's feelings, as well as adult emotions, are involved in day-by-day learning. Acknowledgement of children's feelings is an important part of developing a positive adult role. You may need to let children know that you can see they are frustrated or distressed by their difficulties. You can show your recognition of these feelings just as much as you should be sharing in children's delight when all goes well, or they grasp a skill or an idea that was previously a struggle. The importance of a positive approach to feelings (children's and adults') is also covered in chapter 6 on behaviour.

Constructive feedback

The idea of how to give useful, accurate and supportive feedback has been explored largely within organisational psychology and with application to adults in the work setting. Yet much of this area is equally relevant to children, with some minor adjustments of language.

Children become disheartened and can be resentful of adults who are mainly negative. Whether the focus is children's drawing, their early attempts to write or their behaviour, children are not helped by adults who find fault or for whom nothing is ever quite good enough. The situation is made even worse by adults who are additionally very rude to children, calling them 'stupid' or claiming 'you'll never be any good at this'. The adults themselves, whether parents or early years workers, may genuinely believe they are being helpful – thinking that 'children have to know what's wrong – how else will they learn?' Children undoubtedly need to know what is 'wrong' but always in the context of how to make it 'right'.

Yet, children do not benefit from an undiscriminating stream of positives. If adults always say 'That's lovely' or similar empty phrases, children do not feel that the apparent praise is genuine, because it comes whatever they have done. Also there will be many times when children have not grasped an idea, could manage better with a slightly different technique or have definitely done a calculation or written a word wrongly. Children do not fall apart if their mistakes or misunderstandings are pointed out to them, with warmth and respect. The problem comes if this sort of adult intervention is dismissive and fails to be balanced by plenty of recognition of what has gone well.

Children need constructive feedback, or as it is sometimes called constructive criticism. The main features of this kind of behaviour from adults are that:

● Your positive comments are specific rather than empty 'that's nice' remarks. Children feel supported by adults who draw attention to particular features of what they have done. It might be 'I do like the way you've used the colours in your chalk drawing' or 'I noticed how you helped Andy with his buttons. Thank you.'
● Children's mistakes or misunderstandings are highlighted as a chance to learn rather than as criticisms. Acknowledge what has gone well in addition to 'what you're having some trouble with'. The positives need to be genuine, rather than the faint praise of 'You've done alright but...'

- Explain clearly how children could manage better or where they have got lost. It might be how to hold the craft tool more effectively, how to direct the water into the washing-up bowl without huge splashes or a few of the mis-spellings.
- Adults alert children to the progress they have made – 'Do you remember when you told me you'd never ever be able to... and look at you now!'
- Be ready to support children who are hard on themselves over their mistakes. It might be 'Maybe it's not you. Perhaps I didn't explain very well. Let me try again' or 'It was too heavy for you. We all need help sometimes.'

In a family or an early years centre, where constructive feedback has been established, you will find that the children will start to treat each other this way as well. Perhaps one child tells another 'Well done' or a genuine 'Thank you for helping me' or pays the compliment of 'I like your picture'. This pattern has much in common with the Adlerian approach of encouragement (see also page 147 in chapter 6).

TO THINK ABOUT

Personal memories that may help

Children can be daunted by unhelpful negatives and it is adults' responsibility to ensure that their comments to children are as constructive as possible.

I can still remember the hopeless feeling that came over me as a ten-year-old when my teacher criticised a grid of lines that I had drawn for a project. He told me, in front of other children, that the pattern was 'not good enough' and that I was 'ham-fisted', but gave me no guidance whatsoever on how to improve my technique. As an adult, I can look back on that incident and see how little it would have taken to shift that criticism into a positive direction. He could have helped me to learn something more useful than the belief that I was hopeless in precision work with a ruler. Looking back with an adult's understanding, I can also appreciate that this teacher had a teasing-critical style that he probably thought was constructive.

Think over some incidents from your own childhood, ideally in discussion with colleagues:

- Consider an example when you were given unrelieved criticism. How could the adult have changed his or her behaviour to enable you to learn constructively? What help did you need? Or what did you not understand?
- Look also at an example when you can recall helpful, constructive feedback in your childhood. What did the adult do or say that helped you to learn? If you had gone wrong in some way, how did he or she support your self-confidence while pointing out your mistake.
- Perhaps you, and your colleagues, are coming up with many more examples of negative than positive experiences. Then talk through any ideas about what may have led adults towards this imbalance in their behaviour towards children.
- Talk about your own approach now – how can you ensure that you are not repeating similar mistakes with this generation of children!

A personal opinion – is learning always fun?

I have been struck that early years workers and parents risk being misled by a relentless emphasis that 'Learning must be fun!' The approach summed up by this phrase was a reaction to dry methods of trying to help children learn. But the focus on fun has become a cliché very similar to the old 'Schooldays are the best days of your life'. And, rather like that cliché, risks ignoring children's genuine struggles.

I would rather have an emphasis on helping children find personal satisfaction in all the different types of learning. Their learning will sometimes be enjoyable. But, at other times, the helpful role of adults is to support children as they persevere with a tough task well beyond the point where anyone would give up if the whole point were 'fun'.

- What do you think about the pressure that learning must be fun? Can learning always be fun?
- Why not discuss the issue with your colleagues? And with friends who do not work in early years.
- You might also consider the point that children sometimes do something just because it is fun, not for any clear learning purpose. Some discussions of children's television programmes seem to have muddled the idea that, if learning is fun, then all fun should have a clear educational purpose as well.

The research on mastery and effective learning is also relevant here – see page 133.

5.3 Aspects of children's learning

Learning at home

The idea of children attending nursery or playgroup is relatively new – if you take the perspective of social history. In a 1950s childhood (my own) it was very unusual for children to experience any kind of pre-school setting prior to the first day of school (no prior visits, no settling-in period, your parents very firmly stopped at the school gate). There were some nursery schools but not many, the playgroup movement did not start until the 1960s and the numbers of day nurseries were reduced after the post-war closures.

There was a striking difference between my experience and my own children's 1980s childhood. Living in a city, we had the possibility of drop-in parent and toddler clubs, playgroups, nursery classes and day nurseries. (Not all families either had or now have a range of options since some areas of the country have limited early years provision.) The change brought increased choice for children and their parents and the undoubted enjoyment for many children of the different early years settings. Research into the impact of different pre-school experiences for children has shown some very positive effects, especially for those children from socially disadvantaged families (see page 132). However, an unfortunate side effect has been to imply that children only learn in formal settings and the great potential for children to learn at home has been virtually ignored.

Research about children's family experience has focused much more on their emotional development and the forming of attachments (see page 35). The research on early communication (see page 90) highlights the subtle responses of parents to their babies and very young children. However, the links have generally not been made to how children can otherwise be learning at home. Although educationalists may say that 'Parents are the first educators', developments in the practice of partnership with parents have far more often assumed that parents need to learn from playgroup or nursery, rather than that early years workers could learn from family life.

The prevailing attitude of educationalists is accurately summed up in the opening paragraph of Kathy Sylva's 1994 review of 'The impact of early learning on children's later development' (full reference on page 139). In a very thorough coverage of formal settings for children, Sylva starts with the specific exclusion of home-based learning: '"Early learning" is defined here as learning that occurs outside the home before school entry... Home care and child minders are excluded as their aim is primarily care.' (Page 84.)

Admittedly, there is more research on how and what children seem to learn in specifically pre-school settings, but that is not the reason Sylva gives for dismissing home-based learning.

There have, of course, been some exceptions to this general trend. Barbara Tizard made a firm case for acknowledging that children learn at home and that they learn in a different way from their time in nursery (see page 79). On the basis of another research project in the early 1980s, Tizard and her colleagues offered constructive criticism of approaches to parent involvement that is still relevant now: 'It was generally the case that staff implicitly held a "one-way" model of parent involvement – they wished to change some aspects of the parents' behaviour in order, as they believed, to benefit the children educationally. They did not see a need for school practice to change in response to input from the parents.' (Tizard, Barbara; Mortimore, Jo and Burchell, Bebb 1981: *Involving Parents in Nursery and Infant Schools* page 51, (Grant McIntyre).)

Exploring and learning at home

By talking with parents, Tizard and her colleagues discovered that many were specifically helping children with their learning and that few teachers were aware of what and how much parents did with their children at home.

Margaret Henry has pointed out that developments in an early years curriculum for very young children have largely drawn from the existing curriculum for older children, modified where necessary. There are few examples of curricula that take useful lessons from babies and young children in home settings. In my experience, this imbalance can lead workers to undervalue the necessary physical caretaking routines with babies and toddlers. These routines can be seen as interruptions to children's opportunities to learn through play. Yet the research on early communication, as well as the experience of home care, highlights that the close physical contact and attention of the caretaking routine can be a very valuable time for learning.

Marjorie Boxall's practical work with nurture groups (see also page 137) drew on a positive view of the potential of home learning. Boxall observed how school life presumed that children came with outlooks and ways of behaving that prepared them for group learning. When children had not experienced this type of early learning in a home setting (mainly because of severe stresses on their family), they were very hard to manage in a group. Marjorie Boxall's development of the nurture group experience was an explicit application of 'what a good mother would do with her three- and four-year-olds'.

TO THINK ABOUT

My emphasis on learning at home in the above section is to encourage you to think about an unhelpful bias in approaches to children's learning. As I explained at the beginning this chapter, most of the research looks at early years settings, so take this opportunity to think about the home setting.

- Early years settings like nurseries can offer opportunities that may not be possible at home. But what can home settings and family life offer that you cannot easily re-create in a formal setting?
- Talk with the parents of some of the children who attend your setting. What do these parents feel they have taught their children, what have they shown them within ordinary family life?

The impact of early experience

What and how children learn in their early years does affect their later development but the impact is subtle.

Pre-school programmes for children

During the 1970s, there were many programmes designed to help children from socially disadvantaged backgrounds through early intervention. These projects were assessed by differences in measures of intelligence (IQ tests) between children who had attended special programmes or had not. When there was a difference found between the two groups, the boost to the IQ of the special group did not last longer than the early years of school and the gap between the two groups typically closed. This apparent 'wash-out' of the IQ difference dashed hopes that children's early educational experience could change their prospects in the long term.

What then happened was that some of the best-organised (and funded) American projects continued to follow up the children over all the years of their schooling and they found a long-term impact of the early experience. The detailed findings of these longitudinal research programmes have pointed to what factors in an early learning experience work best for children in the long term.

The successful programmes had a clear structure for children's learning, an active role for children in the day and some elements of parent involvement. One example was the High Scope programme with its plan-do-review approach. The 'graduates' of the well-organised programmes showed greater competence in school. They were less likely to be assigned to special education classes or to be kept down a year (a common option in American schools when children are struggling). By early adulthood the young people had higher aspirations for employment, the girls were less likely to be pregnant and both sexes less likely to be in trouble with the law. The young people were staying in school, were not dropping out and were making a success of their adult lives.

What seemed to have happened was that the high quality pre-school programmes had kick-started a positive outlook in the children, and their parents. They viewed school as a useful experience and themselves as people who could achieve and overcome difficulties. The exact programme of pre-school activities seemed to be less relevant than specific adult effort to develop positive attitudes to learning in children, to boost their self-esteem and to show them how to focus on tasks and persevere.

A sense of mastery

The research into the long-term effect of pre-school programmes has pointed to the great importance of how adults encourage children to view learning. The results are equally relevant whatever your setting or your professional background, because the research did not come out with simple answers that a particular kind of pre-school setting or specifically trained adult was best for children. What matters is what adults do with the children and the impact that exerts on the children's outlook.

In order to make sense of the pre-school research, Kathy Sylva draws on research on mastery behaviour in children carried out by C.S. Dweck and her colleagues in America. In her studies of children and learning, Dweck interpreted important differences by describing two orientations, which children had also learned.

The mastery orientation

Children who had taken on a **mastery approach** had learned a perspective that saw new learning tasks as a challenge rather than a threat. Their outlook when faced with a difficult problem, or one at which they initially failed, was to look carefully at their strategy and try another approach. In interviews with the researchers, children with a mastery orientation showed that they believed effort usually paid off and did not think that difficulties arose because they were stupid. The children had a sense of persistence, of a problem-solving approach and an outlook of continuing to learn. They felt good about themselves and their capacity to learn.

The helpless orientation

In contrast, children who had learned what Dweck called a sense of **helplessness**, were far more likely to view new or difficult tasks as a threat to be avoided. When the experimental tasks became difficult or children experienced initial failure, this group did not persevere or try alternative strategies. They started to chat or engage in other kinds of off-task behaviour. In interviews, these children expressed beliefs that failure showed you were 'no good' at something. They felt negative about themselves and so wanted to get out of the situation. The children had taken on an idea of innate ability: that people are either naturally good at something or useless, and practice will not help. They felt badly about themselves and their capacity to face new or initially difficult challenges.

Practical application

Mastery and helplessness are not absolutes (either-or) but continuums (a stretch from strong through to weaker orientations in either of these outlooks). It does not seem to be the case that children are fixed as mastery-oriented or helpless. Children and adults show greater or lesser degrees of the one orientation. The two orientations were not linked with measurable intelligence. A child could be potentially very able and yet feel helpless and hopeless about his abilities. You can see that this is another example of how different aspects of children's development relate together: children's intellectual grasp, their actual experience but also the sense they make of what happens to them and their feelings about experiences of success or failure.

Dweck and her team are not proposing that children should be encouraged in unrealistic optimism about their capacities. It is rather that an objective assessment of current strengths can go hand-in-hand with a desire to learn more. This practical area of research has implications for a positive role for adults in children's learning:

- The research suggests that adults can help children to develop a mastery orientation if children are encouraged towards **learning goals** – a focus on the satisfaction in learning a skill or gaining more knowledge. Adults can alert children to the sense of continuing to learn.
- On the other hand, when children's learning is weighted towards **performance goals** – this particular task in front of them now – children may learn more to focus on what they can or cannot do currently, with less sense of continuing to learn.
- Early years settings and school need to focus on nurturing positive beliefs about their talents in children, help them to acquire resources for dealing with mistakes and failure, and to think of achievement as reached by effort more than innate ability.
- Children need to develop persistence in the face of difficulties and to deal calmly with errors, misjudgements or misunderstandings. They are unlikely to learn this outlook without a very positive approach from adults towards mistakes. Adults who focus very much on what has gone wrong can instil in children a stronger fear of failure than excitement at the prospect of success.
- Children who come to your setting already convinced that they are 'stupid' will be especially vulnerable to criticism. It will be crucial that you built up their self-confidence. At the same time, you can persistently encourage a view of learning as a satisfying challenge, at which the children can succeed, rather than a threat that will expose them to ridicule.
- Constructive feedback to children will help (see page 127) as will a continuously encouraging approach (see page 147). A positive approach is needed in dealing with mistakes, but not pretending to children that all is well when it is not.
- Children need focused help rather than general exhortations to 'try'. Adults should create positive circumstances for success and satisfaction for children. But it is not usually helpful to simplify a situation so much that mistakes are impossible, since you want children to learn a constructive view of mistakes as opportunities to learn rather than being afraid of 'failures'.

SUGGESTED ACTIVITY

You may have noticed that a great deal of research on children's thinking and learning explores those situations when children do not understand. Intriguing research by Elizabeth Robinson and Peter Robinson focused on what happens when adults are puzzled, when children were not getting their message across to the more mature partner in the exchange.

They found that, when adults did not understand what children meant, the most frequent response from the adult was to ask for a repetition with 'Pardon?' The next most common adult reaction was to ask questions to encourage more information (What? and Who? questions). Some adults would make a guess about what the child meant, or they would repeat and expand the child's message or ignore it. The least frequently used response was for adults to tell children directly, 'I don't understand what you mean' or similar phrases that alerted children to communication failure.

In a series of experiments, it became clear that children did not realise adults had failed to understand unless those adults said so directly. Children are often cooperative with adults in following the route of repeating themselves or answering adult questions. But it seems to be more helpful if any of these strategies are combined with honesty about lack of understanding.

You could explore these ideas in the following ways:

- Keep alert to how you handle times when you do not understand what a child says.
- Try letting children know that you are confused about what they are telling you. Use any questions in this context.
- Listen in to your colleagues. Do many of you have a pattern of asking children to repeat or answer your questions when it is you who does not understand?

An early years curriculum
Learning through play

It is a central tenet of early years practice that children learn through play. This development has a long tradition and the phrase 'learning through play' runs the risk of becoming accepted wisdom that is neither properly discussed nor challenged. This aim of this section is to help you to stand back from the idea and to place the positives of learning through play in a broader context.

Children's play has a long history and children around the world engage in play, unless their childhood is curtailed by working or very poor health. Generations of children have played in gardens, open spaces and their local neighbourhood. The emphasis on children's learning through play was brought into early years settings very much as a reaction to highly disciplined early education which focused on a narrow range of skills.

The very positive side of the focus on children's play is the scope that it provides for children to be active participants in their own learning and creative users in play of whatever is available. Children's play is an important part of their lives because, in their play, children can step outside the restrictions of their real everyday lives. In imaginative play, they can be who they wish, and can integrate props and settings to create what they wish to explore. In physical play they can develop their skills at a rate and in the context that makes most sense for them.

There are plenty of books that promote learning through play in a fairly uncritical way, so my aim here is to give you some thoughts along the lines of 'Yes, children do learn through play but...':

- The approach of 'children learn through play' becomes less positive for children if adults conclude that they have only a limited role in children's activities (look back through section 5.2 for this topic).
- Play is not the sum total of children's activity and they can be very interested and motivated to have an active role in how an early years setting is run

day by day. They learn a great deal from helping out – a point made by Margaret Henry and supported by observations in home settings.

- Children also want and need time to spend with adults. An exclusive learning through play approach can reduce the opportunities for children to learn from direct coaching from adults (Margaret Donaldson's point, see page 126) and from relaxed conversation with adults (the work of Barbara Tizard, page 79).
- Babies and very young children enjoy play but adults can take a wrong turn if they see this activity as time-bound to adult-determined playtimes. An effective very early years curriculum (see below) takes account of the entire day of very young children and looks about what they can and do learn during times of physical caretaking.
- Adults in early years settings need to be honest about their approach to play. They do not give children complete choice in what and how they play. Discussions of practice in early years settings include 'structured play' or 'play with a purpose' which promote certain types of learning but also bring adult purposes to children's play (a similar point to the comments on page 126 about a child-centred environment).
- Ground rules are set and certain types of play that children like, for example, play fighting (see page 159) are definitely discouraged. Such guidance from adults is legitimate, often a responsible approach and also part of children's learning. But adults should be honest about what they are doing.

Helping very young children to learn

Margaret Henry reviewed a number of approaches to work with very young children and concluded that three dimensions were appropriate:

- *Responsiveness*: a warm and affectionate relationship with children that demonstrates the adults' high regard for the children. Adults needed to be engaged with and attentive towards the children.
- *Involvement*: an active support of children's learning, which encourages exploration and achievement. An example of appropriate involvement would be that adults talk with children and not at them.
- *Control*: a positive approach to control, characterised by consistency and explanations and which encourages children to independent action. Positive control in action works through both responsiveness and involvement.

Henry and others have stressed that an appropriate early years curriculum for under-threes cannot be a simplified version of what is usually proposed as good practice for over-threes. Henry emphasises the importance of what she calls 'by the way' teaching of young children, that much of their learning arises from daily events and domestic routine rather than planned play activities with a clear adult purpose. Several themes emerge from a focus on learning and very young children:

- That a very early years curriculum should reflect lessons from home-based learning as well as formal settings for older children. This theme links with the practical concern of avoiding an artificial split between 'care' and 'education'.
- Babies and very young children do not rate activities in a hierarchy of possible learning experiences. They can learn much during the care routines that may seem very mundane to adult carers. Lessons from research into early communication (see page 90) highlight that close contact and affectionate communication is a vehicle for detailed early learning.
- Children under three are active participants in their own learning but the meaning they assign to their experiences and feelings is largely dependent

on the meanings given them through the responses of key and familiar adults. A useful concept is that of **social referencing:** that babies and very young children often look towards a familiar adult, to see that person's reaction and expression, in order to make some sense of a new or ambiguous situation.

- The daily experiences of babies and very young children are just as important as the outcomes of the experience. Robin Leavitt has stressed that concern for what adults want children to become can take precedence over who they are now and their current experience. In practical terms, adults may feel that very young children are less interesting because they appear not to do much or are not yet talking. Again the research into early communication and emotional relationships shows how much is happening before the conventional developmental milestones.

Heuristic play

Elinor Goldschmied has studied the exploratory play of babies and toddlers – the way in which they make choices and often examine objects with great concentration. She calls this kind of play 'heuristic' (from a Greek word) because the very young children's activities enable them to discover and reach an understanding of their world and what is in it. Goldschmied developed her **treasure basket** idea as a result of observations of very young children in day care settings in England and Italy. The wide basket has a generous array of objects that vary in size, shape and feel, but which are safe for infants. None are conventional toys and many are safe but ordinary household objects.

The heuristic play approach has been developed for day care settings with under twos and draws on aspects of home learning when children are allowed safe exploration of objects such as saucepans and wooden spoons. The adult role is to share children's pleasure but not to direct them. Adults remain as a presence but do not intervene or suggest. With heuristic play sessions for toddlers, the young children are encouraged to be involved in tidying up at the end.

When you watch a heuristic play session, it can be a valuable reminder of how fascinated and absorbed young children are by ordinary objects. If you want to follow up the ideas of learning through heuristic play, you can see the play sessions in two videos: *Infants At Work* and *Heuristic Play* (available from the National Children's Bureau, address on page 213).

Nurture groups

The artificial split between what adults have called 'care' and 'education' has never made much sense if the process of learning is approached from the perspective of young children. Children's ability to cope in schools – with large groups and limited adult attention – is built through early experiences which are supported by caring and attentive adults.

The work of Marjorie Boxall in developing her **nurture groups** within primary schools highlighted the needs of children whose early experiences had not prepared them for the school setting. In her work as an educational psychologist during the 1970s, Boxall was dealing with many referrals of children whom teachers judged to be hard to manage in the classroom. Her observations led her to develop small groups for such children in order to develop the skills and outlook that they needed to manage in classes. The main characteristics of the groups were that:

- Numbers were deliberately kept low so that children could learn to relate to a small number of other children sharing the same space and adults (a teacher and assistant).

- There was a focus on pre-school learning activities which the children had largely missed. However, choices between activities were deliberately limited since the children were overwhelmed by too great a range of choice.
- How the group was run was just as important as the activities provided. Specifically, the group leader offered a regular routine in which children could learn about predictability as well as variety in daily events. Children were warned of any changes and visitors kept to a minimum. The overriding aim was to combine the nurturing of family life with the structure enabling children to manage in a group (taking turns, making choices, seeing an activity through to completion).
- Interaction with the children was directed towards encouraging them to develop positive feelings about themselves and towards adults as useful resources. Many of the children needed to learn to trust adults.

Marjorie Boxall's work is a good example of practical work in which the skills of observation combined with a strong sense of what was missing for children who were already failing in the school system. The project combined the lessons of wisdom as well as evidence, a distinction made in section 1.5.

SUGGESTED ACTIVITY

This chapter has focused on how children learn and how adults can best help. Use your skills of observation to highlight these two sides of your work.

Focus on two children over the period of a week and note down what you judge these individuals have learned over this time.

You may be noting quite small steps, but recognise that these may be important in this child's learning. Take a broad sweep at learning. Perhaps one child has managed to persevere in circumstances when she would

previously have given up. Or perhaps another child has learned a specific skill.

- How did you, or any of your colleagues, work to support these children as they learned, or to help the children to recognise and celebrate what they had managed?
- What have you learned about these individual children?
- What have you learned about yourself and your approach?

The nature of early learning

Adults involved with young children are part of a process that stretches into the future. You will see many changes and achievements but children also have a considerable amount still to learn after their time with you is complete. You can make a positive difference to children while they are with you in your setting. You can support their learning in specific areas and help them to develop a positive outlook on learning.

For most children, their parents are the only adults who will accompany them through the whole experience of childhood learning. For this reason, good practice in any early years setting has to include a respect for parents, what they have already done with their children and what they will do in the future. Partnership with parents should include opportunities for them to understand or become involved, if they wish, in how your setting promotes learning. But, partnership must be two-way, with an acknowledgement that your setting is not the only place where children learn. They are also learning with their family at home.

Reading on . . .

★ Bennathan, Marion and Boxall, Marjorie 1996: *Effective Intervention in Primary Schools: Nurture groups* (David Fulton). A description of Boxall's work which highlights the underlying assumptions about how children will cope with group life in school.

★ Bredekamp, Sue 1987: *Developmentally Appropriate Practice in Early Childhood Programmes Serving Children from Birth Through Age 8* (National Association for the Education of Young Children). A practical book on planning an early years curriculum.

★ Donaldson, Margaret 1992: *Human Minds: An exploration* (Allen Lane). Stimulating ideas about children's learning and the approach of adults in settings like school. The broader philosophical framework that Donaldson attempts to create makes for difficult reading in some chapters.

★ Henry, Margaret 1996: *Young Children, Parents and Professionals: Enhancing the links in early childhood* (Routledge). A focus on the learning of very young children. A positive emphasis on how practice in early years settings has much to learn from family life with babies and toddlers.

★ Leavitt, Robin Lynn 1994: *Power and Emotion in Infant-toddler Day Care* (State University of New York Press).

★ Leavitt, Robin Lynn and Eheart, Brenda Krause 1985: *Toddler Day Care – A guide to responsive caregiving* (Lexington Books). Both of these books focus on the specific needs of very young children. The first book describes relevant research and the second looks at implications for practice.

★ Laishley, Jennie 1984: *Taking Responsibility for Young Children: Who? Where? When?* (NNEB Discussion Paper 1). A summary of research and the underlying assumptions of investigations of family life and early years settings.

★ Mayall, Berry 'Children in action at home and at school' in Mayall, Berry (ed) 1994: *Children's Childhoods: Observed and experienced* (Falmer Press). A sociological approach to children and childhood. Some of the other chapters are also thought-provoking, for instance, on children's health and health services.

★ Pascal, Christine and Bertram, Tony 1997 (eds): *Effective Early Learning: Case studies in improvement* (Hodder and Stoughton). A description of the EEL project and detailed examples of how the approach works in action.

★ Robinson, Elizabeth and Robinson, Peter 'Ways of reacting to communication failure in relation to the development of the child's understanding about verbal communication' in Donaldson, Margaret; Grieve, Robert and Pratt, Chris 1983: *Early Childhood Development and Education: Readings in psychology* (Grant McIntyre). Description of the results discussed on page 135 of this chapter. Other chapters of the book are equally interesting to read for an insight into children's learning and how adults can help.

★ Sylva, Kathy 'The impact of early learning on children's later development' in Ball, Christopher 1994: *Start Right: The importance of early learning* (Royal Society of the Arts). A detailed review of the relevant research and the implications for practice.

★ Tizard, Barbara and Hughes, Martin 1984: *Young Children Learning: Talking and thinking at home and at school* (Fontana). Research contrasting the experiences of young children in the different settings of home and school. There are plenty of examples and thought-provoking comments about practice in early years settings.

★ Wood, David 'Aspects of teaching and learning' in Richards, Martin and Light, Paul 1986: *Children of Social Worlds: Development in a social context* (Polity Press). A discussion in detail of the ideas described on page 124.

6 The development of children's behaviour

This chapter covers:

- theories about children's behaviour;
- moral development;
- the development of prosocial behaviour;
- a focus on adults' behaviour.

This chapter focuses on children's behaviour but you can only make sense of what children do within the broader context of their development. So, you will find discussion of how children think as well as what they do. This area of development is also one that throws into sharp relief the impact of children's experience, a large component of which is how adults behave.

6.1 Theories about children's behaviour

The different approaches to describing and explaining child development take varying views on how and why children are likely to behave the way they do. The ideas outlined from the different theories are not mutually exclusive. You do not necessarily have to choose absolutely between them or reject some out of hand. My own view is that there is something to learn from all the approaches. I find some more practical than others and, as hard as I try to be even-handed, by the end of the chapter you will probably realise which approaches I prefer.

Theories of personality
Individual differences

If you observe several children, within a family or an early years setting, it will not be long before you notice that individual children do not behave in the same way faced with what look, to an outsider, like similar events. If you watch the same children some years later, you will almost certainly notice that the child who looked confident and was central in the play is still very much a social leader. The child who stood on the sidelines or who clung to an adult may not cling so much, but probably still seeks more reassurance, especially in a new or anxiety-provoking situation.

The term **personality** is used to explain enduring individual differences in behaviour. You can observe and describe the behaviour; you cannot, of course, see someone's personality. But theories that approach development in this way take the line that you are seeing the effects of individual personality in action.

Psychodynamic theories

Psychodynamic theories usually explain how children behave in terms of the kind of person they are becoming. This group of theories tends to see personality unfolding through sequential stages (that is, that separate stages follow one another), although there is disagreement over the nature of the stage. Another common theme is that behaviour (children's and adults') is influenced by unconscious processes as well as conscious thoughts.

Sigmund Freud

'No, Tanith. Not the video.'

Freud believed that the basics of personality were laid down by the age of five years as a direct result of how children emerged from a series of **psychosexual** stages of development (see also page 21). Later theorists in the psychodynamic tradition and those outside it have challenged Freud's claims about the sexuality of children. The evidence for his psychosexual stages rests on a small number of therapeutic case studies and Freud's interpretations of this material have been criticised.

The Freudian approach views later actions as driven by unresolved conflicts and anxieties rooted in early childhood. Patterns of behaviour are determined by the relative balance between:

- the **id** – raw emotional demands and needs;
- the **ego** – the conscious self;
- the **superego** – the demands of society, which operate as a conscience.

Freud's view of individuals as a battleground between the id, ego and superego has been a stimulating idea but cannot be proven one way or another (like, to be honest, many interesting ideas in psychology). Study of children's behaviour has addressed how children can learn self-control, which includes an awareness of 'I want to' tempered with 'I'm not going to do it because...'

Erik Erikson

Erikson disagreed with Freud's emphasis on sexual drive and placed an alternative emphasis on the development of a personal identity through a sequence of **psychosocial** stages. Erikson viewed behaviour as fuelled by the series of basic tasks, or dilemmas, that children face at different ages. Erikson made sense of development through how children resolved these tasks. He described the stages as follows:

- From birth to one year, babies face the dilemma of basic trust versus mistrust: of the predictability of the world, of babies' ability to affect events and the behaviour of key people around them.
- From two to three years, the dilemma is to weigh up autonomy versus shame and doubt. The toddlers' increased mobility enables them to act more independently (autonomy from others). But this development is balanced against the reaction of others to toddlers' actions and the need to learn some wariness and self-control.
- From four to five years the task is to resolve initiative versus guilt. Young children's physical and intellectual abilities allow them to take the initiative and be creative. But this energy and activity has to be balanced with

learning limits, from a growing sense of conscience and boundaries set by adults.

- From six to twelve years children are dealing with a dilemma of industry (or competence) versus inferiority. With the onset of schooling, children face specific learning tasks in which they may learn a positive sense of competence. Children also have to learn to deal with problems in their learning and balance a realistic sense of their limitations at any time with avoiding a negative sense of inferiority.
- From thirteen to eighteen years young people explore and re-examine their personal identity in a dilemma of identity versus role confusion. They have to resolve the possibilities facing them at this time of change and emerge with a sexual and an occupational identity.

In Erikson's theory, children's behaviour will be shaped by how they balance the competing possibilities of each dilemma and reach some degree of resolution. Balance is a key issue since young children need, for instance, some level of wariness. Total and undiscriminating trust would not be a psychologically healthy outlook. Erikson's series of dilemmas stretch into adulthood since he viewed development as an on-going process and not one that stopped essentially in early childhood.

Alfred Adler

Adler also diverged from Freud's very individual focus and placed an alternative emphasis on children's life within their family, partly the impact of birth order on how they experienced childhood. Adler believed children's behaviour (and later that of adults) was shaped by their interpretations of what happened in their interactions with others, initially in the family. Children developed a belief system about themselves and their sense of self-worth, which in turn influenced children's abilities to relate to other people in a sense of shared social interest.

Rudolf Dreikurs further developed the concept of an interplay between children's emotions, their interpretations of how life works and their observable behaviour. He described the 'four mistaken goals of behaviour' in which children's feelings led to purposeful behaviour which could be disruptive or irritating to adults. These mistaken goals were: to gain attention, to show superiority or power, to get even or seek revenge and to avoid defeat by appearing inadequate. Adults could shape children's outlook and behaviour in a more positive manner once they recognised the purpose behind the behaviour.

Dreikurs and others in the Adlerian tradition have explored practical applications such as use of consequences of behaviour and the role of encouragement. These ideas are the basis of a number of parenting programmes. You will find more on these ideas on page 147 within the section on behaviourism. The Adlerians would not see themselves as behaviourists, but their ideas are a practical response to some problems in applying behaviourist principles in child care.

In summary

Explanations of children's behaviour that start from the perspective of the developing self or personality have some practical application for early years workers. There is no need to take a view that children's personal characteristics are fixed, but recognition of individuality is important. Some psychodynamic theories link mainly with therapy, but other approaches offer frameworks that make sense for adults working alongside children in daily early years settings.

Biological theories

An alternative group of explanations of behaviour looks at the biological basis to what we do – inborn reactions and tendencies.

Differences between the sexes

A note about terms

Apart from all the other difficulties of discussion on this topic, use of words can be a confusion. The word 'gender' and 'sex' are sometimes used as interchangeable terms. Some writers reserve 'gender' for those aspects of sex differences that are the result of social beliefs. But some use the word to cover genetically determined differences. There is no easy way out of this dilemma because of the inconsistency between writers and usage is also changing over time. I have decided to use only the term 'sex differences'.

Sex differences are sometimes explained by inborn biological differences between males and females. An alternative view is that observable differences are learned through the socialisation of girls and boys within their social and cultural settings.

For at least a couple of decades it has been unacceptable even to suggest that there might be some biological basis to sex differences. Such a strong reaction was unsurprising, given the many years in which the approach of psychology and other social sciences was to take boys and men as the benchmark and to view any female patterns as deviations or signs of problems. There is now more chance of a balanced discussion, in which differences are viewed as evidence of diversity rather than deficiencies. Research on possible sex differences still needs careful interpretation, allowing for an interaction between possible biological beginnings and the process of socialisation. (See page 172 for further discussion.)

Temperament and behaviour

The term **personality** tends to be used in discussion of adults, whereas the study of temperament has focused on individual differences in childhood. The word **temperament** is used to mean in-built tendencies for children's reactions and behaviours that probably build the basis for a more enduring adult personality. The two concepts are both attempts to describe and explain continuities in how the same child, or adult, tends to approach and deal with their experiences.

Variety in temperament

Different researchers into temperament in childhood do not propose the same types, or call individual variations by the same term. However, there are some shared themes of individual difference which make sense from experience of a range of children.

- *Active-passive*: some children are physically mobile and react in a vigorous way to the possibilities in their environment. Some are considerably less active and may prefer sedentary play activities. Some may react passively, waiting for experiences to come to them.
- *Sociability*: individual differences between children in how they relate to people and to new experiences or objects. Some children are keen to make contact or explore, some are less enthusiastic and out-going.
- *Wariness*: a tendency to react with fear or to withdraw from new experiences and people. Children vary in the level of this kind of behaviour

and it is often summed up by the word 'shy', but the wariness is not only about people.

- *Negative emotions*: children differ in their tendency to react to experiences with anger and irritability. All children have feelings and most feel annoyed at some point. But some children seem to have a very short fuse, such that minor frustrations can lead them into upset or loud complaining.

- *Effort and persistence*: children vary in how well they are able to focus on what they are doing and to persist despite distractions. There is undoubtedly developmental progress in the ability to attend, but some children continue to find it harder to manage their concentration.

Individual differences in temperament need to be seen as tendencies and not absolutes. Temperament operates as a built-in bias, as possibilities that may be strengthened or weakened through children's experience. Whether children's temperament is experienced as difficult by themselves and by the key adults in their lives will depend a great deal on the adults' reactions. Some temperamental inclinations may be regarded by adults as appropriate, or inappropriate, for this child's sex. For instance, a physically very active boy may be seen as a 'real boy' whereas an equally active girl as too much of a 'tomboy'. The reverse judgement may be made of a boy and girl who are given to swift expressions of emotion.

Research has established that children rated by adults as having a 'difficult temperament' (getting upset very easily, finding it hard to settle and so on) are far more likely to show behavioural problems. But it not the case that a 'difficult' temperament inevitably leads to later problems. Studies have shown that newborn babies who cried a lot more than average do not necessarily grow into irritable, easily upset toddlers. Babies with mothers who were rated as highly responsive were crying less by 5–6 months. But babies whose mothers were observed as less sensitive to their babies crying were still experiencing a great deal of crying at the half-year point. In a similar way, crying babies seem far more likely to develop into cross and defiant toddlers when their mothers had reacted in an angry and punitive way to the early crying.

The research findings highlight that in-born temperament is responsive to different kinds of adult treatment but studies do not conclude by blaming mothers. Generally speaking, mothers were more able to be responsive to their crying babies if they had the support of family and friends. Mothers who had stressful lives found it very hard to dredge up that extra needed for a fretful baby and matters were made worse if mothers had experienced punitive approaches in their own childhood.

So, the study of temperament is a good example of how some research into child development has attempted to trace the pattern of influences and reflect the complexity of daily life for children and families. Temperament may make some children more of a challenge for adults to deal with in a positive way, but the types are better thought of as leading children to be more and less vulnerable to the impact of experiences.

TO THINK ABOUT

The idea of match or mismatch

Some adults – parents and carers – may feel a sharp difference between their own inclinations and the way that a child reacts. A naturally outgoing adult may be baffled by a reticent toddler who seems to approach new situations and people as sources of fear and not of exciting possibility. If adults react in an irritated

way or push the toddler beyond her comfortable distance from a kno
then they may end up strengthening this child's wariness. On the other hand,
adults who take time with the toddler, encourage her but allow her to take social
risks at her own pace may help the toddler towards a less wary outlook.

Questions
1   Can you think of examples of match and mismatch between children and
    your natural inclinations. How are you working to tune into the child
    rather than expect him or her to adjust to you?
2   Think over how your setting is organised – how do you reduce distractions
    for children who find it hard to concentrate? Are wary children saddled
    with the label of 'shy'?

Behaviourism

Behaviourist theories started from the study of animals and the processes of
classical and operant conditioning (look back to chapter 1, page 19 for a
reminder of these ideas). Radical behaviourists still take the line that the basic
principles of conditioning are enough to explain variations in personality and
behaviour. However, social learning theorists, such as Albert Bandura,
emphasise how children learn ways of behaving through observation and that
they think about what they observe (a cognitive component to the process).

The behaviourist theories are not the only ones to focus on what adults
and children do. As described earlier in this section, some of the psychodynamic
theories have a lot to say about behaviour. The particular characteristic of
the behaviourist approach to children's behaviour has been to study what is
actually going on in a situation: what adults are really doing, in contrast to
what they meant or intended to do.

Basic ideas of behaviourism

The behaviourist focus on patterns of reward can be useful once the complex
patterns are recognised. There are two basic propositions in behaviourist
learning theory:

1   Behaviour is strengthened by reinforcement.
2   Behaviour that is reinforced on a partial schedule is stronger, more resistant
    to stopping altogether, than behaviour that has been reinforced every time.

The social learning approach adds two more propositions:

3   Children learn new behaviours mainly through the process of modelling.
4   As well as actual behaviours, children also learn ideas, expectations and
    develop internal standards.

So, the explanation of behaviourism is that reinforcement increases the
likelihood that behaviour (of children or adults) will be repeated. Behaviour
may be strengthened by positive or negative reinforcement.

- **Positive reinforcement** is the experience, the addition to the situation, of
  something pleasant. Reinforcement might be tangible rewards, like sweets
  or a prize. But, with children, it is just as likely to be a smile or hug and
  words of praise. When positive reinforcement is present after an action
  it increases the likelihood of that action.
- **Negative reinforcement** is the removal of something unpleasant or
  unwanted from the situation. For instance, perhaps a child does not want

to tidy up her toys. She whines and moans and deliberately makes a mess of tidying up. Her carer persists for a while in saying 'Tidy up!' but then gives up and lets the child go. The whining reaction to requests to tidy up is likely to be strengthened because it has been reinforced (negatively). The unwanted adult demand to help has been removed.

- **Partial reinforcement** is a pattern in which behaviour is not reinforced (positively or negatively) every single time. Ordinary life for children tends to follow this pattern, since even adults who try to be consistent do not achieve total consistency. Learning on the basis of partial reinforcement is stronger, since individuals persist some time in a behaviour because their experience has been that reward does not occur every time.

Reinforcement strengthens a pattern of behaviour – increasing the likelihood. On the other hand, punishment may weaken the pattern.

- **Punishment** is the removal of something pleasant from the situation (refusal of sweets, cancelling treats or privileges) or the addition of something unpleasant (criticism and nagging, making children do disliked chores, insisting on silence or physical punishment such as hitting). Punishment is intended to stop behaviour, although the results are unpredictable. So, punishment is *not* the same as negative reinforcement. (I stress this point because I have found the two ideas muddled in at least one child care and education book.)
- **Extinction** is a term that describes the complete removal of a pattern of behaviour; it no longer occurs.

Practical applications

In real life, interactions between children and adults are not only those in which the child does something of which an adult approves, the adult reinforces the action and everyone is happy. Adults have to take a broad perspective on what could be rewarding to children – the child's perspective is not always that of the adult.

Unintentionally rewarding children

A child who only experiences an adult's full attention (a reward) when he is behaving in a disruptive way in a group, tends to continue his actions despite the fact that the attention seems like punishment to the adult (telling off or shouting).

In a similar way, adults who are inconsistent can unintentionally reward the exact behaviour they are trying to discourage, because the adult pattern acts as an experience of partial reinforcement to the child. For example, a young child may wake at night and cry to be taken into the parents' bed. On the first few occasions, the parents stand firm and settle or take the child back to her own bed. Then exhaustion or exasperation takes over and on the third or fourth cry the child is taken into the parents' bed. Inadvertently the parents have shown the child that persistence pays off and their experience will be that much harder the next night. Helpful programmes for parents whose children wake at night often use these principles to guide in the management of the problem. Any truly helpful programme has also to acknowledge how hard it can be for tired parents to be consistent.

When rewards backfire on adults

There is anecdotal evidence from families and early years settings in which using rewards appears to have reduced a particular behaviour in a group of children. When children are given prizes for activities or paid to do specific tasks, they do not necessarily increase this behaviour when given a free choice.

The claim is sometimes then that 'reward does not work' or that 'it does not have a long term effect'. In fact, the reward clearly has had an effect because the children's behaviour has changed. The use of tangible rewards has shaped children's expectations and thoughts about this particular activity. Instead of developing a sense of internal satisfaction (I do this because it's fun or because I enjoy helping), children view the activity as one they do for the reward (I only do this if I want to get a prize or I ought to be paid to help out).

The Adlerian approach to using encouragement rather than tangible rewards or spoken praise was a practical response to this type of dilemma for adults. Rudolf Dreikurs and other writers within this tradition stress the difference between praise (and reward) and encouragement.

- Praise focuses on the end result whereas encouragement is freely given for effort and improvement.
- Praise or rewards stress a fixed quality about a child but encouragement focuses on what a child has done ('Well done' rather than 'Good boy').
- Encouragement focuses on feelings: of the adults when they express appreciation for help and on the children by acknowledging their pleasure in a job well done or finished despite the difficulties.
- Encouragement taps into children's feelings of satisfaction and their strengths while patterns of praise and reward tend to be unforgiving of mistakes or times when children do not feel like being 'good' or 'helpful'.

Reinforcement for adults as well as children

Negative reinforcement is an unpleasant event that, when it stops, the cessation acts to increase a particular behaviour. Giving in to a child's yells and whines for a packet of sweets will probably quieten the whining. So parents may be inclined to react in the same way next time – the effect of negative reinforcement (the cessation of the yells) on their learning. However, the adult is not the only person in this situation. In terms of operant conditioning, the child has been positively reinforced for yelling and whining; this behaviour resulted in the sweets. So he is likely to try yelling again in the future – the effect of positive reinforcement (the sweets) on his behaviour. In practical terms, parents and other carers have to be ready to view the situation from the child's perspective as well as their own if they are to grasp the full pattern of reinforcement in operation.

The unpredictable effects of punishment

Although some adults are confident, even enthusiastic, about the likely success of punishment to change behaviour, this method is not a reliable way of dealing with behaviour you would like to reduce. The reason seems to be that children are far more sophisticated than the rats or pigeons of the animal studies. Also, ordinary adults do not behave with the single-mindedness of a scientific researcher, and it would be very disturbing if they did.

Punishment may appear to stop a pattern of behaviour but sometimes what children learn is simply not to let the adults see them doing what is forbidden. Alternatively children whose experience is largely negative may act so as to attract the adult's attention, even though the consequences appear to be unpleasant – any attention is better than being ignored. The learning dilemma for young children is also that punishment does not direct them towards what they could do, it only communicates 'don't'.

Studies suggest that punishment works as one way of shaping children's behaviour if adults act in the following ways:

- Parents or other carers react early on within a sequence of misbehaviour from a child. For instance, that a toddler is removed swiftly from his explorations of the waste bin, and not after a great deal of ineffectual 'Don't do that' from the adult.
- Adults deal with the incident with as low a level of emotion as possible, avoiding screaming matches or attempts to make children feel guilty. Yelling at children muddles the lesson that the adult is trying to communicate and increases the chances that the child will simply learn to yell back.
- Adults use the mildest level of punishment possible and do not increase the negatives because they are angry or embarrassed. Nor should adults drag out punishments beyond the time span of the incident, whether the punishment is withdrawal of privileges or nagging children about their behaviour.
- Adults are generally warm in their dealings with children, consistent and clear about the rules involved.

The Adlerian approach to guiding children's behaviour offers a useful way of side-stepping the difficulties raised by the word 'punishment'. Dreikurs talked about the value of using the consequences of children's behaviour. He distinguished between using **natural** and **logical consequences** as a way to deal with misbehaviour and to encourage children to take on the responsibility for their own actions. Natural consequences are those results which are built in as part of a sequence of action. For instance, a child who throws a tantrum about coming home from the park may delay her arrival back home so that she misses her favourite programme. Logical consequences are pre-warned and applied consistently by adults responsible for safe rules in a setting. An example might be that children who behave in an unsafe way on the climbing frame are removed for a short period of time. The Adlerian approach to using consequences follows all the general rules about effective use of punishment.

In summary

Behaviourist theories can offer explanations of why children behave differently in different situations: the patterns of reinforcement have been different. The approach is also optimistic in the possibility of changing children's behaviour, since adults need to alter the pattern of reinforcement they are giving through their actions. A social learning perspective adds the dimension of learning through copying and of building ideas relevant to later choices in behaviour. The approach does not have a developmental perspective since the learning processes are assumed to work in much the same kind of way regardless of children's age.

Cognitive theories

Cognitive explanations of children's behaviour focus on looking at children's understanding and their mental representations of what is going on, as well as what they actually do. The approach links children's behaviour and the changes in how they act as they get older with the sense that they make of their social world. In the cognitive approach, children's ways of thinking, and the current limits on how they are able to reason, lead their behaviour. So children's behaviour is studied not only through their actions but also meaning and intentions. They are learning not only what people do but why they do it.

The cognitive approach has been very influential in the exploration of children's moral development – more on this topic from page 150. Cognitive approaches to the development of behaviour do not only focus on how individual children think but on the interaction between children, other children and key adults in their everyday social environment.

Research in families, for instance by Judy Dunn, has highlighted the sophistication of learning about behaviour within the home. Dunn has described how actions, allowed and not allowed, are learned within a context that is given sense by the emotional link integral to family relationships. Dunn observed how children as young as 18–24 months had a good grasp of the family ground rules, to the extent that they could talk about them with parents or siblings and deliberately break rules as a source of joking.

6.2 Moral development

Understanding and behaviour

As adults, our approach to children's behaviour has to be grounded in reasonable expectations of their ability to grasp moral issues within their own social world. Children's understanding develops steadily and they can be more sophisticated sometimes than we expect (see also the chapters on thinking and communication). But children still do not see matters through adult eyes and it would be most surprising if they did.

Without positive relationships with others, moral development has very little meaning. Moral values are relevant to how we treat other people, or how we expect to be treated in our turn. So a consideration of children's moral development is intertwined with their social, as well as their intellectual development. There are three main aspects of moral development:

- *Behaviour* – the ways in which children behave or what they learn not to do. Children may behave in line with ways that gain adult approval, for instance, taking turns in the playgroup, without fully understanding the idea of 'sharing' that the adult is explaining.
- *Understanding* – grasping the different concepts that underpin behaviour: what adults mean by 'cooperative' or 'spiteful', ideas of right and wrong.
- *Judgement* – coming to a conclusion about other people's behaviour (children and adults) on the basis of moral concepts: that one should or should not do certain things or that a particular behaviour is wrong, but perhaps excusable under given circumstances.

TO THINK ABOUT

As you read this section, bear in mind individual children who you know. Young children are at a different point in their understanding of moral issues than adults and they have a great deal of learning yet to come. Often, adults responsible for young children need to be satisfied that the children will follow the adults' wishes in what they do. It is usually unrealistic to demand that children understand or agree with the ideas underlying what adults ask – whether the concepts are about sharing or other behaviours that make a group run more smoothly.

The development of social relationships

In the first eight years of life children develop a network of social relationships with other people: adults and children, within the family and outside, children of their own age and those older or younger. Children develop qualitatively different relationships with these different people and they come to recognise the different expectations and constraints of different settings and the key people. It is not unusual for children to behave differently in response to different expectations.

The development of a moral sense

Babies are born morally neutral but inherently social. They do not have the knowledge to be naughty, although some adults act as if they do. Toddlers who are physically more competent and mobile start to discover the 'don'ts' in their environment. Curiosity and their drive to explore take them to things they should not touch or to consequences of their actions that they cannot foresee – or that they overlook in the heat of the moment. Young children do not understand the adult moral judgements of 'messy' or 'destructive', but they grasp adult disapproval and preferences. Older children start to understand guidelines to behaviour, rules and judgements about the behaviour of others. By five and six years, children can have a clear view of ground rules that apply beyond their immediate setting.

Social cognition

Part of children's development is their use of their growing powers of thinking and reasoning. These strengths are not just applied to intellectual learning, but also to people and what children observe in the social setting. The same head that is coming to grips with the meaning of number or that some squiggles are meaningful writing, is also trying to make sense of social situations and the behaviour of others. So, to look at moral development, you have to bring children's sociability together with their powers of thinking and reasoning. This area of children's development is called **social cognition**.

Children's abilities of moral reasoning develop along the following lines:

- Children move from direct observation to making some inferences. Younger children focus on what they can do or have personally experienced. Whereas older children have learned to look for more general principles or causes – under the obvious surface.
- Their judgements move from very definite to more qualified. The rules expressed and followed by younger children tend to be more fixed. Further experience, thinking and talking leads to more 'ifs' and 'buts' and 'it depends'.
- Children become more able to move from a very personal outlook to taking a broader perspective. Young children look and think from their own point of view but they can learn to look through others' eyes and build up a more general framework.

Amongst their many other interests, children think about other people: what they do, might do or should do. They also think to an extent about how other people feel or should feel. This curiosity can be provoked by events unfolding in front of the children, or by characters in books and television programmes. Four-year-olds are often able to discuss why other people, especially their peers, behave the way they do, their intentions as well as their actions and spoken reasons. Children try to an extent to 'read' other people, to anticipate what they may do or could want. They seek some level of predictability in their lives and can be concerned when friends or adults behave out of character.

Children develop working assumptions about familiar adults and about how the social world works in general. At first, they assume that their own experience is universal. Then children discover that some of their peers, and adults, have a similar outlook but that others definitely do not. These assumptions shape up their purposes in what they do. So children's behaviour is also the result of their own thinking and not just a simple cause and effect pattern from what adults do or say.

It is important not to place adult frameworks over children's minds, but it seems likely that adults underestimate children's power of thought more often than not in moral issues. Adults especially overlook the fact that children watch them and learn from what has happened and adult reactions, whether adults intend to be communicating a moral point or not.

Thinking about what people ought to do – moral judgements

Babies and very young children react directly to adult approval and disapproval, both for their own actions and for making sense of the behaviour of others. By three to four years children's powers of thought enable them to build some framework but they tend to focus on what happened, rather than allowing for intentions. The actual consequences of an act are seen as the same as intentions. In a similar way, the wrongness of an act is judged from the direness of the consequences, so a major mess means a naughtier act.

From my observations of children and adults I have concluded that this pattern of thinking is not only because of children's immature thought processes. Adults often get more angry about bigger messes and certainly do not always pause to explore children's intentions before criticising the consequences. So the thought processes of young children may also be supported by their daily observations of how adults behave.

Young children tend to believe that the rules that govern moral judgements are absolute and universal – everyone follows them. (Even adults still have elements of this kind of thinking.) By six or seven years of age, children are able to think in a more sophisticated way. Their ideas about intentions and consequences include considerations of 'I didn't mean to ...' or 'She didn't know that....'. And experience outside the family, in playgroup or nursery shows them that other children, and adults, do not all follow the same rules.

A sense of fairness and natural justice can develop so that, by about seven years, children may express general rules of their own, some of which will be applied to judgements about the behaviour of familiar adults. For example, that it is not fair to let one child do something and not another or that adults should obey their own rules (like not running in the school corridor).

The development of moral reasoning

Lawrence Kohlberg studied the moral reasoning of children and young people. He built on Piaget's views to develop a stage theory of moral development, supported by research into how children of different ages resolved a series of hypothetical dilemmas ('What if..' problems). Kohlberg's stages depended not so much on the choice that children made in such problems but the way they reasoned their choice. Kohlberg proposed three levels of moral development, with two stages in each. In brief, the steps are:

Level 1: pre-conventional morality
- Stage 1: punishment and obedience orientation. Children decide something is wrong if it is punished. They value obedience but follow adult rules because the adults have power.

- Stage 2: instrumental morality. Children follo[w]
  immediate interest. Other people are recognise[d]
  fairness is a matter of equal exchange.

Level 2: conventional morality
- Stage 3: Mutual expectations within relationsh[ip]
  good' as worthwhile for its own sake, because it
  matter. They stress the importance of living u[p]
  significant groups such as their family.
- Stage 4: Social system and conscience. The source of morality moves into
  a broader social context, including the laws of society.

Level 3: Principled or post-conventional morality
- Stage 5: The social contract. There is an awareness that rules may not be
  absolute, but that moral behaviour takes account of the good of the many
  and not only individual wants.
- Stage 6: Universal ethical principles. Individuals have developed a personal
  system of moral principles that guide their actions.

Kohlberg proposed a stage theory, like Piaget's view of child development, in
that children are expected to move through the stages in order. Kohlberg did
not claim that everyone passed through all the stages and he did not relate
the steps to exact ages. Kohlberg's studies and those of other researchers found
that pre-conventional reasoning (level 1) is dominant in childhood.
Conventional moral reasoning (level 2) develops during adolescence and
continues to be the most common pattern of reasoning in adults. Principled
moral reasoning (level 3) is fairly rare, even with adults. Kohlberg later
expressed some doubts about stage 6 – whether it was the logical end to the
developmental sequence and whether many people truly reached and operated
at such a stage.

Kohlberg claimed that his stages were universal and research has mostly
supported this claim, although of course the rules of different societies vary.
Some writers have disagreed with Kohlberg's system and the unspoken values
that underlie the hierarchy of stages. Carol Gilligan, for instance, challenged
Kohlberg's claim that justice and fairness were key features of mature moral
reasoning. Gilligan argued that an equally valid basis emerged from an orientation
of caring or of connectedness. She predicted that girls were more likely to be
socialised towards a care orientation and boys towards the justice perspective.
Research so far has found some sex differences in the direction that Gilligan
proposes, but only for adults' moral reasoning and not for girls and boys.

At first sight, Kohlberg's approach seems to contradict the observation
that young children can behave in an altruistic way (see page 157). This
apparent contradiction is a useful reminder that Kohlberg is talking about
the reasons that children give to explain why somebody ought to behave in
a particular way.

Nancy Eisenberg looked at how children explained considerate behaviour
by giving them hypothetical dilemmas in which there was a clash between
self-interest and helping someone else. Younger children (under fives) might
choose the prosocial (helping) option, as did the older children but their
reasoning was different. The younger ones were more likely to help (or choose
not to help) for reasons of self-interest (if I help out now, this person might
help me another time). This orientation shifted to a focus on the other person's
needs, that s/he would feel better if helped. Adolescents, not children, were
the ones who might reason on the basis of general principles (it's good to
help, or society is better if people help each other).

The work of Kohlberg, Eisenberg and others is a useful reminder to adults who work closely with children that they should bear in mind the different way in which children think about moral issues.

- In guiding behaviour, much as with other areas of your responsibility with children, you are sowing ideas that will not come into flower for some time yet. To go with the planting image, you may well see some buds but it is no use to children, or to your well-being, to try to force an unrealistic growing span.
- A practical approach is to focus on what children do and to guide them towards more considerate behaviour, without demanding mature reasoning for why they act this way.
- A consistent approach by adults, with clear rules, sows the seed of understanding about how rules support a considerate social setting. Be encouraging if children follow the rules and do not fret if their compliance is because they like you, rather than an abstract internalising of the rules.
- Children recognise the existence of social rules, will follow them and often persuade their peers to follow a group rule (like tidying up). But this behaviour occurs some time before the children can explain the rules with any sophistication.
- By all means explain, simply and linked to concrete events, why you want children to behave one way rather than another. But do not give such lengthy or complex explanations that the main message is lost.

From thoughts to action

Studies of moral reasoning can be thought-provoking, but they are not a full explanation of how people actually behave when faced with a choice. Studies, as well as a wealth of anecdotal evidence, support a view that few, if any people, behave consistently in line with expressed principles (beliefs about what one should do). There is a relationship between moral reasoning and actual behaviour but it is not one of 100% predictability.

In daily life with children it is important to remember that there is not a neat link between principles of what is right and wrong and what children actually do, faced with a situation. Children may behave in a way that gets them into trouble with adults for a number of different reasons, for example:

- Young children succumb to the pressures of the moment or strong desires – 'I know I shouldn't but I just want to'. Older children become increasingly vulnerable to group pressures from friends and acquaintances.
- Children may be forced to choose between two incompatible rule systems – perhaps home and school. Or else the environment has not been organised by adults to enable children to follow the rules. For instance, children who are willing to try non-aggressive ways of handling conflict can be put in an impossible position, if adults do not adequately supervise areas like playgrounds.
- Children may have experienced unexpected consequences of their actions, for instance, mess and spillages that resulted from a helpful act that went wrong.

- Children genuinely did not know that an action was not allowed. For instance, a child is allowed to do something at home that grandma or the childminder does not allow.
- Children sometimes rethink a 'wrong' action as acceptable, for instance, that hitting their sibling is excusable because of his unforgivable action earlier in the day.

TO THINK ABOUT

Children may know very well what is expected of them but, for various reasons, be unable to control their impulses.

In one research project, Carol Hayden and Derek Ward interviewed children who had been excluded from primary school. The children (all but one were boys) usually had a clear idea about what was and was not acceptable behaviour in school. They knew they had crossed the boundary, although sometimes felt that the precise incident that had led to exclusion was not necessarily that bad, or as bad as some of their previous exploits. They had knowledge of the rules and what they should and should not do. Their difficulty lay in controlling their own behaviour, in resisting doing what they knew they should not. So motivation and impulse control were the problems and not a lack of knowledge or mis-understanding of the rules. (This research was reported in the journal *Children and Society*, December 1996 volume 10.)

Questions
- You may be working with children younger than primary school age but take some time to think about whether you are placing your efforts too much sometimes towards assuming that children do not know the rules.
- Sometimes your adult input may be better aimed at helping a child to resist an impulse or to learn alternative ways of dealing with explosive situations.

he development of prosocial behaviour

Responsiveness to the feelings of others

Kohlberg's research on moral development focuses on how children think about moral issues. The research into prosocial behaviour provides the necessary balance of what children do.

Observational research of children in different settings has established the possible development of two strands important in moral development: empathy and altruism.

- **Empathy** is the ability and willingness to tune into the feelings of others – children or adults.
- **Altruism** means acting with a selfless concern for the well-being of others.

The combination of empathy and altruism is also called **prosocial behaviour.** The key features are that children show intentional, voluntary behaviour which is intended to benefit someone else. The ability to empathise and the willingness to act atruistically is something that children can learn as the result of their experience. It is a potential development, not an inevitable happening. Equally, the events of their early years may teach children just as strongly not to develop such an outlook and pattern of behaviour.

Children's relationships with others will be shaped by their ability to recognise and respond appropriately to other people's feelings. Piaget's theory of children's cognitive development led to the firm assumption that children under four or five years had very limited grasp of the perspectives and emotions of others. However, careful observational research, often within families, has challenged this view of the egocentrism of young children.

Observations have established that under threes are aware of the feelings of others. Babies tend to join in others' emotions in an infectious way – laughing with those who show merriment and crying sometimes when other babies start to cry. But in the time from one to three years, children show increasing discrimination between emotions and respond in individual ways to that emotion. For example:

- One- and two-year-olds are visibly distressed by arguments between their parents and sometimes move to comfort one parent or to hit the parent who is judged to be at fault.
- Toddlers have developed a sense of other children as separate individuals. They often notice the distress of other children and may initially offer what would comfort themselves, but they soon show evidence of knowing the other child's preferred comfort object.
- Toddlers and young children also seek to bring help to other children by calling an adult's attention to that child's distress or physical hurt (a wish to bring help to that child). You can observe this behaviour in group settings as well as in families.
- Under twos recognise the delight in others and often use clowning about to make others, children or adults, laugh.

Children do not behave in an altruistic way all the time. Very young children understand what will annoy, upset or grab the attention of other children they know well. The needs of adults to handle the self-centred incidents seem to overshadow their observations of the potential development of selflessness. The examples in the following box illustrate that awareness of the feelings of others is a double-edged sword.

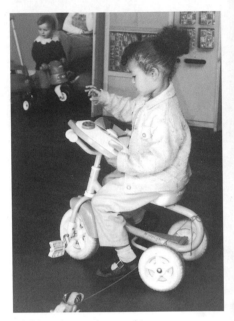

Children learn about taking turns

EXAMPLES

Children use their perceptiveness and knowledge of others both to comfort and to wind up siblings or friends.

- Judy Dunn, in research in families with Penny Munn, noted that teasing of the older sibling was noticeable from when the younger child was 14 months old. She describes how a younger sibling had, by 24 months, learned to tease her older sister by pretending to be that child's imaginary friend. As Dunn points out, this action may not have been very friendly, but it shows great sophistication on the part of the younger one. She had imagined herself into another identity and observed what would seriously annoy her sister.
- In my own family, I noted that at 16 months Tanith brought Drew his quilt and monkey (his personal comfort objects) when she saw he was sad. Nobody ever told Tanith to do this; her actions resulted from her own observations and a wish to comfort. But she used the same objects to provoke him into playing with her when he wanted to sit and look at his books. Tanith would take the quilt or the monkey, stand at the door to the room and wave them at Drew until he chased her (in annoyance).

Questions
- Can you recall times when a young child you know well showed a similar level of subtle understanding of the feelings of another child? What happened?
- It is important that your concern, as an adult, about the wind-ups does not make you overlook examples of a child's prosocial behaviour based on the same knowledge.

SUGGESTED ACTIVITY

Watch out for examples of prosocial behaviour in your own early years setting. If you are observant, you will see examples of young children who show concern for others – children and familiar adults – and behave in a comforting or helpful way. Children may follow a request from an adult but also behave spontaneously in this manner. For instance, I have observed children in nursery classes take steps to make another child welcome and to protect them as they settle in.

You could watch out for:

- The reactions of young children to the distress of others. What do even very young children do in order to offer comfort?
- A sophisticated understanding of how to wind up other children. You may need to step in to deal with the consequences but try to see the developmental side as well as the less attractive aspect to teasing behaviour!
- Adults have to be cautious about guessing children's feelings but, with care, think over what you may have seen about one child's insight into the other's feelings?

If you want helpful and altruistic children...

The research into prosocial behaviour has led to very practical applications for family or early years settings. Study of prosocial behaviour in children is a good example to remind adults that children's development is not the result of the months passing but of the experiences they have had. Children have the potential to develop a prosocial outlook and behaviour, but such a development is far from automatic.

If adults want to encourage prosocial behaviour from young children, then the adults need to:

- Create an affectionate and warm environment for children, whether within the family or an early years setting.
- Give children rules and explain why. It is less effective when children are simply told 'Don't hit your sister'. Prosocial behaviour is far more likely

to be encouraged when such rules are explained in terms of the consequences for another person. For example, general rules such as 'You mustn't hit people' are supported in particular incidents by 'When you hit Sally, you hurt her.' As far as possible, rules should be stated positively, as a 'do'.

- Create opportunities for children to do helpful things – at home or in early years settings. Adults can ask and encourage children to help but allow them the space to choose not to help. Children who are coerced into helping are likely to construe their 'helpful' action as 'Mum made me do it' rather than 'I enjoy helping'.
- Acknowledge and thank children for their helpful behaviour but avoid trying to make children feel guilty if they are not helpful. Trying to induce guilt with 'Don't you think that was a nasty thing to do?' or criticising a child with, 'You've got to share with your little sister, don't be so selfish!' has unpredictable consequences and is certainly not the most effective way to encourage altruistic behaviour.
- Model thoughtful and generous behaviour – possibly the most important aspect. Effective adults behave as they wish the children to behave and a set of clear and positive rules will be undermined if adults fail to show that they follow them. (This practical point makes sense in terms of Bandura's social learning theory and the importance of children's learning through observation.)

The research on prosocial behaviour confirms what has been shown in more general studies of learning, with adults as well as children. The most effective method is a combination of **tell-show-do**. Simply telling children they should be 'nice' to each other or they 'ought to share' is often ineffective for two reasons: children do not always understand exactly what adults mean and there is little incentive to follow these vague demands. Children are better helped by being shown, through adult modelling and guidance between options in a given,

---

SUGGESTED ACTIVITY

If 'good' behaviour is 'caught and not taught', then adults have to work together to encourage the behaviour that they would like from children.

With colleagues, please explore the following perspectives through discussion.

1 What do you want young children to do in your setting?
- What kind of helpful behaviour are you all trying to encourage from children? Please be as specific as you can.
- If you use a word like 'considerate', then discuss some examples of what considerateness from children looks like in practice.
- How do you ensure that your expectations are reasonable for the children's age?

2 How are you working to achieve your objectives?
- What ways do you use to direct and guide children's behaviour?
- What works best on the whole?
- How do you keep aware of your own behaviour, rather than just focusing on what children are doing? How do you handle inconsistencies between workers?

Generally speaking, young children want to be helpful because they enjoy the satisfaction of having that role of helper, especially when it gives them close contact with a friendly adult. So, if children are not involved helpfully in your setting, you really need to look objectively at what the adults are doing, or not doing. Adults create the circumstances for children to learn to be helpful. Problems cannot be explained away by saying there is something the matter with the children.

immediate situation. Finally, as with any pattern of skills, children need a chance to practise. So the setting, whether home or an early years centre, needs to be organised by adults so that children have plenty of chances, as well as adult encouragement, to behave in this way. This kind of pattern is what people mean when they say 'good' behaviour is 'caught and not taught' or that you 'guide' children towards an understanding of 'right and wrong'; you don't teach them.

If you want aggressive children....

There are no hard and fast rules about causes of children's behaviour. However, some patterns of adult behaviour are more likely to lead to aggressive behaviour in children.

Margaret Manning and her colleagues observed different types of hostility in nursery school and at home. They judged behaviour to be hostile if the child on the receiving end was visibly distressed. Manning distinguished three types of hostile action between children in nursery school:

- *Specific hostility* which was provoked by some immediate annoyance, such as having a toy taken by another child or frustration, for example, that a child was breaking nursery rules. In these instances, the aggression was a means to a goal.
- *Harassment* was a pattern in which the child showing hostility had not been provoked and he or she seemed to relish the distressed reaction of the victim.
- *Game hostility* was a pattern of largely physical and very rough behaviour in the course of play.

The three types are a useful reminder that aggressive behaviour from children is not all the same and so adult reactions have to be responsive to exactly what is happening. Equally interesting is that Manning's research was spread over four years and included consideration of the children's home life. The pattern of hostile actions were relatively consistent four years later when children were in primary school. The children seemed to have learned a way to deal with social interaction. The children who tended to react to specific frustrations with hostility came from relatively happy homes. However, the children who indulged in harassment tended to have either very dominating siblings, in which case these children were more likely to use verbal harassment of other children; or else they had mothers with a very controlling style, in which the harassment was more physical. These children, who were often quiet and well-behaved at home, let out their frustrations in the nursery and primary school setting. The children who used play as an aggressive vehicle were more likely to have negative family relations as a whole and the child was also often not the mother's favourite.

Of course, aggressive behaviour from children cannot be completely explained by their family experiences. Some group settings are organised in such a way that children learn it is not worth waiting or taking turns. The adults do not intend for children to become more aggressive in how they handle everyday problems, but the setting has not been organised so that children can learn an alternative. Some practical studies have looked in detail at how adults can guide children towards non-aggressive approaches – more on page 161.

Making sense of play fighting

Early years workers and parents encounter play fighting – very physical games between children (more usually boys than girls) in which the play develops into wrestling and close body contact. Play fighting provokes mixed reactions and deserves more thought in early years settings than a straightforward ban.

Mechthild Schafer and Peter Smith showed children and primary school teachers video footage of play fighting incidents. They found that:

- Children and teachers broadly agreed on how to tell the difference between play fighting and real fights (from facial expressions and the actions) and they also agreed that play fights could turn into real ones. But there the agreement ended.
- Teachers' estimates were that about 60% of fights were play and over a third real and that up to a third of play fights would turn into real ones.
- The children's estimates were that the overwhelming majority of fights were play and that very few turned into real ones.
- It was fascinating that the researchers' observations supported the children's claims.

The explanation seemed to be that teachers were generalising from the small number of children whose behaviour was habitually aggressive and whose play fighting often turned into real fights. These children's behaviour was not typical of the pupils as a whole, a fact that the other children knew from observation and experience. Schafer and Smith view play fighting as potentially positive. They stress that play fighting is one way that relationships are formed and friendships gel, especially with boys. It is an enjoyable activity and, in the main, low risk. Their conclusions are especially interesting because Peter Smith has also undertaken studies of bullying. As a researcher, he is well aware of the significance of genuine playground troubles to children.

TO THINK ABOUT

There are some intriguing and difficult issues arising from the research about play fighting. Think over some of the following and use some questions to fuel a discussion with colleagues.

- Play fighting is much more common as a boys' pattern of play than with girls. Think about how this difference may arise (some ideas on page 172 about theories of child development).
- Now, put to one side possible reasons why boys are more enthusiastic than girls about play fighting. Simply focus on the reality that boys are more likely to start these games and that they are also likely to be discouraged from this kind of play in early years settings. What is the reasoning for discouraging them? Is it sound?
- Females considerably outnumber males in early years settings and primary schools. How far do you think that women run the risk of being too concerned about play fighting and over-estimating the risks because it is a kind of play that we do not understand? (I definitely include myself in this 'we'.)
- If you are fortunate to have a mixed staff or student group, then explore this issue with the help of a male perspective. Your male colleagues will probably be in the minority, so do not put them in the position of justifying the entire male perspective. Just listen to their personal views.

If you wish, you can read the original research: Schafer, Mechthild and Smith, Peter 'Teachers' perceptions of play fighting and real fighting in primary school' in *Educational Research*, vol. 38 (2), summer 1996.

6.4 A focus on adult's behaviour

You will have noticed how frequently thinking about children's moral development takes you directly to what adults do and how they appear to think.

Saying and doing

Adult actions and reactions are important raw material from which children learn. Some adults seem blithely unaware that children are so observant and persist with a view that children only notice what adults want them to notice. In fact, perhaps someone should study adult social cognition in their relationships with children and not only the development of children's social cognition. Many adults seem unaware that children think about moral issues and by seven years are well on the way to some firm pronouncements themselves.

Bandura and his colleagues, in studies of learning through modelling, found that, when adult behaviour did not fit with adults' words, then children were most likely to copy what the adults did. So, research does not lead to any optimism about adult approaches of 'Do what I say, not what I do!' Observational research strongly suggests that children consider what they are told and turn it over in their mind. Children do not simply accept a behaviour rule, especially if the adult's behaviour is not in line with that rule.

Ronald Slaby and his research colleagues have looked at applications of the research on prosocial behaviour. Their concern also arose from a goal of re-directing children away from aggressive patterns. A central theme in this highly practical project was to approach the area as an adult task of coaching children in specific social skills. So the project team worked to identify the kinds of behaviour that children needed to learn if they were to develop, for instance, an assertive way of dealing with conflict rather than turn to aggressive methods. There is an emphasis on considering what adults were doing and how they could shift from telling and directing behaviours ('You must share') or stepping in on behalf of children ('Let him have a go'). Attention was paid to how an early years setting operated on a daily basis – was it relatively easy or hard for a child to take the prosocial option? But strategies were also developed to create adult behaviour that modelled the prosocial options and find ways for adults to coach children in how to handle situations themselves.

Styles of parenting

Research has considered broad patterns of adult behaviour with children. One way of categorising adults' approach is the relative balance between control and warmth. The general options are then:

- harsh control and little warmth;
- little control with or without warmth;
- reasoned control and warmth.

The first two options in general adult behaviour are linked with aggression from children observed in the playground. The combination of reasoned control and warmth seem to work best to encourage children towards learning to control their own behaviour without recourse to hostility towards other children. A considerable amount of this research has been undertaken in families, looking at how parents behave. The findings and ideas are equally applicable to finding the positive adults' role in early years settings.

Diana Baumrind observed families with young children and looked at the combination of four aspects to patterns of child rearing:

- warmth or nurturance;
- level of expectations, which she called 'maturity demands';
- the clarity and consistency of rules;
- communication between parent and child.

She described three parental styles:

- An authoritarian style – high in control and expectations of children but low on nurturance and communication. Authoritarian adults believe they have the right to tell children what to do because of their adult status. They do not have to explain and any steps they take (including physical punishment) are because they know better. Adults are owed respect and attention from children (not the other way around) and obedience without any back chat.
- A permissive style – high in nurturance but low in expectations of children, control and communication. Permissive adults are uncertain about their rights and responsibilities as an older person. They are unwilling to set out boundaries and maybe concerned that guiding and sometimes stopping a child will inevitably be negative.
- An authoritative style – high on all four aspects. Authoritative adults accept that they have responsibilities as an older person, that they have an active role in guiding children. But this is applied with respect for children. Adults set boundaries and keep to rules but explain their reasons. They act as an adult, not a big child. This is not a new idea, it is a style that has been known at least from my own childhood as ' firm but fair'.

Eleanor Maccoby and John Martin proposed three styles similar to Baumrind's, but they described a fourth style: that some parents were mainly uninvolved and neglectful of their children. The authoritative style is the most positive for children's healthy psychological development and the uninvolved style is the most negative.

Study of families and parenting style has produced some common patterns between ethnic groups but also some unique features. Ruth Chao, for example, showed how Chinese-American parents could appear authoritarian since they valued obedience in children. They therefore agreed with those items in the questionnaire. However, the families were consciously guiding children in their behaviour with a clear view of 'training' children to take their place within the family and culture. The expectation that children would obey family rules was in the context of caring about the children and explaining why particular behaviour was required. Current generations of Western parents do not usually view their job so explicitly as raising their children to take their place in society.

SUGGESTED ACTIVITY

In discussion about handling children's behaviour the options are far too often polarised between what is seen as strong adults laying down the law as opposed to weak adults letting children run wild. Baumrind's research on parenting styles in families where parents are involved with their young children have distinguished three options, rather than two. Think over the three styles.

1 What evidence of the different patterns can you recall from your own childhood, from experience in your family or at school?
2 In what ways are you following an authoritative pattern in your setting? Give some examples.
3 In what ways might you work more towards such a pattern?

TO THINK ABOUT

Cultural tradition is not something that just happens to other people. Everyone is influenced by their own traditions. You can learn a great deal about the often unspoken assumptions within a culture by how children are treated, by what parents or early years workers are ready to do and what they resist doing. There has been a strong cultural tradition in Britain that it is acceptable to hit children as a form of discipline. Some people disagree strongly with this view but you will hear and read many examples of people who do agree.

- What do you think could be the sources of a cultural tradition that promotes hitting children but mainly disapproves of adults who hit each other?
- What do you have to believe about children, and about the rights of adults, in order to approve of hitting children?

Emotions as well as intellect

An over-simple view of handling children's behaviour tends to err by saying you can either handle the behaviour or you can deal with the emotions. The implication is that addressing children's emotions will be a time-consuming task, perhaps better suited to therapy. Children whose early experiences have left them emotionally disturbed may well need the help of a therapeutic situation. But, for most children, a recognition of their feelings is a relatively straightforward development in treating them with respect as a whole person.

John Gottman has been involved in longitudinal research with parents in how they deal with emotions within family life and relationships with children. He interpreted his findings about the psychological and physical well-being of children through making sense of the different parental styles of handling the 'negative' emotions of anger, sadness, envy and so on. He distinguished four styles in parents' overall approach, which are equally applicable to any adults responsible for children:

- A **dismissive** approach was taken by some parents. They ignored or trivialised children's negative emotions. Children took the message that their parents did not notice their feelings or that such feelings were silly and unimportant compared with proper adult concerns.
- Some parents were actively **disapproving** of children showing negative emotions. They criticised and punished them.
- Another style was a **laissez-faire** approach by parents who were accepting of their children's negative emotions but failed to guide their children in the expression of strong feelings and did not set limits to behaviour.
- A fourth group had developed a style that Gottman calls **emotion coaching**. These parents accepted their children's expression of strong or negative feelings and let the children know that their emotions were heard and understood. However, unlike the laissez-faire approach, the parents who took an active role with their children's emotions also explored what children might do about the situation that had provoked the strong feelings. On other occasions such parents might acknowledge the emotion yet guide children towards ways of expressing the feelings that were less harmful of others.

Through an approach of **emotion coaching**, Gottman observed that some parents were supporting their children in three important areas of their emotional development:

- understanding their own feelings;
- having empathy with others;
- being able to control their own impulses.

He describes five steps within emotion coaching, that parents;

- become aware of a child's emotion;
- recognise children's expression of these feelings as a time of potential learning and of closeness between adult and child;
- listen with empathy and affirm the child's feelings;
- help the child to find words to name the emotion;
- set limits while exploring strategies to solve the current problem.

The idea of emotion coaching has links with other areas of applied psychology for children. The approach is a direct attempt to help children to develop a sense of self-worth and to help them to understand feelings. Adults are more honest about their own and perhaps share their feelings, in a simple and appropriate way. You will also see the links to the importance of allowing for feelings in how you support learning and deal with mistakes (see page 128). The approach is not one of spending ages talking with children about their emotions – you will lose young children very quickly. Gottman quotes some long exchanges from family settings but often a simple acknowledgement may be key: 'I can see that you're cross about...', 'You're sad today...' 'I can see that you want...' or 'You don't like that, do you. Is it that it makes you frightened?'

There are links between Gottman's explanation of emotion coaching and the practical approaches from the Adlerian tradition, for instance in separating the child as a person from the behaviour (an honest acknowledgement of 'I like you, I don't like it when you...'). An adult acting as an emotion coach does not manipulate feelings of affection to coerce good behaviour (as in 'I won't like/love you any more if...').

SUGGESTED ACTIVITY

Be especially aware for a couple of weeks of how you and other people around you react to children's expression of strong emotions. What evidence can you observe of patterns of dismissive, disapproving or laissez-faire adults? You could use these observations to throw into relief what the emotion coaching approach would look like in practice. For instance, watch out for :

- Adults who dismiss any possibility that children might have strong feelings about an experience ('children that young don't care about....' or 'they don't notice').
- Adults who directly deny children's feelings that the adults do not want to have to handle ('That doesn't hurt') or who belittle them ('You're making a fuss about nothing').
- Adults who decide they know what children are feeling without asking them.

Use your observations to reflect on your own practice and talk ideas over with a colleague. If you are honest, do you tend to assume children will get over an incident quickly because it is easier for you? Or because you believe that acknowledging children's upset feelings will encourage them to be more upset in the future? (The opposite seems to be the case.)

Reading on . . .

★ Chao, Ruth 1994 'Beyond parental control and authoritarian parenting style: understanding Chinese parenting through the cultural notion of training', *Child Development*, 65, 1111–1119. A description of the research discussed on page 162. The article raises more general issues about culture and the study of child rearing than the specific focus on Chinese families.

★ Dreikurs, Rudolf 1981: *Happy Children: A challenge to parents* (Fontana). A practical book on taking a positive approach to children's behaviour. This book and other material on the Adlerian approach is available from: Adlerian Workshops and Publication, 216 Tring Road, Aylesbury, Bucks HP20 1JS.

★ Dunn, Judy 1993: *Young Children's Close Relationships Beyond Attachment* (Sage). Description of research and discussion of ideas that highlight just how much children's social development is intertwined with their cognitive and language development, and so with their behaviour.

★ Eisenberg, Nancy 1992: *The Caring Child* (Harvard University Press). An exploration of prosocial behaviour and the role of adults in promoting this development.

★ Gottman, John 1997: *The Heart of Parenting: How to raise an emotionally intelligent child* (Bloomsbury). A description of the research discussed on page 163 of this chapter, with practical suggestions for parents and other carers.

★ Lindon, Jennie 1997: *Working With Young Children* (Hodder and Stoughton). Part Three has a great deal more about the practicalities of a positive approach to children's behaviour than I have covered in this chapter.

★ Manning, Margaret; Heron, J. and Marshall, T. 'Styles of hostility and social interactions at nursery, at school and at home' in Hersov, L.A. and Berger, M. (eds) 1978: *Aggression and Anti-social Behaviour in Childhood and Adolescence* (Pergamon). A description of the research discussed on page 159 of this chapter.

★ Miller, Judy 1997: *Never Too Young* (National Early Years Network). A practical booklet considering the many ways that young children can be involved in the daily running of an early years setting, and how these opportunities support positive development.

★ Slaby, Ronald; Roedell, Wendy; Arezzo, Diana and Hendrix, Kate 1995: *Early Violence Prevention: Tools for teachers of young children* (National Association for the Education of Young Children). Discussion of the relevant research and practical suggestions for promoting assertive and prosocial, rather than aggressive, behaviour in young children in early years settings. Available in the UK from the National Early Years Network, 77 Holloway Road, London N7 8JZ, tel: 0171 607 9573.

7 Children in society

This chapter covers:

- children within a social and cultural context;
- children and their families;
- families within the broader community.

7.1 Children within a social and cultural context

You will have noticed that many of the theories about child development focus closely on individual children without a great deal of the social and cultural context in which children live and learn. Consequently much of the research, although not all, has tended to filter out many of the aspects of daily life for children.

Psychology developed as a subject for the study of individuals, although social psychology (my own professional background) was always more concerned about individuals within their social settings. Increasingly, some psychologists have become dissatisfied with an unbalanced individual focus and explored ways to place child development within a more realistic context.

The ecological approach

Urie Bronfenbrenner studied the relevance of children's social environment through his approach of the ecology of human development. Bronfenbrenner wanted to describe and study the impact of children's environment, without losing the importance of children's individuality. He saw the influences of heredity and environment as interacting; there was no need to argue whether one or the other were more important.

Bronfenbrenner viewed children as at the centre of their personal world, a world that was influenced by many factors outside a child's or the family's direct control. Instead of treating the social environment as a single whole, Bronfenbrenner described the different aspects that influenced children in more and less direct ways. He developed a model which is presented visually as a series of layers, or a pattern of concentric circles (see the following diagram). The innermost circle is that part of the environment that makes children's (or adults') daily life and their direct, personal interactions. Then, the series of circles moves further away from the individual experience and towards broader social factors.

The microsystem

The innermost circle of the **microsystem** encompasses children's immediate personal environment. This includes their family, peers and friends. It also includes settings of which the child has direct experience: early years centres, schools or places of worship for families with religious beliefs. Children's socialisation occurs within this setting. Socialisation includes the whole process of children's learning what is expected of them as individuals within their social environment. Most child development research is undertaken in this area.

CHRONOSYSTEM

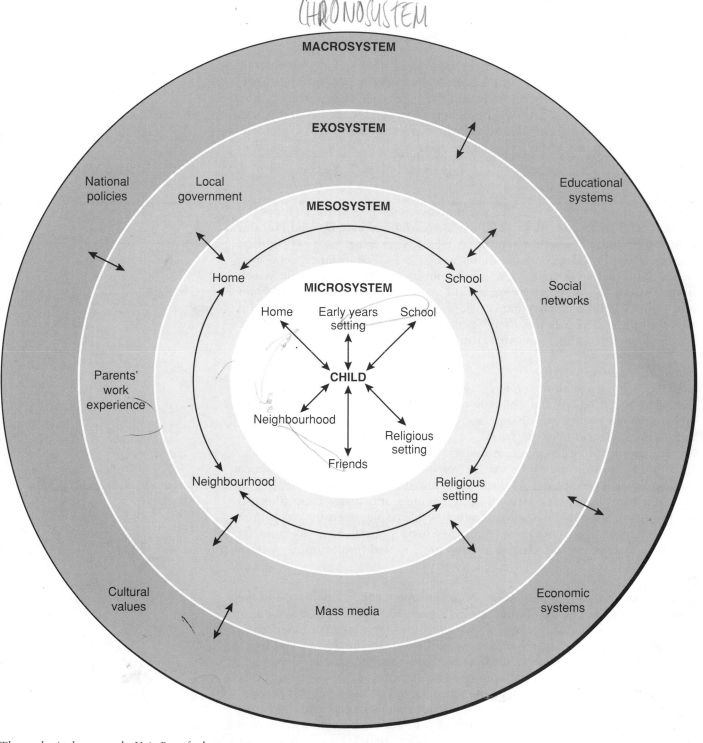

The ecological approach: Urie Bronfenbrenner

The mesosystem

The different aspects of the microsystem do not exist separately. The **mesosystem** is a term Bronfenbrenner uses to describe the relationship between the different settings that children experience during their development, for instance, the match or mismatch for children between the requirements of family and of school, or of their parents and the pressures from children's peers. Some child development research has looked at the experience for children when they face conflicting demands or how adults might ease the children's transition from one setting to another, for instance, starting school.

The exosystem

Bronfenbrenner calls the next layer the **exosystem.** This includes all parts of the social system that have an impact on children. The impact may be direct, but can also be through their family and the experience of important adults in their lives. Important aspects can be the neighbourhood, local social networks including their parents' friends and the world of work, which affects children through their parents' experiences of the pressures of a job or the disruption of unemployment.

The macrosystem

The outer layer or circle is called the **macrosystem.** This circle includes the broad social structures, such as education, economic systems and cultural values. What may sound like remote social ideas nevertheless affect children because these broader systems influence their lives. For instance, economic policy may result in the relative wealth or poverty of the child's family, which in turn affects the stresses on parents and the child's life prospects. The child and family's ethnic identity gains meaning from the predominant cultural values of the society. Are this family's culture or religious beliefs respected or are they an undervalued minority group?

The chronosystem

Bronfenbrenner sets all the circles in what he calls the **chronosystem**, which describes the broad social changes over a child's whole life. Patterns of environmental events will change and broad social changes may affect the nature of childhood over the years.

All the other circles operate against the backdrop of socio-historical factors. An example would be that between two generations there has been a technological revolution. As a result of miniaturisation and falling prices, children now have access to computer, video and other technological equipment that would have seemed unbelievable to the generation for whom a computer occupied an entire room. My own interests as a psychologist include a fascination with social history and you will find examples within this chapter.

Research to study the subtle effects of environment can be complex and the most likely influences are of interactions rather than linear patterns of cause and effect. For instance, parents' approach to child rearing (as influenced in part by family and cultural tradition) will exert an impact on children's behaviour and their approach to adults and peers in other settings. Depending on the match or mismatch between the expectations or rules of these other settings, children may be at ease in the setting or fail to find a role. Or perhaps they manage to integrate at the cost of dissociating themselves from some of their family loyalty. Pressures on families – financial, lack of friends or a dangerous neighbourhood – may in turn reduce parents' capacity to cope or give their children time. And so the complex interaction continues, with broad environmental influences wound around individual differences.

One advantage of the ecological approach is the attempt to grapple with social structures, the many influences on children's development and the complex interactions. This advantage in a thoughtful approach and trying to be realistic is something of a liability in research, since it is very difficult to design studies that take account of the real complexity of everyday life. Some studies have tried to weigh up how different factors interact – see page 182.

SUGGESTED ACTIVITY

It can be difficult to design good research that takes careful account of the different aspects of children's daily life. On the other hand, you can have a very stimulating discussion about how everything may interact, since you do not have to prove any of your suggestions.

Take the following scenario and think through what might be happening. Discuss your ideas with a colleague. You might also find a diagram a useful way to gather your thoughts.

Scenario
Dave and Julie have two children of 2 and 4 years old. Dave has been made redundant from a job with a good salary. He has only been able to get part-time work on short contracts. The firm for whom Julie works is expanding and she has been given a promotion that means longer hours, more travelling and sometimes staying away overnight. Their children attend a local private day nursery. Until recently Julie handled all the organisation of child care and ran the home, only asking for Dave's help if she was really over-loaded. The family cannot continue to run as before.

Dave and Julie have friends in the neighbourhood, most of whom also have young children. With the exception of one set of friends, Julie is the only mother who has returned to full-time work. Dave's family live a few miles away. His mother worked as a teacher throughout Dave's childhood, whereas Julie's mother gave up her career when she had the children.

Possible questions
- How are the two children likely to feel about the changes in their family? What circumstance might make the children feel secure about the changes? If you think they may be troubled – in what way? And for what reasons?
- How might each of the parents feel about this change in earning power and domestic responsibility? Think about Dave and Julie separately. What circumstances could lead them to feel confident about the change? What might lead either of them to feel uneasy?
- What else would you ideally like to know about this family if you were going to make predictions about how well they will manage this change and what, if any, problems they will experience?

A socio-historical perspective

Children's pattern of development is undoubtedly shaped by the cultural traditions that they experience through family life and other settings influenced by the predominant culture, such as early years centres and school. But cultural traditions are not fixed for ever, they can change over time. Some knowledge of recent social history can help an understanding that there can be changes *within* a culture and well as differences *between* cultures that co-exist within a diverse society. Within-culture differences and changes in social values over time may lead to conflict between generations within a family.

Advice on child care
Christina Hardyment, a social historian, undertook a survey of child care advice from 1750 to the mid-1990s. She documents the changing themes in

how mothers were told to treat their babies and how advice was often grounded in the current view of children and childhood. Were children wilful little creatures who had to be firmly trained from the first days? Or were they individuals needing security and care that was timed to their own needs? Reactions to the firm training and schedule approaches of Truby King and other writers of the 1940s and 50s gave way to the 'trust your instincts' approach of Benjamin Spock. Conviction that this approach has created over-permissiveness with children led to concerns about how to combine affection with setting sensible boundaries for children.

Surveys such as Hardyment's are very useful for providing a window on to prevailing social values, or the co-existing and conflicting values for a given generation of parents. Of course, parents do not always follow the advice of books nor of health professionals. So historical research of this kind does not provide a basis for saying that during such and such a decade, parents behaved, or did not behave, in a particular way. The other advantage of a grasp of recent social history and child care is that it discourages any over-confidence that current ideas are absolutely right and will not change. Changes to current approaches and reactions are inevitable.

A view of childhood

Sociologists have become more interested in childhood and their approach sometimes includes a historical dimension as well as looking at children's experience grounded in their social settings. Berry Mayall is one of several writers who have studied childhood as an experience that is **socially constructed**. This idea is that children's experience is shaped partly by adult views about children and the nature of childhood. Mayall questions, for instance, the nature of 'child-centred' settings in early years and primary school. She takes the challenging view that such a philosophy does not necessarily produce settings that are genuinely attuned to children's needs, since adult priorities are usually dominant (see also page 127).

Some events of relatively recent history highlight views of children as completely subordinate to adult definitions of their best interests. Margaret Humphreys documented the emigrations of children from residential homes to America and Australia, which only finally stopped in 1967. These were mass movements of children, purportedly to provide them with a better life, in which the children's welfare and emotional well-being were strikingly ignored. There was no follow-up of the children, many of whom experienced harsh, sometimes abusive, conditions. Most of the children were given no information about themselves, such as their birth certificates, and there was no thought that the uprooting and loss of identity might adversely affect children's later development. Changes in beliefs about children's need for a personal identity have led to significant changes in adoption procedures. It is now usual that children's adoptive parents hold material for them about their birth family and young people have the right to trace their birth family after their eighteenth birthday.

Another mass movement of children during the twentieth century, the evacuations during World War Two, also seemed to be undertaken (admittedly for reasons of safety) with very little official recognition that being moved away from home, and sometimes also from their family, might upset children. Some writers on the wartime evacuation of children have speculated that many of the government officials were likely to have experienced boarding school from a young age, possibly preceded by care by residential nannies. They may have had very limited understanding of the emotional distress of children whose families had taken full responsibility for their care.

The meaning of childhood is affected by time and place

TO THINK ABOUT

We all bring something of our own childhood to how we relate to children, whether as an early years worker or a parent. One way of thinking about the layers of experience is to say that we can experience four slightly different and interlocking 'childhoods'. I explain the idea in this way:

1   We have our parents' memories of our early childhood. In this way we hear about and integrate into our own memory events that we cannot recall directly. In families that share many conversations about children's early lives, it can become difficult to be sure what you recall directly and what has become a fresh memory through your parents' reminiscences.

2   We have our own childhood directly experienced during the years of being a child. Sometimes emotionally strong experiences are laid down in great detail. A trigger later in life can release the memory as fresh as ever. These may be pleasant memories but might also be unhappy experiences.

3   Childhood is re-lived and re-construed through memories during the adult years. Some adults use these re-worked memories as proof that childhood or children are different now. The comparison may be with regret or criticism.

4   The possible fourth childhood is experienced by adults who have responsibility for children, either as a parent or an early years worker. You bring your own childhood into your work and re-experience that time through your current involvement with children. An experience of the past entering the present can be very positive, perhaps reminding a carer how hard it is for a three-year-old to wait for her favourite bike. Obviously, re-worked memories may be problematic if carers are reliving unresolved problems of their own childhood through the children. It is also unhelpful if adults assume that their own childhood concerns and interest will necessarily be shared by all other children now.

Think about how childhood is not a one-off experience for any of us.

- Can you, and your colleagues, think of well-worn phrases that have popped out of your mouth without warning? Perhaps you've even repeated a cliché that annoyed you as a child.
- Inaccurate, nostalgic memories of 'how children used to be' are not usually helpful. But can you think of changes in children's environment that have perhaps changed the possibilities of childhood, although children themselves are much the same as always?
- Our own memories can help us to look through children's eyes now. Collect some examples of when your own memories helped you to understand how a child was probably feeling or why she was having difficulty.

Families within a culture

All families raise children within a given culture with prevailing cultural and religious traditions. Parents may view their parenting role as explicitly passing on their own beliefs and traditions. But some parents will be following a cultural pattern without consciously thinking ' this is the way of my culture'. The approach will be more that 'this is the right or normal' way to raise children.

Study of families within different cultures has shown variations as well as shared patterns. Any research of this nature has to be very carefully planned since there is a great deal of difference within cultures as well as between them. Additionally, families of a particular cultural background live in different social settings. The life of a family living in a disadvantaged area and in poverty may be better explained by the financial and other stresses on this family than on cultural traditions.

Cultural traditions shape the pattern of family life. All children start off with potentials and then are shaped by what they learn as well as the impact of their own individuality. You will recall from page 94 that babies are able to make any of the sounds in human languages; but that they swiftly lose the ability to make sounds or sound combinations which do not appear in the language(s) they hear at home.

Beatrice Whiting and Carolyn Edwards studied family life in several different cultures. They stressed that all children begin with the potential for a wide range of behaviours. Cultural forces act on children through the adults who care for them. Children are guided in particular directions by various aspects:

- Adults' expectations of children are influenced by the dominant culture and/or religion.
- Expectations are put into daily life through adult choices about what they give children most opportunity to practise. These choices reflect adult values of what is more important or appropriate for children
- Adult reactions show children those behaviours which are meaningful and the value that is placed upon them.

TO THINK ABOUT

All families live and make decisions within a cultural framework. In a multi-cultural society, parents and carers of the most dominant culture may not even think of their choices for children as reflecting their own culture. Decisions may be seen as the 'normal' way and cultural traditions as something exotic, that other people experience. Much of the research into child development has been undertaken in a Western context (the United States and Europe). But some researchers have considered different patterns and how far ideas are applicable in different cultures. You will find some examples in this chapter. Look also at the section on bilingualism on page 104.

The development of boys and girls
The cultural context

In their survey of different cultures, Whiting and Edwards observed that young boys and girls showed similar patterns of behaviour. They were both inclined to:

- react in a nurturant way to babies who were still small enough that they were supported on someone's lap;
- behave dependently towards adults, looking for guidance and help;
- respond in a playful and challenging way towards their child companions.

From these similar beginnings, boys and girls were then set upon different paths by adult behaviour that treated them differently according to the cultural values. In particular:

- boys and girls were allowed different amounts of autonomy (their freedom to determine what they do);
- they were given different patterns of responsibility;
- limits and constraints were placed on the company they kept.

All cultures take some stance on the ways in which boys and girls, women and men, are treated differently. In some societies, for reasons of culture or religious belief, the social expectations and requirements are significantly different for the two sexes. In other cultures there is more overlap, although firm views may still exist on the more acceptable behaviour and aspirations for boys and girls. In Britain we have seen a change within the dominant culture over the last three generations. A co-existing change has been the growth of a multi-cultural society in which some groups have different, perhaps conflicting views on this issue.

Research on differences between boys and girls

Research in a social context

I mentioned on page 143 that discussion can become very heated over differences in the development or abilities of girls and boys. There are two related problems:

- Any differences have frequently been interpreted as deficiencies: that one sex is 'better' than the other. So, it has been very difficult to discuss what appears to be a tendency for one sex without getting into arguments about whether such a difference is positive or negative. The social climate seems to have changed enough that there is now a chance of seeing differences as evidence of the diversity that any society needs.
- Sex differences have also been entangled in the argument about a biological basis to differences or the impact of socialisation on children – another version of the nature-nurture controversy. The resistance to considering any possible biological base to sex differences was grounded in my first point. Any differences were so often interpreted in a negative way for females.

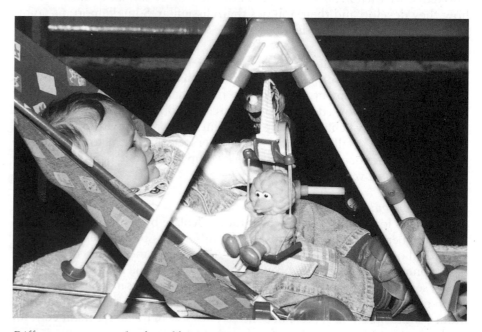

Different treatment of girls and boys may start very young

Additionally, a claim that such differences arose from biology left girls and women trapped in an inferior role. Again, the social climate seems to have changed enough that some biological basis to behaviour can be considered because learning through the process of socialisation is also considered.

Psychology, and other social sciences, carry some responsibility for the problems. For decades they reflected the views of society as a whole and often studied males as if they were the entire human race and any female patterns were oddities. For example, male aggression was interpreted as a positive quality of leadership, yet evidence of other emotions in female response patterns were seen as evidence of weakness or lack of objectivity. Practical applications showed a biased interpretation. For instance, girls' struggles with maths and science were often seen as proof of the sex's problems with logical thinking. Yet boys' relatively greater difficulties with language work, especially reading, were seen as evidence of the need for remedial help.

Are there any consistent differences?

Girls and boys are clearly not identical, in that there is a sex difference, determined at conception. The sexes are biologically and physiologically different and those differences are accentuated during puberty when girls make the move into becoming young women and boys into young men. There are two main questions for research in child development:

1   Apart from puberty, are there areas of development in which the sexes are consistently different?
2   To what extent do any of the differences arise from the sex difference (biology) rather than social learning?

1   Are there areas of development in which the sexes are consistently different?

The answer to the first question is that very few consistent patterns of differences have been found between boys and girls in aspects of their development. There is a great deal of variation *within* each sex as well as *between* boys and girls. Looked at as a whole, boys and girls are much more similar to each other in how they develop and their abilities than dissimilar. Some important points to understand are now outlined.

Any differences are small

Most frequently, no sex differences have been found in children's abilities within their development. Some of the firmly held beliefs, such as girls are more helpful than boys, do not stand up to careful observation of how children as a whole actually behave. Where consistent differences have been identified, they are usually small. Even when the differences are clear, for instance, in males' greater tendency to aggressiveness compared with females, the average difference is still very small.

Statistics provide averages

Researchers look at **averages**, which they calculate by testing or observing a large number of children. In most of the differences found there has been a great deal of overlap between boys and girls. For instance, study of language development has shown that, on average, girls tend to talk more and in slightly longer sentences in early childhood. This difference persists into later childhood when girls are slightly better than boys (on average) at verbal reasoning and brain teasers based on words. In contrast, boys seem to have a slight edge for intellectual problems based on numerical reasoning.

You notice that I keep saying 'on average'. Some boys have great difficulty with numerical reasoning and not all girls, by any means, are confident in their use of language. There is a wide variation in each sex. Almost without exception, each sex has the full range of a given ability or tendency in which there is an average difference. One of the very few exceptions is the finding that boys are more likely than girls to show almost all of the different kinds of extreme physical, emotional and intellectual vulnerability to stress.

Groups and individuals

Group statistics on small differences do not give a firm basis for predicting about individuals. For instance, groups of adolescent boys so far have produced better average scores on mathematical reasoning than girls. But this information cannot make you confident that a given individual boy will be competent at this kind of reasoning any more than you can predict that individual girls will have problems. Nor is there any reason to suppose that the slight differences now will necessarily hold in ten years' time.

In the same way, if you were working with a reception class of children, you could fairly predict that, on balance, more boys in the class will struggle with their reading than the girls. But you will need your skills of observation to determine which boys are having trouble and whether any of them are showing signs of possible dyslexia (three to four times more likely for boys than girls). But many of the boys in your group will become confident readers and some of the girls will have persistent difficulties.

Some differences do not last

Studies that have found small differences between the sexes when children are young do not necessarily find a similar pattern as children get older. For instance, some studies have shown a pattern of slightly greater cooperativeness in girls of pre-school age than the boys. However, even this small difference fades away when older children are studied. The one remaining difference into the older age groups is that children who are judged to be extremely uncooperative at home or school are more likely to be boys than girls.

2 To what extent do any of the differences arise from the sex difference (biology) rather than social learning?

Research suggests that some combination of biology (inborn differences) and socialisation accounts for the few consistent differences that have been found. Some of the variation, and for some differences perhaps quite a lot of it, arises from adults' twin convictions that boys and girls are different, and should be different. As a consequence children are treated differently according to their sex, even from babyhood (the socialisation process).

For instance, up to about eight years of age, girls tend (on average – again!) to be slightly better at arithmetical computation (adding, subtracting, counting) than the boys. But in the following years this gap closes. Then the boys' average scores tend to be higher on the more complicated maths problems that children and young people start to tackle in the latter years of primary school and then secondary school. There could conceivably be some biological basis for relative strengths in different kinds of mathematical ability, although I have not encountered a good explanation of that kind. Studies have demonstrated, however, that adults' (parents and teachers) beliefs that girls are less good at maths appear to shape their treatment of the sexes. Some parents (not all, of course) seem to accept girls' struggles with maths as an inevitable part of being female, which no effort will be able to counteract. Some teachers have been observed to pay more attention to the boys in maths and science classes. So, there is a strong basis for saying that this sex difference is affected by social learning, and any biological basis is interacting with socialisation.

Another example is provided by the studies on aggression in children. Many studies on this topic (but not all of them) have shown a pattern that from a young age boys hit and insult each other more than girls behave to their own sex. The boys also tend to react faster and more strongly if they are hit or insulted. Boys also engage more than girls in play fighting and rough and tumble games (see also page 160). Boys emerge, on average, as more aggressive in their behaviour than girls all the way through into adulthood. There is the possibility of a biological basis to this difference because the pattern emerges at a very young age and there seems to be some link between sex hormones and level of aggression. Yet, observation of adults shows that many encourage, or tolerate, different patterns of behaviour in aggressiveness and dominance depending on whether the children are boys or girls.

SUGGESTED ACTIVITY

This section gives you a brief description of the research into sex differences and sums up that there are very few consistent differences between boys and girls as a large group. Of course, this does not mean that boys and girls are all the same – clearly they are not. Yet many adults show through their words and their behaviour that they expect children to differ in particular ways because of their sex.

Over a couple of weeks, collect examples of adult assumptions about how boys and girls will act, or how they ought to behave. Discuss your observations and thoughts with a colleague.

- Watch out for how people selectively interpret what they see. An incident that supports their existing assumptions is seen as proof ('Look at Jamie building that castle. Boys are so good with their hands'). But an event that challenges assumptions is dismissed as something out of the ordinary ('Harry is so helpful. It's odd isn't it? It's usually girls who want to help').

- Perhaps you observe a parent, or almost catch yourself saying to a girl, 'Let me help you up the climbing frame. It's a bit high for you', when a boy would be allowed to try.

- Maybe if parents ask you for advice, they are worried at an earlier stage if a girl is hard to manage, but seem to tolerate more disruption from a boy before his behaviour is seen as a problem.

7.2 Children and their families

Families as social groups

Families are sometimes discussed as if they are a collection of separate individuals. More accurately, families are social groups in which individuals live their lives and children develop and learn. Adults also have their own concerns within the family and their own adult relationships. The view of family life as the life of a social group highlights the observation that all families develop patterns to deal with issues of:

- family rules;
- roles within the family;
- boundaries to family life.

Rules in the family

Family members might not voice it in this way but family life shows the unspoken patterns. All families have some pattern of rules, if only that 'we don't have any firm rules here'. The family rules may be expressed out loud or remain unspoken and affect daily interactions and communication (see for example the section on dealing with emotions in the family on page 163). The setting and negotiating of rules show the patterns of authority within a family.

Roles

All families develop a pattern of **roles** for different family members and the extent to which there is possibility of change. A role includes expectations about how an individual will behave, but there is also a sense of an overall framework within which he or she reacts. So, perhaps three children, in different families, are expected to help to tidy up after a family meal. However, in one family the child is expected to help because his parents believe that even young children should be active members of the household. In the second family, the child is expected to help because she is the eldest and a girl as well. In the third family, the child is expected to help because he is 'the considerate one' in this family. His siblings make a fuss about tidying up and their parents do not press them.

Adult family roles develop over whose job it is to discipline, encourage or protect. Cultural traditions will shape family choices and perhaps influence how roles are decided on the basis of sex or age. Family dynamics are affected by the pattern of roles and individual family members may feel empowered or restricted by the role assigned to them. For instance, children may feel they are not allowed to behave differently from their particular role in their family, but are forever the 'strong' one, the 'awkward' one or the 'disorganised' one. In some families the assigned roles can be very fixed, other families have more tolerance of change and adjustment.

A 'shared history'

The view of families as a social group, with a past as well as a future, makes sense in terms of research into close relationships within the family, for example, by Judy Dunn. In families, as with children's friendships, there is a shared history for the relationship. Exchanges between parent and child or between siblings (and between friends) only make full sense with some understanding of what has gone before. The current, observed exchange may be following a general pattern set out very early in the life history of this relationship.

Alternatively, the exchange between, for example parent and child, may be so charged with emotion precisely because one person is challenging the pattern established to date.

Boundaries

Social groups also develop boundaries, and family life is no exception. The family's rules and roles shape the boundaries to family life and how much flexibility is allowed. Observation of different families can highlight how far family members are allowed to stray before others step in or how strong are the boundaries around this family. Families also develop patterns of support within and outside the family. Some have strong systems of support, some have very little. Families also develop boundaries about acceptance of support – within the immediate family, the extended family, friends, the extent of acceptance of non-family members.

The cultural tradition in which families operate will influence the development of rules and family roles. There are broad differences between cultures but also great variety within any single culture. Differences also develop within the same culture over time.

TO THINK ABOUT

Turn your thoughts to your own family. Looking back on your childhood, can you see how your family worked with roles for different individuals and some family rules?

- How were you expected to behave? What seemed to your family to be usual for you and what kind of behaviour surprised them ('Now, that's not like you, is it? You're such a .... girl/boy.')
- What kind of boundaries did your family operate? What was acceptable and what was not alright?

There is no need to share these personal thoughts unless you and a colleague both wish to do so.

The family as a social system

Family members, adults and children, are part of a network of interrelationships. They affect one another through each other's actions and beliefs. Views of child development have expanded to encompass the idea that children affect their family just as much as parents affect their children. Neither research, nor daily experience for that matter, suggests that parents or other carers can impose their pattern on children in a one-way relationship. A more subtle model of family life has been offered by **systems theory**.

The basis for this approach is the model that any system is more than just the sum of the separate parts. So, systems theory would say that families cannot be described only by talking about each individual family member. Family life is created by the relationships between parents, children and any other close relatives. The experiences of individuals within any family are influenced by the way this family operates. Systems theorists, like Arnold Sameroff, often take the analogy of music. You cannot possibly appreciate a piece of music by listing all the separate notes. The unique tune is created by how those notes are set together, whether they merge in harmony or clash.

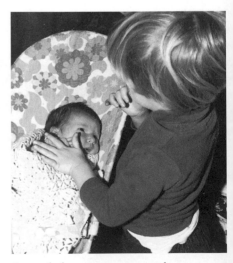

A new baby means everyone has to adjust

The other defining feature of a system like a family is that the system adapts to change in the same kind of way that Piaget describes for children's cognitive development (see page 66). Families can be resistant to change (some more than others) and if possible they will absorb some new feature into family life without major re-adjustments (Piaget's idea of assimilation). But sometimes, family life becomes very stressful unless particular re-adjustments are made which shift how the family runs (Piaget's idea of accommodation).

Families as self-balancing systems

Families establish a way of coping that for them defines normal family life. The main ideas from a view of families as social systems are that:

- All families act so as to achieve a balance in their relationships.
- Family members help to maintain this balance overtly and covertly.
- Family communication patterns help to maintain this balance.
- If equilibrium seems precarious, family members exert effort to restore it.
- Sometimes, equilibrium may be maintained by one member or members imposing on others in the family.
- Changing the balance, or having change thrust upon a family, can be stressful.

Much depends on previous family experience of dealing positively with adjustments. The balance for some families is very dependent on people not changing. Having children is an enforced experience of dealing with change and subsequent children bring about greater or lesser change in the existing family. Alfred Adler made the point that each child is, in effect, born into a 'different' family because they face a different configuration of people and existing roles than either an older or a subsequent child. Children are themselves active family members, responding and reacting to the family system. They make alliances with or feel resentment towards individual parents, siblings or other relatives in the close family.

Systems theory and any view of families as social groups raise the potential for conflict in families.

- In a social group with several members, preferences and perspectives will not always coincide. This is as true for families as any other small group.
- Family conflict is not necessarily substantial but, in many minor issues, not everyone's first choice can prevail.
- How to handle conflict and resolve relative power between members is an issue for all families and different families face compromise and negotiation with different styles (see page 161 on parenting styles).
- The potential for conflict takes you inevitably to an uneven balance of power in families – between adults, between different children in the family and between adult and child family members.
- Finally, families do not operate in a vacuum. They are all affected by the ways in which the surrounding community judges their actions and creates expectations that may put further pressure on families as well as offering support (Bronfenbrenner's idea of the mesosystem).

What would be healthy functioning within a family?

A great deal of discussion, and media interest, focuses on families that are judged to be dysfunctional. No family will be happy and calm all the time. There will be disagreements and clashes of viewpoint that disturb periods of relative calm. What matters most is how upsets are handled and that every family member avoids harking back once matters are relatively friendly once more. Psychologically healthy families are not free of conflict or adjustment difficulties, or have no painful or negative feelings. Rather they deal with negative feelings, acknowledge and express them in a sensitive manner.

Studies of families (often from the therapeutic side) have pointed to the features of those who pull together as a more cohesive and supportive unit, rather than experiencing life as full of conflict. In contrast with families who experience a great deal of conflict, families who are more supportive to each other show these kind of characteristics:

- Family members spend more time together in shared activities – in comparison with the more conflict-filled families.
- They put more effort into spending time together and so avoid or withdraw from each other less.
- Parents and children have many more warm exchanges and less hostile or critical interactions.
- There tends to be full, honest and accurate communication between family members.
- Family members tend to think well of each other and there is a lower level of criticism than in the families which are full of conflict.
- Family members tend to believe that the others think well of them.
- Parents and children believe that members of the family care about one another, although there are different ways of showing affection – not all families are physically demonstrative.
- People are pleased to be part of this family and optimistic about the future stability of the family.

These kinds of studies have usually been undertaken with families who are part of Western cultural traditions. So, it is not possible to say how far the ideas can safely be generalised to non-Western cultures. (See for instance, the different perspectives on parenting styles on page 162.)

TO THINK ABOUT

Many early years centres try to work in partnership with parents. In a family centre, the balance of the work will definitely include time spent with parents for their own adult concerns. When your work, or concerns, are focused very much on the child, it can be hard to think why some families might resist help with their children. Yet, studies of family work highlight the significance of considering how a family may be functioning, and not only the development of a child – as important as that is.

When families resist your help, or the kind of help you are currently offering, they may have any one of a number of reasons:

- This family may not want to admit to having difficulties. Perhaps they see it as a sign of failure or they are wary of authority.
- The family genuinely does not see this as a difficulty – perhaps the approach is 'boys will be boys' or 'our family is full of late talkers'.
- The child's misbehaviour or other problem is deflecting attention away from other issues in family life that adults do not wish to address – perhaps their own, adult relationships or an even more worrying problem with another child.
- Perhaps the parents are very resistant to any approach that indicates an effort to change on the part of adults. It is far easier to say everything is the child's fault and responsibility.

● The overall level of family stress is too great to make any space for the needs of the child.

Think about families with whom you are working or have contact because of concerns about the child. How far do any of these ideas help you make some sense of parents' resistance? Even when parents are cooperating with you, think about how they may be coping as individuals to accept that their child needs some help. The experience may be difficult for them.

Families within society

Families run their lives within a broader society. Bronfenbrenner's ecological approach is a reminder that any family social system, however strong the boundaries, will be affected by other events and pressures. Mary Pipher's work is also a counter-balance to an excessive focus on families and their influence on the children. (Pipher works as a child and family therapist in the United States.) She argues for a greater awareness of the impact on family life from external events such as the pervasive effect of the media, the sub-culture of school life and high pressures of jobs that force parents to choose between work and family. Pipher's concern is to avoid placing all responsibility (and blame) on families for their children's behaviour or problems. In a consumer-oriented society, strong messages reach children and young people that their identity is formed by what they own. Pipher has also explored how girls' positive identity is undermined by a school sub-culture that values looks and tolerates offensive behaviour from the male pupils.

Different kinds of families

Currently in Britain the overwhelming majority of children live in a two-parent family – 82% of them according to the 1991 Census. This fact is worth recalling when you encounter media reports suggesting that the two-parent family is a dying breed. Social patterns have changed, however, in that all these families are not composed of two married adults with their birth children. In some two-parent families, the adults have chosen not to get married. And an increasing number of these families include step-parents as well as biological parents. This family pattern also introduces step- and half-siblings. Step-families are not new, but several generations ago they would most likely have been formed after widowhood. Now one or more parents is far more likely to have been divorced than widowed.

The 1991 Census reported that approximately 19% of families were headed by a lone-parent and the majority of these families are headed by a mother (90%). Some of the families counted as lone-parent families at the beginning of the 1990s will now be step-families, since many divorced lone-parents re-marry. A relatively recent change in the composition of lone-parent families has been the growth of lone mothers who have never been married (24% of the lone-parent families in 1991). Study of this phenomenon explains it partly by a cultural tradition for women of Caribbean origin. But lone-parenting by choice or lack of male support is also a feature of some socially disadvantaged areas, for women of a range of cultural backgrounds.

Very strong views are expressed about the proper family circumstances in which children should be raised. Confident claims are made that children need two parents for healthy sex-role development, that children in lone-parent families will be disadvantaged and that children raised by homosexual rather than heterosexual couples will be emotionally damaged. Undoubtedly the quality of family life does matter to children but a clichéd approach that a two-parent family is the only safe environment is not supported by careful research. Nor would such a rosy view, that all two-parent families necessarily benefit their children, survive a reading of the files of the NSPCC or your local child-protection team.

Lone-parent families

If you take a global perspective, there are many different ways of raising children (see the comments on page 41), but undertaking this challenging task alone is not a common family system. However, lone-parenting has become more usual in countries such as Britain and the United States.

The difficulty in studying lone-parent families is that being a lone parent is often inter-linked with other social factors that do not usually support positive outcomes for children's development. In terms of Bronfenbrenner's ecology of development (see page 167), lone-parent families are a good example of how careful research can tease out that there are few easy answers.

Large surveys of children raised in lone-parent households show that, on average, the children do less well in school, are more likely to have behavioural problems and to become teenage parents. The research certainly does not say that all children of lone parents will have low achievements, any more than studies claim that living with two parents is a certain protection. But the research points to the risk factors of being raised by only one parent:

- Study of the social and financial circumstances of lone parents highlights that they are far more likely to be poor than two-parent families. Low income reduces a family's options and raises the emotional stress for any parents. Women who become lone parents through divorce are likely to experience a significant drop in the family income. Never-married mothers are significantly over-represented in very low income groups. So a major part of the negative effect on children's development seems to be the result of poverty and the resulting social disadvantage for the family.
- Parenting is an emotionally demanding task and research into lone-parent families, even those with fewer financial worries, produce descriptions of parents who have to face all the normal demands of children from their own emotional resources. An important factor is to what extent a lone parent is genuinely on her, or his, own. Some lone parents have considerable support from their family.
- A considerable number of lone-parent families are created by divorce, an experience that creates its own stresses, emotional as well as financial (see the next section).
- It is obviously important not to assume that every two-parent family has two, fully involved adults available to the children. Fathers of two-parent families may work very long hours or some effectively absent themselves from close involvement with their children. And studies of dual-career families sometimes paint a picture of two parents losing the struggle to balance ambitious and time-consuming careers with the emotional and intellectual demands of children.
- Never-married mothers are also much more likely to be young mothers, still teenagers when they had their first child. Apart from managing on a low income, studies of these young women suggest that many are emotionally ill-equipped to raise a young child. Frank Furstenberg's research (in the United States) describes patterns whereby very young mothers spent less time talking and playing with their children (compared with older, married mothers). The consequences were that the pre-school

children of the young lone mothers were more likely to behave aggressively and less able to control their own behaviour. They were also less advanced in their cognitive development than the children of the older, married mothers.

It is right to be concerned that lone-parent families should not be stigmatised or subject to stereotyping. But, such an awareness should not lead to avoidance of the uncomfortable findings that children raised by one parent can, on average, have less positive development than children from two-parent families. The research certainly does not justify any claim that lone parenting causes the pattern of developmental disadvantage. Some children raised by lone parents achieve well in school and adulthood, but these are far more likely to be from families who are not trapped in poverty.

Divorce and children's development

Divorce, like lone parenting, is a striking social change of recent social history. Children now are far more likely to experience the break-up of their family through divorce than previous generations. The experience of family breakdown is a major contribution to the creation of lone-parent families, although such families often change again, with the remarriage of a parent, and form step-families.

Stress, of all different kinds, leads parents to be less nurturant towards their children, more likely to resort to physical punishment and less consistent in their dealings with children. The stress involved in divorce spreads over a period of time and is likely to lead to styles of parenting that are less beneficial to children. Adults who are absorbed in their own distress and conflict have fewer resources to give to their children.

Neither divorce nor children's reactions to it are a single experience. There is often a pattern of family conflict before the divorce and difficulties of adjustment afterwards. Divorce and family break-up is a distressing experience for children and often has some negative effects on their development, at least in the short-term. However, careful studies of the impact of divorce on children's development have highlighted the complex pattern of the experience for children. Studies have led to practical suggestions to help children.

- Children whose parents divorce often have emotional difficulties that are visible in their behaviour, play and achievements in school. The children's upset is most marked in the first year after divorce but these difficulties do not usually last. Mavis Hetherington showed in her research that the question 'does divorce affect children' has different answers depending on the time scale after the divorce. The impact on children's development becomes far less marked, but interviews with children and young people show that the whole experience can leave an effect. Children have not forgotten distress, may still wish that their family had not broken up and wonder about their own future relationships.

- Boys seem on average to have more troubles and a lot depends on their relationship with their father, who is usually the non-custodial parent. Studies support the pattern of boys' greater vulnerability to stress. They are likely to show greater emotional impact at the time and to take longer than girls to re-adjust.

- Children in families where parents eventually divorce have sometimes shown developmental or behavioural difficulties in the previous years. One possible explanation would be that parents who are in conflict have less emotional resources for their children. Adults under stress tend not to offer warm and consistent parenting. This area of research is a useful reminder that conflict in the family can damage children's general development, whether the family remains intact or not.

- Children may also experience a parent's re-marriage and the creation of a step-family. Children often take time to adjust to the new family set-up. Studies have suggested that girls experience more difficulties with the remarriage of their mother, whereas boys are more likely to react positively.

- A finding in several studies of step-families is that children tend to show more problems when the new couple's relationship is very close. The opposite is found in non-divorced families. This effect is especially striking when the mother and children have lived in a lone-parent family for some time. So, a possible reason for children's difficulties is that the re-marriage forces new relationships and their mother's clear affection for her new husband disrupts old bonds even more. (Look back at page 178 on systems theory.)

- Children will be affected by their parents' divorce but the research suggests that the best outcomes will be in families where parents reduce conflict to a minimum, where they show agreement over how they treat children and where, after divorce, both parents are easily accessible and involved in children's lives.

- Children need no more disruption than is absolutely necessary. Children who do not have to change schools often find some respite from having at least one setting in which nothing has changed. Friends and teachers may also be a source of positive support.

CASE STUDY

Katie and Jon were six and four when their parents divorced. They moved to a smaller home with their mother and their father visited them every other weekend and sometimes during the week. In the two years before the divorce, their parents had quarrelled a great deal but believed the children were unaware because they only argued after Katie and Jon were in bed. Their disagreements about money and the father's long working hours continued after the divorce. He sometimes cancelled his visits at short notice because of work commitments. Their mother took a job to supplement their income and the children were given chores to help out. They did not mind these responsibilities because it was time spent with their mother and she showed appreciation of what they did.

Four years after the divorce, their father remarried and within the year there was a new baby. He cut back his working hours and was able to have Katie and Jon to visit him on a regular basis. Six years after the divorce, their mother re-married and they moved into her new husband's house. He had a daughter who was then fourteen and Katie was asked to share a bedroom with her.

Questions
What do you think could have been the experience of Katie and Jon at different stages over the last eight years – in the last years before their parents' divorce up to and including their mother's remarriage? Use ideas from the summary of research to help your thoughts.

- What kinds of adjustments have been asked of Katie and Jon – at the time of the divorce? during their life in a lone parent family? in the new step-family? Use the ideas of families as social groups and systems theory from pages 178–79.
- What will be important at each stage if the adults involved are going to support Katie and Jon?

7.3 Families within the broader community

Families live within a society and use a range of services. Some of these services are specifically for children, such as schools and the different kinds of early years centres. Families also use services that are available to the whole community, such as the health service.

A child focus in services

The research on how children form attachments has raised many issues about children's well-being within the family (see chapter 2). But the studies have also had an impact on what is regarded as good practice in services, especially hospitals, residential care and day care.

Children's experience of separation

The process of attachment was studied partly by following children who had been separated from their families on a temporary or more permanent basis. In the early research, children's experience of separation was interpreted almost entirely as one of **maternal deprivation**. This term was used to mean the negative consequences on children's later development of having been separated from their mother, usually at what is seen as a crucial, young age. Subsequent research has allowed for the more complex nature of the disruption of children's relationships with their family. However, research into two kinds of separation – hospitalisation of children and removal into residential care – have led to changes in practice beneficial to both children and their families.

Studies documented the distress of young children separated from their parents and placed in an unknown environment, such as a residential children's home or hospital. (These studies were undertaken when parents were not

In some areas there will be a wider choice of services

allowed to stay with their children on the ward.) Children's distress was sometimes extreme and prolonged. For some time, children were inconsolable, but some then slipped into a depressed state when they no longer even bothered to protest: When children were reunited with their parents, they showed a range of emotions indicating the loss of a sense of security: lack of welcome for the parents, renewed distress and later clinging and refusal to let parents out of their sight even for very short separations.

In the 1960s James and Joyce Robertson made a series of films which demonstrated the distress of young children on separation. In one film a child went into hospital, in another a young boy was cared for in a residential home while his mother was in hospital having a second baby. The films are upsetting to watch as the young children move from overt distress, to a visible despair and then to a kind of detachment from their surroundings. This distress was largely interpreted by the Robertsons as evidence of the crucial importance of mothers to their children. But the children in the films were separated from their entire families and removed from their home environment.

Although the interpretation of the children's experience would not now focus so exclusively on loss of their mother, the power of the Robertsons' work for children should not be underestimated. The films and other similar work led to significant changes in practice regarding children and their families.

Changes in hospital practice
Previously, parents were often regarded as a source of infection and interference, as people whose presence upset their children. Medical staff, who were unaware or unwilling to address children's emotional needs, had taken the convenient view that young children who had stopped crying were no longer distressed.

Faced with clear evidence of children's despair, hospital practice steadily changed to be more welcoming to parents: visiting hours were less rigid and arrangements began to be made for parents to stay in hospital with their children. A measure of this change is that the organisation Action for Sick Children now has a publication to advise on good practice when children stay in hospital without one of their parents, since this has become the less usual situation.

SUGGESTED ACTIVITY

Explore how hospitals approach health care for children. In what ways are health services adjusted for the age and needs of young children?

There are two possible approaches and it would be ideal if you could follow both of them.

- Find out from your nearest hospital how they organise to offer good quality health care for children. You can gather any written material and leaflets and obtain a copy of the NHS Patients' Charter (Services for children and young people). If possible, make an appointment to talk with a member of the medical staff on a children's ward or children's out-patient services.

- Take the opportunity to accompany parents you know with their child when the child needs a hospital procedure (out-patient or in-patient). It is important that both the parent and child are happy for you to accompany or visit them. Look at the experience from the perspective of the child: waiting time and waiting areas, the approach of medical staff to children, play opportunities for in-patients, the approach to uncomfortable, painful or upsetting procedures.

The organisation Action for Sick Children is also a good source of material on this topic. You can contact them at Argyle House, 29–31 Euston Road, London NW1 2SD, tel: 0171 833 2041.

Residential care

Research documenting children's distress in impersonal forms of residential care also had positive consequences. The great value of the work was to highlight children's feelings and that they were affected by adult behaviour reflecting the organisation within residential homes.

An overhaul of practice for residential care led to much smaller groups and more personalised care, with the aim of helping children to form relationships with familiar workers and reducing moves for children and disruptions in their living patterns. Research by Barbara Tizard in the 1970s confirmed the findings of other studies that young children could have experienced a tremendous turnover of caretakers. In one study Tizard reports that, between four months and four-and-a-half years, a group of children had experienced an average of fifty caretakers in their residential home. The continued disruption of relationships seemed to disturb the ability of some of the children to make further relationships.

Although the large, impersonal residential homes have gone, some problems still remain in putting principles into practice within residential care, and the outcomes for many 'looked after' young people are not promising. Staff turnover within residential homes can still be high and it is questionable whether methods of organisation provide sufficient continuity for children.

Children and day care

Initially the concern about maternal deprivation focused on extreme forms of loss and separation. But gradually the threads of argument became focused on temporary separations such as occur when women who are mothers go out to work and seek out-of-home day care for their children, especially for under-threes.

Up to the mid-1980s, many studies were planned in the expectation that any kind of non-maternal daily care would have negative effects on children. The underlying reasoning was the firm belief that working mothers inevitably caused their children to be deprived. Yet, reviews of the many studies from the United States and Britain established that there was no clear-cut, consistent link between maternal employment and damage through day care. Contrary to expectations, day care did not, in itself, harm children's development. Some forms of day care, with favourable adult-child ratios and clear learning programmes, had a measurably positive effect on children's later development, especially when those children were from deprived backgrounds.

In a second wave of research, studies began to be designed to look for positive as well as negative consequences. The details were planned with the recognition that all day care settings were not the same, any more than home-based care was the same in all families. The focus moved to trying to identify the features of good quality day care.

The same negative assumptions were then built in to studies of day care for the very young, specifically under-ones. The particular concern was that children might fail to develop a sufficiently strong attachment to their mother if they are cared for by others for noticeable lengths of time – the most common cut-off point being taken as more than 20 hours a week. Some studies found apparently less secure attachment to mothers in some young children in day care lasting more than 20 hours per week. But this was not a consistent finding and, on the measures used, the majority of young children in full day care were securely attached.

Research evidence does not support a negative view that day care, even for the very young, is inevitably harmful. However, there is no doubt that the quality of care for young children is important. Children in poor quality day care can have unfavourable outcomes in terms of their intellectual and social development. Where children have to compete for the attention of workers, there does seem to be a risk that, not surprisingly, some of them learn disruptive forms of behaviour in order to gain attention. Behavioural problems are not caused by the experience of day care itself but by some features of organisation within some settings.

Quality of care

Children's attachments

The research and theory on attachment and separation is a complicated, and often emotive, area (more in chapter 2). Strong beliefs about the right way to ensure children's well-being have resulted in assumptions colouring the planning and interpretation of research. Several themes emerge, despite the complexity of the topic.

- Babies and young children need to develop stable and affectionate relationships within and outside the family.
- Parents need to develop their own sense of attachment to their young children but this is a process that stretches over time.
- Children are not indifferent to who cares for them and they need to relate to a small number of people. However, mothers are not the only ones who are equipped to provide an important early attachment and the care giving.
- Early experience does matter for children's later development but patterns seem to be more important than single events. Explanations for positive or negative outcomes do not follow a simple cause and effect relationship.
- Children have feelings, these are legitimate and should be respected. Distress needs to be addressed and not dismissed as a nuisance or attention-seeking.
- Children are distressed by sudden separations from their family and every effort should be made to ease the experience of transition or unavoidable hospitalisations. The organisation of out-of-home care (daily or residential) should enable children to form attachments.

Organisation in settings

An understanding of children's need to form attachments leads to the practical issues in good quality day care. Children need consistency and continuity created through the routine and the behaviour of carers. Settings need to be organised, especially for the younger children, in a way that enables children to form close relationships. Children should be treated as individuals and not as an undifferentiated group. In day care settings, good practice leads to a **key worker** system in which individual staff take responsibility for named children. Such an approach addresses young children's emotional needs as well as their physical and intellectual needs. Workers are able to relate closely to a small number of children and their parents. Good quality care cannot be provided on the cheap and the balance of quality and cost remain a practical issue.

Culture and services for children

Services for children, schools and all the different early years settings reflect the dominant culture in any society – although differences only become apparent when cultures are compared.

Joseph Tobin and his colleagues studied the pattern of interaction between teachers and children in three pre-school settings. They reported that what the teachers did was different in each culture but what they believed they should be doing was also different. The teachers, like other adults within any culture, were preparing children for their future in a particular society.

Tobin showed teachers in two of the settings, Japan and the United States, videos of a pre-school day in the other culture. Both sets of teachers were critical of some aspects of the other setting. The Japanese teachers felt that the Americans intervened too much in children's behaviour and conflicts. On the other hand the American teachers thought the Japanese were ignoring behaviour from some children that should have been tackled directly. The American teachers were behaving so as to promote what they viewed as independence and self-reliance in the children. Whereas the Japanese teachers stressed the importance of cooperation and a sense of inter-dependence in the group.

Any service for children will reflect in obvious and more subtle ways what is valued by society. When several cultures co-exist within a community then such differences become more obvious. For instance, what one culture values as courtesy (not pressing one's opinion, nor disagreeing with a teacher) may be judged as passive and showing lack of confidence by someone from another culture.

The impact of social disadvantage

Families live within a broader society and the pattern of their lives is affected by social and financial circumstances (Bronfenbrenner's macrosystem). As Rudolph Schaffer has pointed out, 'social class', 'poverty' and any other broad descriptions are labels. The reality of their impact on children comes through their relationships with others, much of it in the family. Children's behaviour and their development is not changed directly by social class itself or by the family income. Children are affected by the attitudes, experiences and stresses that reach them through their parents, and other important adults in their lives.

Poverty affects families by increasing the chances that the children's environment is more chaotic, with greater stress and fewer resources:

- Mothers may have less easy access to pre-natal care which can increase the health risks to mother and child.
- Families with low financial resources are more likely to live in deprived areas with fewer and poorer quality services.
- When both parents have no option but to work, they may have to take poor quality child care.
- Stress in the family is likely to mean that parents have less time with their children, play and talk with them less and use authoritarian methods of child rearing.
- Very poor families may live in areas that are realistically dangerous, so the children's play opportunities and experiences are restricted.

All these features combine to make for more negative outcomes for children's development. But the results of poverty are being filtered through people's behaviour towards children. Arnold Sameroff has suggested that different sources of stress or negative experiences can build up on children. A child may be able to recover from one or two stressful early experiences but when the stresses continue to grow, then their development is almost certain to be negatively affected.

The idea of vicious and virtuous cycles describes a pattern of how negative (or positive) experiences may be perpetuated by the reactions of children and adults. For instance, stress may affect a child's behaviour so that he acts in a challenging and disruptive way. Adults who find him hard to handle respond in a punitive and rejecting way, which confirms the child's view that the world is a cruel place with no warmth for him and his problems. Alternatively positive experiences may prime a child to react well in a new setting. His behaviour is welcomed and adults are positive in return.

A complex picture is drawn also by studies of families and of pre-school programmes for children in disadvantaged areas. Families who live in poverty are not all the same. Studies of parents who felt they had good social support show that these parents feel more able to be supportive and less punitive towards their children. Poor parents with relatively more education are more likely to talk more with their children and support their learning than other families who have equivalent financial problems but less education. Comprehensive pre-school programmes that involve parents are more likely to support families and their children in escaping a poverty trap (see Kathy Sylva's review of the research on page 132).

The characteristics of children themselves are also relevant to how their development unfolds and to their later prospects. After many studies of the disadvantaging impact of poverty and social deprivation, researchers in the 1980s became interested in those children who, against all the odds, emerged to do well in adulthood. Norman Garmezy, Michael Rutter and others developed the idea of resilience and relative vulnerability in children. A series of studies has suggested that particular characteristics of children and their circumstances may help to protect them from social and financial stresses.

An important factor is that families are cohesive (they pull together – see also page 180), parents are loving towards the children and act in an authoritative way (see page 162 on parenting styles). More resilient children felt a strong sense of attachment to parents, which seemed to protect them to an extent in comparison with families who were equally poor, but had problems such as alcoholism, which disrupted attachment. Children with a relatively higher IQ and those who attended effective schools were also more likely to emerge with achievements from their childhood.

In summary, the consequences of poverty and social disadvantage for children are probably an interaction and not a straightforward cause and effect. The amount and source of stress with which children must cope will interweave with the range of competencies or potential advantages that they bring to the situation. Research shows that poverty does not inevitably lead to bad outcomes, but it pushes the balance very firmly against most children.

Children and the media

Children are affected by the media in two ways:

- They are featured in some news reports and television programmes.
- They are viewers of television.

Children in the media

The nature of news about ordinary people is that it has to be something out of the ordinary; famous people are seen as news in their own right. The presentation of children (and adolescents too) in the media of newspapers, magazines and television tends to focus on extreme points in the continuum of normal life.

A few children who misbehave so badly that they are excluded from nursery school will make a news item. But thousands of children who behave well will not be mentioned at all. The few are likely to be seen as the 'tip of an iceberg' and attract further articles and programmes about how the current generation of children is out of control. This faulty pattern of generalising, without basis, from the very few to the many is the same error of interpretation that has been raised in other sections of this book about some research studies.

Unfortunately, ordinary good behaviour is not newsworthy. To achieve media interest, children have to engage in acts of heroism or be battling diseases or serious injury (the 'tragic toddler' news story). This treatment of children in the news media has established the extremes of 'angels' or 'demons' and leaves little in between. Practical magazines for families or early years workers are the section of the written media most likely to reflect the ordinary lives of the vast majority of children and their carers.

The media treatment of incidents involving the injury or death of children has also tended to distort reality and adults' judgements of relative dangers. Tragic incidents involving abduction of children by strangers and subsequent injury or death of the child are very rare. The incidence has not increased over the last twenty years of the twentieth century. But many people believe that the risk has grown and their reasoning is based on high profile cases in the media. Statistics demonstrate that children are many times more likely to be injured or even killed by people that they know, most likely within their own family. Children are also at far greater risk from traffic accidents than from attack by strangers.

SUGGESTED ACTIVITY

For a period of two weeks, cut out any news article about children in your regular newspaper. If you can do this activity with colleagues, you could cover several newspapers.

- What image do the articles give readers about children and families?
- What has made these children or families newsworthy?
- Imagine that these reports were your *only* source of information. What picture would you be forming of children and their place in society?

- Are some kinds of children or families absent from the news?
- Think carefully and discuss with your colleagues. How fair is it to draw conclusions from the newsworthy children or families to others? Fair or not, what sort of conclusions do you think people will draw – especially those who are not involved with children day by day?

Children and television

Adults' view of the world can be shaped, to some extent, by their use of the media. In a similar way, children's viewing of television affects them through the image of the world they experience.

Positive effects

General discussion about television and children tends to focus on the possible negative effects. But studies of programmes that set out to help children learn have shown measurable positive results for the children's development. In America, young children who are regular watchers of *Sesame Street* have been shown to develop larger vocabularies than children who watch less often or not at all. Similar studies have shown that children who watch programmes which emphasise helpful and kind behaviour tend to show more of this type of behaviour in their daily interactions. Of course, television is not the only

---

SUGGESTED ACTIVITY

- Television programmes for young children can be a source of enjoyment at the time, in conversations with adults who show an interest and of later happy memories.

- Share recollections with your colleagues about the programmes you watched when you were young.
- What did the programmes offer to you, as a child? What was your favourite programme and why do you think you liked it so much?

---

influence on children's lives but it is worth noting that it can be a positive support to children's development.

Negative effects

Among older children, long hours of watching television has been linked with lower achievement in school, especially with basic and important skills such as reading, writing and mathematics. Large studies have confirmed that this relationship applies in children from well-educated families as much as in families where the parents have lower levels of education. So, the relationship cannot be explained away by saying that children with less well educated parents are allowed to watch more television. As you might guess, it is difficult to prove exactly what is happening in this relationship between television and children's development. But part of the explanation seems to lie in all the activities that children give up if they sit in front of the television for hours each day.

A considerable number of studies, many undertaken in the United States, have shown a link between children's watching of violence or aggression on television and their own patterns of behaviour. There is not a simple causal link but the evidence is strong enough to take children's viewing habits very seriously. The main themes in the research are as follows:

Television can be a source of imaginative play

- Experiments with children show at least a short-term effect on children's behaviour of watching programmes with aggressive content. The themes of the programme can be observed in their later free play. There is plenty of anecdotal evidence from early years settings of how current popular programmes fuel children's imaginative play. When the imitation and play themes lead to more aggressive play, adults become concerned and intervene.
- American children who watch more television are almost always found to be more aggressive in their behaviour than their peers who watch less. (And surveys of children's programmes has shown high levels of violence in the content.) Careful studies have suggested that this link is partly explained by the fact that children, who are already more aggressive than the average child, choose to watch more television and select the more violent programmes. However, the children who watched the most television within this more aggressive group, emerged as the more violent and delinquent adolescents and adults.
- Another group of studies has looked at changes over time within societies following the introduction of television or increased ownership of televisions. In small communities who previously had no television, there have been patterns of an increase in children's aggressive behaviour in play. Levels of violent crime in several countries have been seen to rise dramatically some fifteen years after television became widely available to children. None of this research points to television aggression as the only cause of more general violence in societies. But the research strongly

indicates that television is a major factor in developing children's views that aggression is acceptable and probably in desensitising them to the real impact of violence.

Parents and children's viewing habits

There are certainly many studies that should concern us about the impact of television of children's development and behaviour. But these are in the context of research that underlines the difference made within a household when parents exert control and guidance over their children's viewing.

Studies of the families of children who watch long hours of television highlight that their parents exerted little control over how much or what the children watched. Their homes had less books and other alternatives to undiscriminating television watching. In contrast, parents who restricted their children's television were also more likely to take the children out to places other than shopping. Research has also confirmed that children absorb more of the content of a programme when their parents watch the television with them and talk about what they have all seen. So, children's television viewing makes sense within the broader context of their family life and how actively their parents are involved in what their children do and learn.

Reading on . . .

★ Bronfenbrenner, Urie 1979: *The Ecology of Human Development* (Harvard University Press). A description of the ecological approach to child development.

★ Buckingham, David 1996: *Moving Images: Understanding children's emotional responses to television* (Manchester University Press). A discussion of how children react to television programmes, supported by interviews with children of different ages.

★ De'Ath, Erica 1991: *Changing Families: A guide for early years workers* (National Early Years Network). A descriptive survey of the different kinds of family common in Western society.

★ Elfer, Peter and Robinson, Ann 1993: 'Day care for children under three' *Highlight* series no. 116 (National Children's Bureau). A brief summary of the research on the effects of day care on very young children.

★ Haggerty, Robert; Sherrod, Lonnie; Garmezy, Norman and Rutter, Michael (eds) 1994: *Stress, Risk and Resilience in Children and Adolescents: Process, mechanisms and interventions* (Cambridge University Press). Discussion of the research and ideas on how children may resist the impact of negative experiences and how this process may work.

★ Hardyment, Christina 1995: *Perfect Parents: Baby care advice past and present* (Oxford paperbacks). A survey of a couple of centuries of advice to parents. The discussion shows how ideas cycle round more than once and is a reminder of the need for humility. This generation of professionals is no more likely to have got it all right than previous ones.

★ Hennessy, E.; Martin, S.; Moss, P. and Melhuish, E. 1992: *Children and Day Care: Lessons from research* (Paul Chapman). Practical implications from the research on children and their experience of day care.

★ Holman, Bob 1995: *The Evacuation: A very British revolution* (Lion). Description of the evacuation of children from Britain's cities during the second world war – a useful insight into another era.

★ Humphreys, Margaret 1994: *Empty Cradles* (Doubleday). An account of Humphreys' discovery of the forced emigration of children from many residential homes to parts of Britain's former empire. A window on to a time when the rights of children (and their parents) were viewed very differently.

★ Lansdown, Richard 1996: *Children in Hospital: A guide for families and carers* (OUP). A practical account of good practice in hospital care.

★ Lindon, Jennie 1996: *Growing Up: From eight years to young adulthood* (National Children's Bureau). A description of the development of children from middle childhood to the brink of adulthood. There is a detailed discussion of sex differences, especially in Part Two.

★ McGurk, Harry and colleagues 1992: 'Controversy, theory and social context in contemporary day care research' in *Journal of Child Psychology and Psychiatry*, vol 34, no.1. Discussion of the research and the complex issues in this area of study and social policy.

★ Miedzian, Myriam 1992: *Boys Will Be Boys: Breaking the link between masculinity and violence* (Virago). A thought-provoking book about the development of male identity.

★ Pipher, Mary 1994: *Reviving Ophelia* (Vermilion).

★ Pipher, Mary 1996: *The Shelter of Each Other: Rebuilding our families to enrich our lives* (Vermilion). Practical and thought-provoking books about the impact of social pressures on families. Pipher, a child and family therapist, is constructively critical about therapy and offers positive approaches to helping troubled children and parents.

★ Phoenix, Ann; Woollett, Anne and Lloyd, Eva (eds) 1991: *Motherhood: Meanings, practices and ideologies* (Sage). A broad ranging discussion and descriptions of research on mothers and families in society. The different chapters cover issues such as becoming a mother, employment, life with more than one child and other real-life issues.

★ Tobin, Joseph; Wu, David and Davidson, Dana 1989: *Preschool in Three Cultures* (Harvard University Press). A description of the research discussed on page 188.

★ Whiting, Beatrice Blyth and Edwards, Carolyn Pope 1988: *Children of Different Worlds: The formation of social behaviour* (Harvard University). An account of research in different cultures, finding shared themes as well as differences.

8 Observation and study of children

This chapter covers:

- planning a study;
- undertaking your study.

8.1 Planning a study

This chapter is different from the rest of the book. In all the other chapters you will have read summaries of research and discussion of ideas from people who spend their professional lives studying children. Readers of this book are most likely to be practically involved with children day by day. The lessons of research should be of use to you, but your own work is more likely to include projects and observations.

This chapter addresses some key issues and questions about undertaking small-scale studies of children or their families. So, the points are important as you build up your portfolio, a common part of many child care courses. However, effective early years workers are people who continue to think as they carry out their job. Observations are not just for students and many early years settings have a system for regular assessment of children. Good practice is also to be alert to what is happening in your setting day by day. There are times when it is appropriate to watch the children, or the adults, with a particular purpose in mind that will add to the effectiveness of your work. You may also be supporting parents, who are unused to observing, as they watch their children and learn. Workers can then, themselves, learn from parents' insights. Consequently, this chapter is not restricted to observations of individual children for a course portfolio. The range of examples is also relevant to alert observation of the children within the course of a normal day in your setting.

Choosing a focus

Any study, whether large- or small-scale, has to have a clear focus. Without some sense of direction any study can become unwieldy, as can any observation planned to support ongoing practice. There is a temptation to add various items of interest along the way or to switch methods for reasons that seem sensible at the time. The end result can be a mass of notes or tapes, but not a great deal that is useful for you to conclude.

So, your first step in planning a small study is to explore the questions of:

- What are my reasons for undertaking this piece of work?
- What do I want to find out?
- What questions would I like to be able to answer when I have completed my study? On what topics would I like to be able to say something of interest?

You have to be realistic, because a small-scale piece of research is not going to answer complicated questions. But, as you will have gathered from reading about research throughout this book, some of the most useful studies have focused with care and then been able to contribute some information and ideas. If you are on a course of study, then your supervisor should help you as you make all the kinds of decisions that are discussed here. For example:

- You will not be able to sit in the garden of a nursery and observe the children's play as a whole. There will be too many children and too many activities. You will need to make decisions, in advance, about how you will focus your observations. You might decide to home in on a specific kind of play, perhaps use of the fixed climbing equipment. Alternatively, you might be tracking a particular child or group of friends and gathering information on how they use the outdoor resources and how they move around the garden.
- Children's development progresses as a whole rather than in separate parts. But, it will not be possible for you to aim to understand a child's total development, especially in relatively short observations. A realistic alternative is to focus on one aspect of a child's development, perhaps his growing language abilities. A careful and detailed observation of this child's current abilities, and how he uses his skills, could give you an accurate view of the child as he is at the moment. You could also have the basis for some supported comments about how his language skills probably relate to other aspects of his development, perhaps in making friends. So, you are placing your observations in a broader context. By talking with his parent(s), you might be able to understand something of how he uses his language at home.

EXAMPLE ONE

Natalie was undertaking a study of different ways for children to eat a healthy and balanced diet. She had taken into consideration the research that suggests that a healthy diet for children is not simply smaller portions of the recommended balanced diet for adults (see the discussion on page 30). Natalie worked in a nursery with children from several different cultural and religious groups and had built into her study plan this opportunity to look at different family patterns of eating. She was almost ready to start talking with parents and noting children's eating patterns.

Then a colleague, Razia, pointed out that Natalie had picked up from someone the phrase 'restricted diet'. Through a conversation with Razia, Natalie realised that she was mainly using this phrase to describe children's diets that did not include foods that she normally ate. She did not use 'restricted diet' to describe the situation when a child's health condition meant he could not share part of his family's normal meals.

Questions
- What is the matter with Natalie's use of the phrase 'restricted diet'?
- How could the assumptions underlying this phrase affect her study of children's eating habits?

Checking your assumptions

A careful consideration of possible assumptions should be part of developing the focus for any pieces of work. Checking your assumptions is also part of responsible interpretation of any observations that you collect, whether as part of student work or observations as an early years worker.

Everyone has assumptions about other people and how the settings of ordinary life will operate normally – life could not go without them. Your task when you are planning, making and interpreting your observations is to be very aware of your working assumptions. You need to be ready to ask yourself questions, or to allow colleagues to challenge your assumptions through discussion. Be ready to consider 'Why am I expecting this?' or 'What

EXAMPLE TWO

Afia was planning observations of Joe over a period of three weeks. She had chosen to observe Joe because he was a child who was frequently told off by the staff in the pre-school where Afia had her student placement. Afia and her colleagues shared a concern that any cooperative behaviour from Joe risked being lost in the general irritation with his aggressive actions towards other children. Afia was well aware that she could not observe Joe under a vague heading of 'aggressive'. She had to have a clearer idea of what range of behaviours the staff judged as aggressive. In conversation with the pre-school staff, Afia heard that Joe was often the 'ringleader' in fights between groups of children, usually the boys, based on popular television cartoon characters. Joe was also judged to have a very short fuse and be intolerant of other children who wanted to join activities that he was leading.

Questions
- Joe's behaviour may be disruptive of the calm of the pre-school, but does it sound aggressive?
- Afia needs to consider the particular interpretation that the pre-school staff are making about the play fights based on the cartoon programme. What might be going on here? (Look at page 159 for a discussion of different types of aggression and of playfighting.)
- What may Afia have to consider about how she plans her observations, if she is to avoid a situation in which her work is seen as evidence of Joe's bad behaviour?

EXAMPLE THREE

Delroy was planning a study of how what children do with parents at home could support their learning in nursery and reception class. His theme was that 'parents are their children's first teachers'. Delroy was planning a series of questions for parents that related to the kinds of activities offered to children in the school where he was on placement. Delroy wanted to explore how parents were already, or could potentially, help their children with self-care skills that would ease their nursery life. He was also interested in how parents could carry on at home with learning themes established in the nursery or reception class.

Delroy had the opportunity to show his draft list of questions to Gill, a parent governor of the school. Gill made some practical suggestions about wording and then commented that the plan seemed rather one-sided. She said, 'It might be better to describe parents as co-educators with teachers. And you seem to be assuming that the only way for children to learn at home is for parents to complete work started in school.'

Questions
- What do you think are Gill's reasons for suggesting parents are 'co-educators' rather than children's 'first teachers'? What underlying assumptions is she challenging?
- In what way could Delroy's project emerge as 'one-sided'? Why would this matter? (Look at the discussion on page 131.)
- In what way might he adjust his plans to acknowledge home-based learning?

EXAMPLE FOUR

Martha wanted to explore the early communication skills of babies under a year old. With the agreement of the staff in the baby room of her day nursery, Martha made detailed observations of three babies with their keyworkers. Her observations were made over two weeks in total and made at different times of the nursery day. Martha was looking especially for the early 'conversational exchanges' between baby and carer and for any signs of contact made between babies themselves. (Look at page 90 and 49 for discussions of these topics.)

Martha presented some of her project findings at a staff meeting. She had many examples of short conversational exchanges between a baby and carer and a few of contact between babies. But what also emerged was that there were stretches of the day with very few such exchanges and Martha felt that valuable opportunities were being lost. Martha's observations showed that, when two staff were in the changing room at the same time, they tended to talk with each other and not with the baby they were changing. Staff had the most exchanges with the babies during the time of the day that was called 'playtime' but sequences of chat with babies were often interrupted if an adult spoke.

Questions
- What do you think is happening in Martha's day nursery? (You could look also at page 135 for comments on a very early years curriculum.)
- Martha's study of early communication raised uncomfortable questions in her day nursery. But the discussion around her work could be very useful to the nursery in the end. What would be important circumstances that would support nursery staff to make positive use of her findings?

EXAMPLE FIVE

Tamar became interested in sleep and waking patterns among babies and toddlers. With the help of a local health visitor, Tamar was put in touch with two groups of parents of young children. One group had asked for help with their disturbed nights by visiting a special sleep advice session at the clinic. The other group had children of similar age but had not asked the clinic for help.

Tamar wanted to explore whether there were any obvious differences between the two groups. She had read a number of books about sleep and waking patterns and had considered very carefully how to make a respectful approach to families who were experiencing problems. But an unexpected twist emerged after Tamar had visited four of the families who had *not* used the clinic for advice. Three of these families were up in the night regularly with their baby or toddler. Tamar realised that she definitely did not have a 'sleep problems' and a 'no sleep problems' group.

Questions
- What might be parents' reasons for coping with a tough problem like broken nights and not asking the clinic for help?
- How might Tamar adjust her project so that she can still emerge with useful information?

makes me believe that?' Perhaps your assumptions are a good basis for exploration, so long as you pose them as a question rather than a fact (see the example about helpfulness of boys and girls on page 176).

Ethics and good practice

Over the last few decades research in social sciences, including psychology, has become more respectful of the people who are being studied or invited to be involved in observations and experiments. It is symbolic that my own professional organisation, the British Psychological Society, requires that articles for its house journal no longer refer to 'subjects' (the impersonal term previously used for anyone being studied). People are to be described in a more personal way as children, students, parents and so on.

Informing and consulting

The idea of informed consent

The ethics committees of organisations such as the BPS are far more concerned than, say, thirty years ago, that anyone involved in a research study should be able to give their **informed consent**. People cannot give their informed consent unless they are given an honest description of the study which they are being invited to join (or asked to allow their child to join). Informed consent means that people must be allowed to say 'No' as well as 'Yes', when they have a full understanding of what is being asked.

So, part of any study, however small, is that the people involved are properly informed and consulted. In different ways, this concern should extend to your colleagues, the children and the parents.

Working with others in the setting

It is sensible and courteous to discuss any plans with your colleagues in the early years setting – whether you are in a permanent post or on student placement. Several practical issues arise and should be discussed:

- What kind of observations or work with the children are you planning to do? What are your aims in undertaking this work?
- How much time is this likely to take? Are there particular times of the day when you would ideally like to do the work? Work out a plan of what you will do and when, including time to write up your notes. Will you need to take individual children into a quiet corner or another room in order to explore a set of materials?
- Are you seeking the involvement of any of your colleagues and, if so, what would you like them to do (or not do)?
- If you are on student placement, check on any guidelines or procedures in this setting. There may be particular ways in which you should approach parents for their permission.
- Discuss the kind of circumstances in the setting when you would stop your observations and help out (perhaps minor but normal crises).
- Discuss how you will share your findings with your colleagues (perhaps in a slot created in the staff meeting).

Partnership with parents

Your setting may have a general agreement with parents about students working with their children or with staff making regular observations. However, it is good practice and courteous to talk with a parent when you are planning to focus on his or her child.

- Explain what you plan to do and why. There may be a reason for your choice of this individual child, so explain.
- If you are hoping to make observations in the child's own home, then you need to discuss with the parents (as carefully as you would with colleagues) what your planned study will entail for them and their time.
- Parents should be able to understand what you are doing in order to give their informed consent. If you are intending to take photos of a child, it is courteous to make an extra copy for parents.
- Tell parents when you will be ready to share your observations with them. Be prepared to show parents a copy of your study. It can be a very positive discipline to imagine the child's parent reading your observation notes and later your conclusions. You can still be honest, but this thought can concentrate your mind on expressing your observations in a positive way and being cautious about interpretations. Good practice in any early years setting is that records should be open to children's own parents.

- You might need to be especially sensitive if you are planning a study of a child with disabilities. Parents will want to feel reassured that you have a good understanding of their child and will approach her development in a positive way. You should ask permission if you wish to consult a specialist who sees the child at your early years setting, perhaps a speech therapist or a physiotherapist.
- Sometimes, your observations might be of more general interest and do not focus on single children so much as a child developmental study. Under these circumstances, parents could be informed by a more general letter, or a parents' meeting, when observations have led to stimulating ideas or a change in practice in the setting.

Awareness of the children

In practice, it will be parents who give consent for the involvement of their young children in any study. But you also need to think about the children's possible reactions to your study.

- If you are observing without involvement in the activity, still be ready to explain simply what you are doing, if children ask.
- If you are working with a child, perhaps asking questions, then be ready with an explanation of why you are making notes. Perhaps you could say, 'I'm really interested in what you do/are saying. But I won't remember it all unless I write it down.'
- If children become uncomfortable or unwilling to continue, then let them return to the group.
- If you are exploring in detail the skills of a number of children, then a few of the children who are not involved may want to know why. Your planned activities may look like an interesting special time. Sometimes you may be able to say honestly, 'I'm looking at how much the younger ones know about letters. You can already read, so this is too easy for you.' Or you can offer to show a child the materials later on.
- You will have discussed with your colleagues under what circumstances you stop your observations. You may say to a child who wants to involve you in play that you are enjoying watching for now but will play later on in the day – and make sure you keep your promise. However, a child who is distressed or hurt should be comforted if no other colleague is immediately available.

8.2 Undertaking your study

Techniques and methods

Research into children's development and behaviour has used a wide variety of methods of study. You may be using a number of these methods for your observations. Section 1.5 includes a discussion of research issues and techniques, but the approach in this chapter is more focused on the kind of project a student might do, or that an early years worker might explore.

You need a <u>clear focus for your observation – what are you observing and for what reasons.</u> But you also have to choose a method of observation from the different possibilities. Some issues and options are now described but the suggestions for further reading on page 212 will be useful for more details.

Your role as an observer

The impact of observing

Ideally, as an observer, you need to behave as unobtrusively as possible. If you are watching a child or a group but are not joining in the activity, then you need to be able to see and hear, but not so close that children or adults remain very aware of your presence.

Adults and children often behave differently when they know they are being watched. But, you cannot predict what direction the change in their normal behaviour will take. Some children become quieter and more reticent. Some play to you as an audience and 'show off'. As someone who has spent many hours observing adults in their work with children, I can confirm that adults vary between these alternatives too. They also sometimes take any excuse to disappear completely from your line of vision! You cannot make people not notice you, but you can increase the chance that your observations do not provoke reactions that are very out of the ordinary:

- Explain to the adults, and if appropriate to the children, what you are going to do and your reasons.
- If you are undertaking your study somewhere that you are not known (in a family home or an early years setting that you are visiting), then allow yourself some time to become a familiar face. Ideally, you should be ready to throw away your notes of a first session of several observations, or perhaps the first half-hour of a long single observation.
- Be as unobtrusive as possible in your note-taking and make sure you have everything you need close to hand. People will recall your presence if you have to keep moving around to find a pen or to see the clock.
- Rest assured that most people swiftly forget that someone is observing and simply get on with their day. Children, especially, soon lose interest unless your work directly involves and intrigues them. They have a tolerance of adults' incomprehensible activities – sitting in the corner with a sheaf of notes is just one more odd thing that adults do.
- It would be rude to ignore children's approaches completely. Be as natural as possible with children, but avoid being interesting in your brief replies.

The participant observer

Not all observations involve sitting away from the action. Another method of observing is as a **participant observer** – meaning that you are also part of the activity that you are observing and noting. Your role has to be different if you are joining in or leading an activity. You cannot freeze the action while you make some notes, so you need to plan your records differently.

Perhaps you would like to explore children's understanding of conservation of number (see page 63 for a discussion of this aspect of children's thinking). So you devise a sequence of activities which you present to individual children. In this situation, you may be able to prepare a sheet of notes with appropriate gaps for how a child reacts to play materials or answers your questions (see also page 207 later in this section about questions).

Sometimes participant observation involves you in the flow of an activity which could take a number of unpredictable turns. Perhaps you are following a theme of exploring feelings through conversation, stories and puppet play. In this kind of study it would be more appropriate to make notes after you have finished the activity with the children.

Writing up notes
Useful and appropriate notes are:

- legible;
- factual;
- written up promptly.

Notes that you make at the time of an observation may not be in your neatest writing, but they have to be readable. If you are working from a checklist, it has to be clear which items you have ticked and which comments relate to which item. Part of planning an observation can be an organisation of the timing that allows you realistic space for making notes (see page 205).

You should write down what you see or hear and not your guesses about what people are feeling or their intentions. For instance, if you have the impression that a child is happy or distressed, your judgement has come from something you have observed. Write down what you have observed ('Marcus frowns. He is staring at the book') rather than your conclusion ('Marcus is confused').

Sometimes you will be writing notes at the same time that you make your observations, but with other kinds of project there will be some delay. The sooner you make your notes, the more accurate they will be. Certainly you should not leave writing up any later than the same day. You could still help yourself with some headings, for instance, of the materials you used, the main themes you believe emerged and what children said or did, as accurately as you can recall.

A longitudinal or cross-sectional design

The longitudinal method
This approach focuses on the same child(ren) over a period of time. You might undertake a child study over a period of months, observing the child on many occasions and in different settings, such as home and nursery.

The advantages of following one child are that you can gain a sense of continuity in development and you see the changes over time. You may see possible patterns in how the child reacts and perhaps the consequences, positive and negative, of earlier experiences. Since you are probably undertaking only one very detailed child study, at most two, you have to be cautious about how you use the information. You cannot generalise broadly to other children's development, but you can have a rich description of how this child's development or behaviour has progressed. You will have noticed during the book that I used the diaries of my own children in this way. At no point do I claim that the exact pattern I observed and noted is common to all children.

But I use what I saw, and enjoyed, to illustrate themes in children's development. A longitudinal child study can bring development alive for you; you can see and hear all the ideas in action with real children.

A *cross-sectional design*

This approach focuses on different groups of children, most likely differing in age. Perhaps you might plan to observe the different ways in which babies and children use wooden building blocks. (Look back to page 70 for a discussion of Bruner's idea of the spiral curriculum.) You might organise yourself to watch, on separate occasions, some one-year-olds, three-year-olds and five-year-olds. The advantage of this method is that you can observe differences in development without waiting for the babies to grow up. You cannot predict with certainty that your youngest group will, in two years time, behave exactly like the current three-year-olds that you observe. But, if you ground your project in reliable material on child development, you will be able to say something useful when you have gathered all your material.

A *descriptive record*

You may build up your material for a study through an open-ended record, like a diary or a descriptive narrative of activities that you have watched or in which you have been involved.

- The advantages of an open-ended record is that the description can flow and a sense of real children and early years activities can emerge from the written material.
- The disadvantages of any kind of unstructured record is that your attention may be pulled from one event or child to another and you end up with muddled notes that do not really tell you much of substance.
- You can work to avoid confusing notes by keeping clear your reasons for making the observation and, if appropriate, having a few headings that remind you of the full range of interest. For instance, a case study on a child would need, over the time of your observations, to cover all aspects

of that child's development. Some reminder headings could alert you to the bias that you have become fascinated with this child's language and developing friendships and are at risk of overlooking his self-care skills.

- One strength of a descriptive record can be the personal nature of the observations and where your interest takes you. This strength can unbalance your observation if you become too **subjective** (focused on your own perspective and the sense you make of what is happening). You need also to be **objective** as you read through your notes: push yourself to look from another perspective: the child, another child who was involved, the parent or colleague. Be ready to question yourself: what is my reason for thinking that? Why do I believe this is so important/unimportant? Sharing your notes with a colleague or the child's parent can also help you reach an objective view.

Sometimes, you might combine several methods in one project. For instance, a case study of an individual child might include a descriptive record, but also some specific activities explored with the child and an interview with his parent.

Using audio or video tapes

A number of different kinds of observation can be supplemented by audio- or video-taped material.

- The advantage of making tapes is that you have an accurate record of what a child said or did. If all goes well, you can later watch or listen to whole sequences of what happened while you were involved.
- But there are technical issues and hitches about taping. Unless you are working in an early years setting that is part of a university, it is very unlikely that the centre is already organised for recording. Without built-in, high quality equipment, you will have to use a tape recorder or hand-held video recorder which is obvious to the children. Some of them will inevitably perform for the camera and some of the adults will run for cover. It will take time before everyone reverts to behaving normally. So, if you would like to make some tapes, allow time for everyone to settle down if taping is not usual in your setting.
- An audio tape recorder needs to be of good quality and the microphone close enough to everyone to pick up what is said. The same issue arises for the microphone of a video recorder.
- Be aware that taping is not an easy option in a project. You will almost certainly have to tape for much longer than the final length of sequences that are useful for your project. Children who normally hold lengthy conversations go silent and other children produce noises and nonsense talk, or pull scary faces for a video camera. People who make films about children and child development (or any other topic) abandon large amounts of footage on the cutting room floor.
- You also need to be aware that transcribing (writing down word for word) audio tapes or watching a video tape step by step (stopping, freeze-framing, going backwards and forwards) is surprisingly time-consuming. Researchers, such as those who study patterns of infant communication (see page 90), spend considerably more time watching and analysing the tapes afterwards than making the recordings in the first place.
- You should always ask the parents' permission if you are going to make tape recordings of their children. All the general points hold (see page 199) and additionally parents should be told who will see the recordings outside the early years setting – perhaps your supervisor or college group. Parents

should be confident that tapes of their children will not be copied or used as general teaching material, without their informed consent. It is good practice never to tape sequences with children that you would think twice about if adults were on camera. For instance, it would be inappropriate to video children changing into swimming costumes for a paddling pool session.

None of these cautionary remarks are a reason to avoid any taping. But do be realistic in your plans and get some technical advice, unless you are experienced with the equipment.

Sampling

There are many kinds of interest in children's development and behaviour that cannot be effectively explored by unstructured observations. Methods involving sampling are one way to ensure that your observations are an accurate reflection of a child or a group. **Sampling** means taking a selection, of possible times of observations or of behaviours, in an organised rather than a random way.

Time sampling

You can sample time in your study and this can be a practical way of organising your observations. You cannot continuously observe a child or group and make accurate notes at the same time – unless very little indeed is happening and that would be a cause for concern. So, you have to pace yourself for watching and noting. Time sampling can be a useful method of observation if you are looking at children's use of language or the pattern of interaction between children at a specific activity.

EXAMPLE SIX

Kate was interested in how the children used the nursery computer, since this was a very popular item of equipment, but Kate had the impression that children were using some programmes more than others. She also was concerned that some children were dominating the computer so that others could not get a turn. Kate wondered if the boys took more turns but she kept an open mind.

After discussion with her colleagues, Kate assigned one hour for observation during two mornings in one week and two in the following week. At each agreed time she sat close enough to see and hear activity at the computer, but not so close that children expected her to be involved. She had laid out her paper in preparation. Her plan of observation was to make notes once every five minutes (timed accurately with a stopwatch). For one minute she watched and then had four minutes to complete her notes. Her reminder list directed her to note down the names of the children at the computer (there was room for two) and any who seemed to be waiting. She also noted the programme on the screen and what the children said and did.

When her four sessions of observation were complete, Kate worked her way through her observations. She built up a chart of children who used the computer, which child tended to work the keyboard when two were sitting at the screen and those children who waited but did not get a turn. She also had a record of the programmes used and an approximate estimate for amount of usage. She was able to support her impression that some children used the computer far more than others, but these were not all boys. The children who had control of the keyboard seemed to make more decisions about use of the programme or changing it. Some of the conversations that she noted made Kate think that the more confident children were those who had access to a computer at home.

Questions
- How do you think Kate's small observation study might be followed up in her nursery. What might be the practical implications?
- Perhaps the study could be extended by asking parents about home computer use. What do you think would be a useful series of questions to ask?

Sampling behaviour

Sometimes it will be appropriate to sample events or a specific kind of behaviour, rather than sampling time. In order to sample behaviours in an accurate way, you need to have a clear idea of the behaviour in which you are interested. If you set out to collect examples of 'cooperative' or 'aggressive' behaviour, you should work out (ideally in discussion with a colleague or your supervisor) exactly what you mean by the term. You can prepare your sheet of notes with a few key headings, such as time of day, name of child(ren), name of adults involved and space for a brief description of what happened. It can be possible to make these kind of notes and still remain responsible for the children.

EXAMPLE SEVEN

Tim was on placement in the reception class of a primary school. With the agreement of the staff, he planned to make observations of prosocial behaviour from the children (see page 156 for a discussion of this topic). His approach was to note down any examples of intentional, voluntary, helpful behaviour by children. The actions could be towards adults or other children. He included in prosocial behaviour children's cooperation in following a request to be helpful in some way, so long as the child appeared willing and did not have to be pushed at all by the adult. Tim included any examples when he would usually have asked a child to help. But he was alert that he did not create opportunities when he would not normally have done so.

Tim kept his notes over a period of two weeks and did not read through them until his observation time was complete. He then worked through his notes, adding up the number of prosocial acts, the children involved and any patterns in the time of day. In discussion with his supervisor he looked at creating some broad categories, such as snack and mealtimes, help through words or through actions, single helpful acts or sequences, fetching help for another child and so on.

Several themes emerged from Tim's observations. Some children were far more prominent than others in showing prosocial behaviour and some did not appear at all. He observed two boys, who had something of a reputation as 'tough', being protective towards the cousin of one of them who had just arrived in the school.

Four adults appeared in Tim's observations: himself, the reception class teacher, the nursery nurse and a playground supervisor. Tim felt that each of the class team, himself included, tended to ask the child nearest them to help rather than look around or walk to another child, in order to give everyone the opportunity to help. The playground supervisor had a habit of calling for 'helpful girls' or 'strong boys' when she asked for volunteers. Most of the helpful acts towards adults were around organised times such as meals when a rota was in operation. Tim had the impression that there could be more spontaneous opportunities for children to help.

Question

Tim's observations were a small project and he, and his colleagues, would have to be careful in how they generalised from his findings. But what might be some themes to explore about practice in the reception class and in the playground?

Using checklists

Sometimes a checklist can be the most effective way to explore a child's level of skill or overall development. The early years setting in which you work may have an assessment record that includes a checklist of skills in the different areas of a child's development. If you are on a course, the college handouts may provide possible checklists.

The advantage of a good quality checklist is that it guides you through a wide range of skills in observation of a child and can ensure that you take a well-rounded look at individual children. Reservations about using checklists often focus on the risk of building a fixed picture of a child and perhaps one that focuses too much on what a child cannot do. Checklists have potential

disadvantages, like any other method of observation and study, but proper use of them can produce a positive record of a child, that still gives a sense of changes yet to come. It is important that you:

- Approach a child with respect and plan carefully how you will explore the different kinds of items in a checklist.
- Some items will be in the form of questions and it will matter how you ask these – see the section on asking questions below.
- You can supplement checklists with some explanatory notes as well. If a child does not manage a particular item, there is good reason to make a note that the child partly managed to complete a task. You might also make a supported comment about where the difficulty seems to lie at the moment. Checklists definitely do *not* have to be used as a pass/fail method.
- It is important not to boost a child's achievements because you like the child or her parents. The information will be much less useful and it is not helpful for the child in the long run. When you approach checklists in a positive way, as outlined in this section, you will be far less tempted to bias your results.
- Keep a balance of children's strengths as well as difficulties as you write up an observation based on using a checklist. Spend time on what the child can manage, what he can nearly manage as well as those areas which are currently outside his capability.

A positive approach to asking questions and writing up your notes can lead to an accurate view of a child at the moment and a sense of how her development will progress in the near future.

Creating an opportunity to observe

Sometimes you will be making observations of children in the surroundings of an early years setting or family home and you will be watching their spontaneous behaviour. Part of normal life for children is that adults often make requests, guide and direct children. So naturally occurring activity at least sometimes includes an active adult role.

Sometimes, an observation may require you to intervene in one way or another but this involvement does not have to be intrusive. You might wish to create a situation to check and explore what a child can do. Perhaps you put out particular equipment or deliberately use a particular book, because you want to observe children's reactions. You might invite a child, or a series of children to join you in an activity, ask them questions or invite their opinions. Children are still exercising choices about what they say or do, but you have nudged the play environment in order to make a particular set of observations.

Asking questions

Asking children questions

Sometimes your method of study will include asking children questions. You might be asking them for their reaction to some play materials, to pick out particular items or to do something with the materials. There are several practical issues that are very relevant to ensuring that your questions lead to useful information.

- Plan in detail what you are going to ask children. Know what you will say and in connection with which play materials, or opinions about what aspect of the setting.
- When you are planning to work with a series of individual children, you should follow the same procedure and wording with all of them, unless

there is a very good reason for change. Your findings could well be muddled if you have swopped around your order of the way you ask the questions, perhaps because you want a change.

- If you are going to repeat the same pattern with a number of children, it is your responsibility to keep yourself fresh. It is irrelevant that this is the tenth time you have asked this sequence of questions. You owe it to each child to look as interested as the first time.

- When you are exploring children's development, it is important not to change the wording of your questions, because that can change your meaning. It matters how you phrase questions to children. For instance, suppose you have a selection of objects in front of you and a child. The two questions, 'What's this?' (holding up the teddy) and 'Where's the teddy?' are focused on the same object and require that the child understands the idea of questions and reply. But otherwise the two questions are asking the child to show different skills. 'What's this?' means that the child has to know and say the word 'teddy'. A question formed by 'Where's the ....?' means that a child can point, look or pick up the relevant toy. The first question is checking the child's expressive language (what she says out loud) and the second taps into her comprehension (what she understands of what you say). See also page 71 for discussion of research and the way children are asked questions.

- Look interested when you ask any questions and as you wait for a child's reply. Never ask a question and then look away, perhaps to another adult or child. This behaviour is discourteous and confusing, especially to younger children who will not continue to focus on the play materials, if your behaviour suggests that you have already lost interest.

- Be aware of your body language as well as what you say out loud. This awareness tends to be especially important if you are exploring children's language or their reasoning abilities. When children are uncertain, they naturally look towards an adult for extra clues. When you are supporting children's learning, all these clues are positive and useful. But if you want to gain an accurate assessment of what a child can do without help, then you have to curb your unintentional help. Perhaps you will have to look in a friendly manner towards the child when you ask a question, rather than at the play materials in front of you. The direction of your gaze may give a clue.

Asking adults questions

When part of your study is an interview with parents your planning should include a detailed layout of the questions, just as much as your plans for children. Several other practical issues arise in structured conversations with adults:

- Adults – fellow early years workers or parents – will inevitably be aware of the impression they are giving. You need to plan your questions as far as possible so that you gain accurate information rather than what the other adult thinks would be a better answer.

- Specific questions are sometimes better than general ones. For instance, consider how you might reply, as a parent, to a question like, 'Does your child watch a lot of television?' As an interviewer you would be better asking a definite question such as, 'What did your child watch on television yesterday?'

- Questions about activities like television, or children's diet, may also be better supplemented by asking parents to keep a diary. A food diary would also benefit from some guiding questions – for a parent or for you if you were keeping such a record. For instance, you would want a record of everything that a child ate and not just the official mealtimes.

- Sometimes it would be sensible to ask an open-ended question. You might ask a parent, whom you are interviewing about her child's move into primary school, for her own views – 'What do you think is most important to help children to settle into school?'

Using a combination of methods

Student projects will often focus on one method of inquiry at a time. But it is possible that a larger project might include a combination of methods. For instance, suppose you were studying the experience of a young child who has a hospital experience (the suggested activity on page 186). You would plan your project in detail, including spending some time to read around the topic. You would gain the informed consent of the parents and the child – unless the child is genuinely too young to understand what you are asking. Your approach in the study could include an interview with the parent, and perhaps the child before and after the experience. You might also, with the appropriate permissions, make some observations of the child in the out-patient situation or on the ward as an in-patient. Another relevant possibility would be to talk with one or two of the medical staff about their approach to children as customers of the health service. There might also be written material from the hospital or clinic.

Interpretations

Any research, whether small-scale or very substantial, has to be interpreted with care. However much information has been gathered, you have to be sure that the sense you are making of your findings is not stretching the material too far. You will have read examples of research in this book for which the interpretations have been challenged – either at the time of publication or later, with a different perspective on the research methods or conclusions. In your own studies you will need to be cautious about what you do with the information you gather.

Support your interpretations

Any interpretations, final conclusions or practical suggestions from your observations must be supported. The key word is 'because...' – whether you write it, say it or think it. Some examples follow.

Focus on what you have observed

Any detailed child study should avoid vague words like a 'good' child just as much as general criticisms like 'poorly behaved'. Focus on what you have observed and bring out the descriptive information. If you believe that a child is 'good at' some activity, then explain why. Use specific examples of what he does and how. If you judge his skills are striking for his age, then refer to some developmental material that backs your opinion.

If you believe there is some reason why a child behaves in a particular way or shows particular interests, then support your view. Remain tentative with 'it is possible that..' or 'my observations suggest that...' and do not draw firm conclusions that you cannot justify.

Afia (the example on page 197) might write up that her observations confirmed the staff's concern that Joe risks being labelled as an 'aggressive' child, with few redeeming features. But Afia would have to balance this view with examples of cooperative behaviour from Joe that appear to be overlooked and a careful analysis of what seems to be happening in the cartoon-inspired play fighting. Taking an objective viewpoint, could the observations she has gathered be presented as either evidence of rich and sustained pretend play or of inappropriate aggressive play? What might be inclining the pre-school team in one direction or another? Afia can avoid a sense of criticising her colleagues by concentrating on the patterns of what may be happening and of possibilities, not assigning blame.

Limit your generalisations

Be careful about how far you generalise from your study. Perhaps a child is quiet in nursery (rarely speaks without being asked, looks on from the sidelines and so on) but you cannot be sure, without checking that she is equally quiet in other settings, such as home. You cannot conclude that she is 'a quiet child'.

In much the same way, you cannot generalise from an observation of one Turkish family to Turkish cultural patterns in general, nor from one step-family to step-families in general. The temptation to generalise about some cultural and social groups more than others is often a sign of broader assumptions that need challenge. I have heard people generalise to 'Asian culture' on the basis of one or two Asian families, when they would certainly not build a working theory about 'people who live in Manchester' from a couple of observations of families who were resident in that urban area. Look also at the discussion on page 48 about myths of only children and their development.

Tim (the example on page 206) might write up his notes to suggest that the reception staff including himself are unintentionally restricting the children's opportunities to be helpful. But he will need to support this perspective with observations. He cannot continue his theme and speculate that this is the pattern throughout the school, any more than he can make generalisations about the approach of all the playground supervisors from the one person he observed.

Distinguish between fact and opinion

A useful study makes a clear difference between information that has been gathered in an objective a way as possible and opinions that are developed or supported by the study. Observations can lead to useful practical suggestions, which are one kind of opinion. But any views of suggestions have to be supported – the step of using 'because...'.

In a similar way, you cannot imply that your observations tell you what is going on in a child's head, their motivations or intentions. You can observe and write up your observation that a child watched another one climb a forbidden tree in the nursery garden and then went to tell a worker what was happening. You cannot conclude from a single incident that 'Kelly wanted to get Priyash into trouble' or that 'Kelly likes telling tales'. Perhaps Kelly was genuinely concerned that Priyash would hurt himself. However, if your observations showed many incidents of watch-and-tell from Kelly, you might have a better basis for supporting a view that she felt responsible for the younger children or that she appeared to seek attention from adults by bringing tales of danger or concern.

Be wary of your assumptions

From page 196 there were examples to illustrate caution about your assumptions at the planning stage of a study. You also have to be careful at the interpretation stage.

Natalie (example on page 196) was stimulated to think about her assumptions before she started her study of children's diets. But without Razia's courteous challenge, Natalie might have collected information on the children's different family eating patterns and then written up the variations through comparisons with what she regarded as a normal way of eating. Without the challenge from Gill, Delroy (the example on page 197) might have overlooked examples of children learning in their family home. He ran the risk of classifying such incidents as not 'real' learning, because of his unchallenged assumption that genuine learning only happens in formal settings like nursery and school.

There is often more than one possible interpretation that can be drawn from the same set of observations and assumptions can unbalance an interpretation. There is an example in the following box.

EXAMPLE EIGHT

Becky, aged 18 months, continuously empties out the contents of the vegetable rack and plays with the vegetables. You can describe her actions as 'Becky looks at the rack, walks over, pulls the rack on to the floor, sorts out the potatoes and so on'. But adults will rarely stop with a blow-by-blow account of what Becky has done; we are keen to make sense of what we see to interpret for meaning. It might be:

1 Becky is fascinated by what objects will do. She is experimenting and has learned that some potatoes roll, that raw carrots are good to eat and that a lot of sprouts can be fitted into her father's slippers.

2 Becky shows evidence of learning from experience. She has worked out how to hook the rack off its bracket and what initially took her ten minutes of hard work is now completed in only a couple of minutes.

3 Becky is a naughty little girl who has been allowed to get away with things. I think her parents have a permissive approach to child rearing and they should give Becky firmer boundaries for her behaviour.

Questions
The three interpretations show different interests and perspectives – what are these?

A good way to check how well you are supporting your interpretations is to ask yourself some pointed questions, or work with a colleague or your supervisor in this way. You might ask yourself:

- What is my evidence for this view or my conclusion? What is leading me to say this?
- Why do I believe that this activity is more valuable than that one?
- What are my reasons for guessing that this child is distressed or that this parent is worsening the situation?
- What are the other possible interpretations of what I have observed?
- What other reliable information can I also use? What about reading, other studies, developmental information and so on?
- Perhaps I do not really understand what is going on in this observation, or this family's reasoning for their approach to this problem. Why am I guessing when I could just say that I do not know the answer or the cause here?

In summary

Any study has to be realistic in what you try to cover, the methods that you use and how you interpret your results. Some of the choices are practical issues about what is genuinely possible with the time and resources at your disposal. Students on courses will also, with the help of their supervisors, be aiming to undertake a number of projects, which will vary in focus and methods. However, some of the important issues are about unspoken assumptions and you should work to make these open to challenge, at the planning and the interpretation stage of any study. Caution about how you collect information and make sense of what you gather will support you in a responsible approach to practice with children in general.

Reading on . . .

★ Drummond, Mary-Jane; Rouse, Dorothy and Pugh, Gillian 1992: *Making Assessment Work: Values and principles in assessing young children's learning* (National Children's Bureau). A practical workbook with many ideas about how to plan and undertake assessments, as well as consideration of the issues underlying how you assess children.

★ Harding, Jackie and Meldon-Smith, Liz 1996: *How To Make Observations and Assessments* (Hodder and Stoughton).

★ Hobart, Christine and Frankel, Jill 1994: *A Practical Guide to Child Observation* (Stanley Thornes). Each of these books offers a wide range of examples showing the many different ways that you can observe and the kind of information that you could gain with varied methods.

★ Lindon, Jennie 1997: *Working With Young Children* (Hodder and Stoughton). Part One gives a discussion of the framework of good practice in which observation and assessment should take place, including report writing and partnership with parents.

★ Schaffer, H. Rudoph 1990: *Making Decisions About Children: Psychological questions and answers* (Blackwell). Examples of what research says, and does not say, on topics of social interest for child development and family life. Useful reminders about caution in interpreting information from any study.

Video material

Some readers may have more difficulty than others in making observations of children, parents and early years settings. Video material can be an alternative way to watch children in action and you can, of course, re-run sequences as you wish. Video can be a valuable supplement to learning even if you have opportunities to observe children.

I have found these two videos to be especially useful for a rounded view of children and child development.

Baby It's You – the double video from the Channel Four television programme of the same name. Available from high street stores. If you have difficulty, the distribution company, Beckmann Communications can be contacted by telephone on 01624 816585.

Tuning in to Children is a joint production of BBC Publications and the National Children's Bureau. Contact the NCB for current prices at 8 Wakley Street, London EC1V 7QE, tel: 0171 843 6028 or 6029.

Final thoughts

My aim in this book has been to make theories and research on child development interesting and accessible to you. Most readers will spend many more hours actually working with children than in tracking down books and articles about the early years. So I have been very aware that studies and theoretical approaches have to earn their worth. They must either stimulate useful ideas or contribute something about helpful adult behaviour with children.

Theories can guide us in making sense of what is happening to children and may offer useful explanations of how children develop. Practical ideas developed from a good theory can sometimes give a perspective that will help you support children in their learning and puzzle out what they do not understand. Yet theories about child development must never become more important than the children themselves. In a clash between what a theory predicts and what children actually do, we must be ready to question the theory and not just the children.

You will also have realised that some theories take such diverse viewpoints that the different groups of supporters will never reach agreement. As practitioners useful to children, you need to keep an open mind and look for what you can learn and use from the different perspectives. Contrary to what some enthusiastic theorists will claim, there is no evidence that any one group has cornered the market in completely understanding young children in all their complexity.

Research studies over the last few decades have considerably extended our understanding of what happens as children develop in all the different aspects of their learning. We have a far greater awareness of how events support or block children's psychological and physical health. We have much more grasp of how the different parts of children's learning relate together – of the whole child that we see day by day. But we do not know everything and it is an unwise researcher, or practitioner, who gives the impression that there is nothing left to learn.

Theory and research is affected by time and place; by the prevailing social values, the culture in which the team is working, the favourite research topics of the decade and not least by the possibilities of funding. Research in the social sciences needs a cultural and historical perspective if there is to be any hope of understanding unintentional bias, unspoken assumptions and what has been overlooked.

In chapter one (page 27) I described the difference between two sources of knowledge about children: evidence and wisdom. You will be able to gain a great deal by learning from the **wisdom** of more experienced practitioners, when they share with you not only what they have learned but the thinking that underpins what they do and why. Years of time spent working with young

children do not automatically become experience. Practitioners have to be willing to reflect on their practice and continue to be open to new thoughts and approaches. You may meet people who reject even the mildest question or challenge with, 'I've been in the job for twenty years so I know what I'm doing.' My usual reaction is to suggest that twenty years (or some other round figure) is definitely long enough to have done some thinking as well as doing, and be able to communicate the results courteously to less experienced colleagues.

The **evidence** that emerges from well-conducted research can challenge assumptions that arise from working in a limited context. And even the most-travelled early years workers will have some boundaries to their experience. Careful studies can document children's development and behaviour in detail that would be well nigh impossible in a normal day of working with children. Research can produce new thoughts and fresh angles that stimulate practice with children. And sometimes, as in the case of the early communication of babies, researchers may be filling in the details of a view that has always been promoted by those who tuned into the life of babies and very young children.

So, you need to combine your knowledge sources of wisdom and evidence in order to be effective in your practice with real children.

- Look at what babies, toddlers and children do and can nearly manage – watch, listen and enjoy what you learn.
- Reflect on what could be going on under the surface but keep an open mind. Even in the most careful research, or time spent with a child you know very well, there will always be some guesswork.
- But also be ready to think about what you do, to question your reactions in a constructive way. Are you looking from the child's perspective enough of the time? Or is there an imbalance to your own, adult viewpoint, or to what you expect to be happening? Be ready to continue to reflect in this way, no matter how experienced you become in your work.
- Watch out for the possibilities of sharing your observations and thoughts with colleagues or with children's parents. And often there will be a chance to share your enjoyment and great interest with the children themselves.

Appendix 1:
Cross reference to child care and education course modules or units

The book will support your study in the following courses. The details include the revisions to NVQ/SVQ units made in autumn 1997.

NVQ/SVQ in Early Years Care and Education
Level 2

C1	Support children's physical development needs
C4	Support for children's social and emotional development
C8	Implement planned activities for sensory and intellectual development
C9	Implement planned activities for the development of language and communication skills
C12	Feed babies
C13	Provide for babies' physical development needs
E1	Maintain an attractive, stimulating and reassuring environment for children
P1	Relate to parents

Level 3

C2	Provide for children's physical needs
C3	Promote the physical development of children
C5	Promote children's social and emotional development
C7	Provide a framework for the management of behaviour
C10	Promote children's sensory and intellectual development
C11	Promote children's language and communication development
C14	Care for and promote the development of babies
C16	Observe and assess the development and behaviour of children
C17	Promote the care and education of children with special needs
C24	Support the development of children's literacy skills
C25	Support the development of children's mathematical skills
E3	Plan and equip environments for children
M7	Plan, implement and evaluate learning activities and experiences
M8	Plan, implement and evaluate routines for children
P2	Establish and maintain relationships with parents

NVQ/SVQs in Playwork

Playwork covers involvement with children from the ages of 4–5 years up to 14–15 years. So, this book is mainly relevant to work and study focused on the younger end of the age group covered within playwork.

Level 2

PA1   Contribute to positive relationships with children and their parents/carers
PA3   Contribute to children's development through play

Level 3

D25   Prepare play opportunities to enhance children's development
D26   Facilitate play opportunities to enhance children's development
D27   Promote children's social and emotional development
E7   Contribute to the maintenance and improvement of a child-centred environment
P14   Establish and maintain relationships with children and parents
P15   Provide for the management of children's behaviour

CACHE Certificate in Child Care and Education (CCE)
Core modules

2   The care and education environment
4   Physical care of the developing child
7   Working with young children
8   Play and the young child
9   Emotional and social development
10   Parents and carers
11   Understanding children's behaviour

Option Module

1A   Caring for babies 6 weeks to 1 year

CACHE Diploma in Nursery Nursing (NNEB)
Modules

A   Observation and assessment
B   Work with young children
D   Foundations to caring
E   Physical care and development
F   Emotional and social development
H   Learning through play
I   Cognitive and language development
J   Children's behaviour
L   Work with babies 0–1 year
U   Early years curriculum

CACHE Advanced Diploma in Child Care and Education (ADCE)
Modules

1   How children learn
2   Language and literacy

3	Feelings and relationships
4	Work with children from birth to three years
6	Early years curriculum
9	Children and families under stress
20	Observation and assessment

BTEC National in Childhood Studies (Nursery Nursing)

Core modules

1039L	Human growth and development
1040L	Practices in child care
1041L	Early childhood learning
1044L	Professional practice
1048L	Psychological aspects of child development
1049L	Sociological aspects of child development
1050L	Learning activities and play

GNVQ in Health and Social Care

Foundation

Unit 2   Understanding personal development and relationships

Intermediate

Unit 2   Influences on health and well being

Advanced

Unit 4   Psycho-social aspects of health and social well being
Unit 17   Psychology in the context of health and social care

GCSE

Home Economics: Child Development

The book will support your study in the child development option within a home economics syllabus, offered by SEG, MEG, Northern Ireland, ULEAC and NEAB.

Psychology

The book will be useful for students following the Psychology syllabus offered by SEG, MEG, ULEAC or NEAB.

A level Psychology

The book will support study in the Psychology syllabus offered by AEB, SEG and NEAB.

Name index

Subject index